Running a Charity

Fourth Edition

Running a Charity

Fourth Edition

Mark Mullen BA (Dunelm.)
of Lincoln's Inn, Barrister

Published by
Jordan Publishing Limited
21 St Thomas Street
Bristol BS1 6JS

Whilst the publishers and the author have taken every care in preparing the material included in this work, any statements made as to the legal or other implications of any transaction, any particular method of litigation or any kind of compensation claim are made in good faith purely for general guidance and cannot be regarded as a substitute for professional advice. Consequently, no liability can be accepted for loss or expense incurred as a result of relying in particular circumstances on statements made in this work.

© Jordan Publishing Limited 2015

All rights reserved. No part of this publication may be reproduced, stored in a retrieval system, or transmitted in any way or by any means, including photocopying or recording, without the written permission of the copyright holder, application for which should be addressed to the publisher.

Crown Copyright material is reproduced with kind permission of the Controller of Her Majesty's Stationery Office.

Crown copyright. The model documents contained in Appendices A to I have been reproduced with the kind permission of the Charity Commission. www.gov.uk/government/organisations/charitycommission.

British Library Cataloguing-in-Publication Data

A catalogue record for this book is available from the British Library.

ISBN 978 1 78473 021 5

Typeset by Letterpart Limited, Caterham on the Hill, Surrey CR3 5XL

Printed in Great Britain by Hobbs the Printers Limited, Totton, Hampshire SO40 3WX

PREFACE TO THE FOURTH EDITION

As at the end of September 2014 there were more than 164,000 charities registered with the Charity Commission for England and Wales alone. These had a combined annual income of in excess of £64 billion, some £10 billion more than in 2010. There are estimated to be about 900,000 charity trustees in the jurisdiction. Just under 70,000 of the charities registered in England and Wales, however, had an income of less than £10,000 per annum. For many charities, therefore, their continued existence depends on the good will and efforts of their trustees, doing what they can with limited income and resources. At the same time, the sector has become ever more regulated and has seen significant reforms in recent years. In England and Wales, charities are now subject to the Charities Act 2011 and regulation by the Charity Commission for England and Wales. There are proposals to extend its powers further. The English and Welsh Commission has been joined by the Office of the Scottish Charity Regulator and the Charity Commission for Northern Ireland established under legislation in those jurisdictions. More recently still, the Charities Regulatory Authority has been established in the Republic of Ireland.

Charity trustees thus face ever more intensive scrutiny and have to keep pace with developments in the law and the regulation of the sector. This book is intended to offer some pointers to them and to non-specialist advisers. It focuses on the law in England and Wales, but refers to the other jurisdictions in the United Kingdom by way of comparison. It is not intended as legal advice and charity trustees should consult the appropriate professionals, or seek the assistance of their regulator, as and when required.

Mark Mullen
Radcliffe Chambers,
Lincoln's Inn

31 January 2015

CONTENTS

Preface to the Fourth Edition — v

Chapter 1
Introduction — 1
1.1   What is a charity? — 1
       England and Wales — 1
       Scotland — 3
       Northern Ireland — 4
       The Republic of Ireland — 4
       Exclusively charitable purposes — 4
1.2   Who is a charity trustee? — 5
1.3   Responsibilities of charity trustees — 6
       Public trust — 6
       Conflict — 6
       Delegation — 7
       Contracts with third parties — 7
       Other duties — 8
1.4   Charitable status – examples — 8

Chapter 2
Constitutional Requirements — 11
2.1   Setting up — 11
2.2   Choosing the legal form — 12
2.3   Registration in England and Wales — 13
       Exempt charities — 14
       Excepted charities — 14
       Registration process — 14
       Name of charity — 14
       Registration number — 14
       Significance of registration — 15
2.4   Registration in Scotland — 15
2.5   Registration in Northern Ireland — 15
2.6   Changing the constitution — 15
       Alteration to the constitution of a charitable company — 16
       Alteration to the constitution of a CIO — 17
       Express power of alteration of the constitution of
           unincorporated charities — 17

	Alternative procedures	17
	Statutory power in England, Wales and Northern Ireland	18
	Scheme in England, Wales and Northern Ireland	18
	Scheme in Scotland	20
	Reviewing aims and procedures	20
	The new governing instrument	21
2.7	Merger	21
	Transfer of assets	21
	Statutory power	22
	Scheme	22
	Amalgamation of CIOs	22
2.8	Winding up	23
	Express power to wind up	24
	Statutory power	24
	Winding up of CIOs	25
2.9	Cy-près schemes – examples	25

Chapter 3
Money and Property — 27

3.1	Accounting	27
3.2	Accounts and record-keeping	27
	Structure	27
	Small charities that are not limited companies	28
	Formats	28
	The annual report	29
	Branches	29
3.3	Independent audit	30
3.4	Tax and rates	31
	Income and capital gains	31
	Property used for charitable purposes	31
	Gift Aid	31
	Payroll Giving Scheme	32
	Gifts	32
	HM Revenue and Customs guidance	32
3.5	Insurance	32
	Fire, other damage and theft	32
	Vandalism and terrorism	32
	Legal expenses insurance	32
	Public and employer's liability	33
	Fidelity insurance	33
	Particular risks	33
	Liability insurance	33
	Other means of financial protection	34
3.6	Investment	34
	Common investment funds	34
	Powers of investment	35
	Statutory powers (unincorporated charities)	35

	Advice on investments	35
	Investment advisers	35
	Holding of investments	36
	Incorporation	36
3.7	Land and buildings	36
	Holding of land	37
	Certificate of incorporation	37
	Land vested in the Official Custodian	37
	Sale, exchange or leasing of land in England and Wales	38
	Proceeding without consent	38
	Formalities	39
	Mortgage of land	39
3.8	Making grants	39
	Objective of grant	40
	Applications for assistance	40
	Policy guidelines	40
3.9	Raising funds	41
	Managing fundraising	42
	Methods of fundraising	42
	Restrictions on fundraising	42
	Fundraising records	43
	Fundraising agreements	44
3.10	Accepting gifts and legacies	45
	Refusal to accept gifts	45
	Gifts subject to conditions	46
	Failure of purpose	46
	'General charitable intention'	46
	Identifiable donors	47
	Avoiding failure	47
3.11	Patrons and sponsors	47
3.12	Trading	48
	Trading activities as an adjunct to charitable purpose	48
	Trading for the purpose of raising funds	48

Chapter 4
Management   **51**

4.1	Choosing trustees	51
4.2	Trustee meetings	52
	Preparation	53
	Quorum	53
	Chairmanship	53
	Minutes	54
	Frequency of trustee meetings	54
4.3	Dealing with professionals	55
	Choosing a professional	55
	Fees	55
	Relationship between adviser and trustees	55
	Effectiveness	55

	Problems with advisers	56
	Mistakes to avoid	57
	Particular specialists	57
	Beauty parades	58
4.4	Employees and volunteers	59
	Interviewing candidates	59
	Security	60
	Annoyance	60
	Encouragement or praise when deserved	60
	Support for weaknesses	60
	Training	60
	Fairness	60
	Remuneration (including pension rights)	60
	Remuneration of trustees	61
	Health and safety legislation	61
	Relationship between director and trustees	62
4.5	Good management	62
	Time	62
	Contract culture	63
	Coherence	63
	Charity consultants	63
4.6	Stationery	63
	Cost	64
4.7	Computers	65
	Websites and social media	65
4.8	Premises	66
	Appearance of premises	66
	Regulations	66
	Listed buildings	67
	Moving premises	67
	Neighbours	67
4.9	Training	68
	Self-help	68
	Academic institutions	68
	Technical skills training	68
	Special courses	69
	Opportunities for staff	69
	Informal training	69
4.10	Troubleshooting	70
	Physical emergencies	70
	Insurance	70
	Negligence	70
	Tenants' defaults	71
	Compensation	71
	Problems	71
	Running out of money	71
	Charity Commission inquiry	72
	OSCR inquiries	73

	Mediation	73

Chapter 5
Europe 75
5.1	How charities fit in	75
	Social economy	75
5.2	European law	76
	Treaties	76
	Regulations	76
	Directives	76
	Decisions	76
	Recommendations and Opinions	76
5.3	European institutions	76
	Council of the European Union	77
	Committees of Permanent Representatives	77
	European Council	77
	European Commission	77
	Directorates General	78
	European Parliament	78
	Committees	78
	European Economic and Social Committee	78
	Committee of the Regions	79
	European Foundation	79
	The Structural Funds	79
	Council of Europe	80
5.4	Interaction	80
	European Commission	80
	European Parliament	80
	European Economic and Social Committee	81
	European Foundation	81
	International non-governmental organisations	81
5.5	Networks and umbrella bodies	81

Appendix A
Charitable Trusts: Model Trust Deed 83

Appendix B
Company Not Having a Share Capital 103
Articles of Association for a Charitable Company 103

Appendix C
Company Not Having a Share Capital 127
Memorandum of Association 127

Appendix D
Charitable Associations: Model Constitution 129

Appendix E
Charitable Incorporated Organisation: Model Constitution for a CIO with a Voting Membership (in addition to the charity trustees)   149

Appendix F
Charitable Incorporated Organisation: Model Constitution for a CIO Whose only Voting Members are its Charity Trustees   187

Appendix G
Charitable Objects   217
Advancement of Education   217
Advancement of Religion   218
Advice and Counselling   219
Animal Charities   220
Carers   221
Community Amateur Sports Clubs   222
Community Capacity Building   223
Community Centre   224
Community Transport   225
Conciliation and Mediation   226
Conservation of the Environment   227
Disasters   228
Elderly People   229
Equality and Diversity   230
The Establishment and Maintenance of a Museum and/or Art Gallery   231
Family Planning   232
Promotion of the Law, Police and Crime Prevention   233
Promotion of Human Rights   234
Racial Harmony   235
Recreational Charities Act 1958   236
Recycling   237
Refugees / Those seeking Asylum   238
Relief of Financial Hardship   239
Relief of Poverty   240
Relief of Sickness   241
Relief of Unemployment   242
Religious Harmony   243
Social Inclusion   244
Sustainable Development   246
Urban or Rural Regeneration   247
Village Halls   248
Young People   249

Appendix H
Model Annual Report for an Unincorporated Charity   251

Appendix I
Model Annual Report for a Larger Charitable Company 263

Index 283

CHAPTER 1

INTRODUCTION

1.1 WHAT IS A CHARITY?

The word 'charity' has a general meaning in ordinary speech and a special meaning in law. Many people are surprised to learn how limited the legal meaning is and this book is concerned with charity in that special, legal sense. It will focus on charity law as it is understood in England and Wales and on the regulatory regime here. Reference will, however, be made to the position in Scotland and Northern Ireland, which have their own statutory and regulatory systems.

1.1.1 England and Wales

Since the time of Queen Elizabeth I and before, certain purposes have been regarded by English law as worthy of favourable treatment. The courts and, in more recent times, the Charity Commission for England and Wales, help to enforce them and prevent abuses. Charitable trusts have certain distinctive features. For example, the rules which place limitations on the term of a trust ('the perpetuity period') and which restrict the number of trustees, do not apply to charities and, because the purposes of a charity must be beneficial to the public, charitable organisations are given favourable tax treatment. The courts and the Commission also have the power, by means of a tool called a 'scheme', to alter a charity's purposes to bring them up to date or to make them workable.

These days, what is and what is not a charity in the eyes of the law is governed by statute. Section 1 of the Charities Act 2011 provides that a charity is an institution which is:
(a) established for charitable purposes only; and
(b) falls to be subject to the control of the High Court in the exercise of its jurisdiction with respect to charities.

There are some other statutes that confer charitable status; for example 'qualifying academy providers' are charities by virtue of the Academies Act 2010 and have their own principal regulator. For most charities the 2011 Act will determine whether or not they have charitable status.

To find out what 'charitable purposes' are, we have to look at s 2(1) of the 2011 Act. A charitable purpose is a purpose which falls within the descriptions of purposes listed in s 3(1) of the Act and is for the public benefit. Those 'descriptions of purposes' are as follows:

'(a) the prevention or relief of poverty;
(b) the advancement of education;
(c) the advancement of religion;
(d) the advancement of health or the saving of lives;
(e) the advancement of citizenship or community development;
(f) the advancement of the arts, culture, heritage or science;
(g) the advancement of amateur sport;
(h) the advancement of human rights, conflict resolution or reconciliation or the promotion of religious or racial harmony or equality and diversity;
(i) the advancement of environmental protection or improvement;
(j) the relief of those in need by reason of youth, age, ill-health, disability, financial hardship or other disadvantage;
(k) the advancement of animal welfare;
(l) the promotion of the efficiency of the armed forces of the Crown, or of the efficiency of the police, fire and rescue services or ambulance services;
(m) any other purposes not within the above categories
  (i) that are not within paragraphs (a) to (l) but are recognised as charitable purposes by virtue of section 5 (recreational and similar trusts, etc.) or under the old law,
  (ii) that may reasonably be regarded as analogous to, or within the spirit of, any purposes falling within any of paragraphs (a) to (l) or sub-paragraph (i), or
  (iii) that may reasonably be regarded as analogous to, or within the spirit of, any purposes which have been recognised, under the law relating to charities in England and Wales, as falling within sub-paragraph (ii) or this sub-paragraph.'

Section 3(2) offers some definitions. A religion includes a religion that believes in more than one god or no god at all. The advancement of health includes the prevention or relief of sickness, disease or human suffering and the advancement of citizenship or community development includes rural or urban regeneration and the promotion of civic responsibility, volunteering, the voluntary sector or the effectiveness or efficiency of charities. 'Sport' means a sport or game which promotes health by involving physical or mental skill or exertion.

Every charitable purpose will come within one (or more) of the categories in s 3(1), but not every purpose which is within these categories is necessarily charitable. Deciding whether a given purpose is charitable depends on legal precedent and analogy from legal precedent. Sometimes, a purpose which was not regarded as charitable in the past will be accepted as charitable as times change. An example of this is the promotion of racial harmony, which was accepted as a charitable purpose only during the 1980s. The opposite can also occur. Even if an organisation is charitable at its inception each charity must ensure that it remains beneficial to the public each year.

The public benefit requirement must be carefully considered. The purposes of the charity must be clearly beneficial in nature and those benefits must be available to the public at large or to a sufficient section of the public. What constitutes a sufficient section of the public for one type of charity may not be sufficient for another and the category of people who are eligible to benefit may not amount to a section of the 'public' even if they are very numerous. The Charity Commission is obliged by statute to produce guidance on the public benefit requirement to which charities are subject and charity trustees *must* have regard to any such guidance when exercising any powers or duties to which the guidance is relevant. The statutory guidance is available on the Commission's pages at www.gov.uk and should be carefully read by anyone wishing to set up a charity, as well as existing charity trustees. The site also has extensive other guidance for charities. Charity trustees are not obliged to consider this other guidance, but most will find it helpful and informative.

Certain decisions of the Charity Commission may be appealed to the General Regulatory Chamber of the First-tier Tribunal. Information on the work of the tribunal is available at www.justice.gov.uk.

1.1.2 Scotland

In Scotland, which has a different legal system the origins of which can be traced back to Roman law, the meaning of 'charity' has traditionally been less technical and, for most purposes, equivalent to the relief of poverty. However, since the Charities and Trustee Investment (Scotland) Act 2005, an organisation must pass the 'charity test' and be registered in order to be a charity in Scotland. All organisations that refer to themselves as charities must be registered, even if they are also registered in another jurisdiction. As always, there are exceptions. A body can refer to itself as a charity without being registered in Scotland if it is established and entitled to refer to itself as a charity in a country or territory other than Scotland and it is managed or controlled wholly or mainly outside Scotland, provided that:

(a) it does not occupy land or premises in Scotland; or

(b) carry out activities in a shop, office or similar premises in Scotland.

If those requirements are met it may refer to itself as a charity as long as it also refers to itself as having been established under the laws of a country or territory other than Scotland.

To pass the charity test an organisation must have one or more of the purposes set out in the 2005 Act, provide public benefit in Scotland or elsewhere, not be a political party or have as a purpose the advancement of a political party and its constitution must not allow its property to be distributed for non-charitable purposes. Further, the activities of the organisation must not be controlled or directed by government ministers.

Information and guidance connected with Scottish charities can be obtained from the Office of the Scottish Charity Regulator ('the OSCR', usually just referred to as 'Oscar'), and it also provides a number of relevant publications on its website at www.oscr.org.uk. In particular, it provides guidance on how it determines whether an organisation meets the charity test.

Many decisions of the OSCR may be appealed to the Scottish Charity Appeals Panel.

1.1.3 Northern Ireland

In Northern Ireland the situation is governed by the Charities Act (Northern Ireland) 2008. This establishes the Charity Commission for Northern Ireland and the Act's approach to charitable status is very similar, but not identical, to that in England and Wales. The 2008 Act also disapplies certain regulatory provisions in the case of 'designated religious charities'. As in England and Wales (but unlike in Scotland), charitable status does not depend on registration. All institutions that are charities must, however, be registered. At the time of writing, existing charities are being called forward for registration in blocks.

Information and guidance on charity issues in the province can be obtained from the Northern Irish Commission. It has a number of relevant publications on its website at www.charitycommissionni.org.uk. It too produces statutory guidance on the public benefit requirement and charity trustees in Northern Ireland are again obliged to have regard to it.

Certain decisions of the Charity Commission for Northern Ireland may be appealed to the Charity Tribunal in Belfast.

1.1.4 The Republic of Ireland

Charities in the Republic of Ireland are governed by the Charities Act 2009 and regulated by the Charities Regulatory Authority. Reference should be made to the regulator's website at www.charitiesregulatoryauthority.ie for more information as to the operation of charity law and regulation in the Republic.

1.1.5 Exclusively charitable purposes

A charity, whether in the form of a trust or some other organisation, must be established for exclusively charitable purposes. It is not enough that some of its purposes are charitable if other purposes are commercial, political or for the benefit of private individuals, or even if they are simply 'good causes' that do not come within the legal concept of charity.

As long as the purposes are exclusively charitable it does not matter what form the trust or organisation takes, or what assets it has, or how many people are involved in running it. Charities come in all shapes and sizes. Of course, there are tried and tested forms of organisation and, depending on what the charity aims to achieve, the activities it is involved in and the resources available, there are optimum numbers for the governing body, staff and so on. There is also a relatively new form of charity known as a charitable incorporated organisation ('CIO'). The legislation in Scotland and Northern Ireland introduces such organisations in those jurisdictions, but the provisions are not yet in force in the latter.

These matters are discussed in more detail in Chapter 2.

1.2 WHO IS A CHARITY TRUSTEE?

The expression 'charity trustees' is defined in s 177 of the Charities Act 2011 to mean the persons responsible for the general management and control of the administration of a charity. The Scottish and Northern Irish legislation use the same definition. The definition encompasses the trustees of a charitable trust as well as the board of directors of a charitable company. Sometimes the constitution of a charity will describe such persons as the charity's 'governing body' or 'trustee board'. The function of this body, rather than the name given to the body or its members, determines whether its members are charity trustees. In this book, the expression 'charity trustees' or 'trustees' will be used as a shorthand expression for all those who constitute a charity's governing body, whether they are described as trustees, governors, feoffees, committee members, council members, directors, board members or some other name. It does not include employees of the governing body, although much of what is said about trustees is directly relevant to the responsibilities of senior staff and officers of a charity.

Some charities have more than one tier of responsibility within their governing structure. For example, the function of holding the legal title to property is often allocated to a body or group of people separate from the decision-makers themselves and (confusingly) the property-holders may be called 'trustees' in the charity's constitution. It is also not uncommon for day-to-day management decisions to be delegated to a small number of the governing body, often called the 'executive committee'.

Anyone who becomes involved in a formal capacity in the running of a charity should be quite clear from the outset whether or not he or she has the responsibilities of a charity trustee. In cases of doubt, the Charity Commission or a professional legal adviser will be able to clarify the position. All charity trustees have a duty of care and must ensure that its finances are used appropriately, prudently, lawfully and in accordance with its objects.

1.3 RESPONSIBILITIES OF CHARITY TRUSTEES

A trustee shares responsibility with his or her co-trustees. Unless there is a specific provision in the governing instrument requiring a different proportion, decisions are taken on a simple majority vote of those present at a meeting, usually with a casting vote for the chairman of the meeting. All the trustees are bound by a decision properly taken. Attendance at trustees' meetings is, therefore, one of the main responsibilities, and someone whose other commitments do not permit regular attendance should not be a trustee. Many charities have constitutions which provide for a minimum number, or 'quorum', of trustees to attend meetings in order for them to be able to act.

1.3.1 Public trust

Trusteeship of a charity calls for a high degree of integrity. It is essential that all decisions are taken in good faith in the interests of the charity itself. People who have been convicted of offences involving deception or dishonesty (unless the convictions are spent), or who have been disqualified from acting as company directors or removed involuntarily from previous charity trusteeships by the court or the regulator, or have been made bankrupt or entered into a voluntary arrangement with creditors, are generally disqualified from acting as charity trustees. They cannot lawfully become charity trustees and may suffer criminal penalties if they do. A professional legal adviser or the Charity Commission will clarify the situation in case of doubt if given the full facts. In suitable cases, the Commission will waive this restriction. Similar provisions apply in Scotland and Northern Ireland.

1.3.2 Conflict

A trustee who stands to gain, however innocently, from a decision of the charity's governing body, or who finds that there is any conflict between his or her duty to the charity and his or her personal interests, should disclose this and take no part in the decision. If the conflict is sufficiently serious or is likely to be prolonged, the trustee concerned may have to avoid attending meetings for a time, or even resign his or her trusteeship. If, however, the trustees as a whole are convinced that the resignation would not be in the charity's interests, they may seek a special dispensation from the regulator. If a trustee is found to have impermissibly benefited from his or her position as a trustee, he or she may be required to restore to the charity any private gains enjoyed. If a trustee appears to be able to offer services to the charity, the charity may enter into a contract for the trustee to provide those services and receive remuneration provided that the relevant requirements under the charities legislation are fulfilled or it is authorised by the regulator or the court.

Conflicts can also arise between a trustee's duty to the charity and some other public obligation. This is not uncommon because those who are willing to shoulder responsibilities usually tend to have further responsibilities placed upon them. Charity trustees are often local councillors, school governors or trustees of other charities. Alternatively, trustees may be appointed by outside bodies which have an interest of their own in the area in which the charity's work lies. If the trustee is appointed by, or a member of, another body, he or she must remember that, as a trustee, his or her duty to the charity overrides all other obligations. If an irreconcilable conflict arises, he or she may have to avoid taking part in decisions of the charity, or attending meetings or, in extreme cases, to resign from one or other position.

1.3.3 Delegation

Trustees must not delegate their responsibilities, except insofar as is permitted by the governing instrument of the charity and by the general law. Thus, trustees take personal responsibility for all major decisions made in their name and, if they allow someone else to decide something on their behalf, they are legally responsible for that decision. They must know, therefore, what is going on within the charity at all times, and have workable procedures for dealing with emergencies.

Many charities employ staff to carry out the day-to-day management of the charity and employ specialist managers to take care of property or investments. It is vitally important that staff and managers should have clear policy guidelines to work to and ready access to the trustees should the need arise. Good practice is for the trustees to decide in advance what their policies should be and to decide on written policy documents.

1.3.4 Contracts with third parties

Contracts made with third parties on the charity's behalf are the legal responsibility of the contracting parties. Where the charity is an incorporated body, such as a limited liability company, the body itself, as a legal person in its own right, is the contracting party and individual members of the body will not, generally, be personally liable. There is an exception where a company is operating whilst technically insolvent. Where, however, the charity is unincorporated, the trustees themselves will ordinarily be the contracting parties and if the charity is not able to meet its commitment, the trustees will normally be personally liable. Contracting as a trustee does not, itself, limit a trustee's potential liability. This underlines the need for trustees to take care not to enter into any commitment on the charity's behalf which the charity's resources will not meet, unless the trustees are prepared to underwrite it personally.

Other situations and activities, such as ownership of property, operations on land or buildings, the employment of staff or fundraising events can also give rise to legal liabilities or other costs. It is wise, in order to protect both the charity and the individual trustees, to insure fully against all usual risks.

1.3.5 Other duties

The law imposes a number of more specific duties on charity trustees, for example the requirement to keep accounts and to produce an annual report, to supply certain information and documents to their regulator, and to seek their regulator's consent to certain transactions or acts. These specific duties are dealt with in detail later in this book.

Finally, it is worthwhile for every trustee to bear in mind that the charity has a reputation of its own, which is dependent on the conduct of its trustees and their staff. A charity may be a landlord, an employer, a neighbour or a provider of services. The law does not permit a charity to operate otherwise than in furtherance of its purposes, but there is nothing to prevent it from acting efficiently, fairly and reasonably in its relations with the rest of the world while doing so.

1.4 CHARITABLE STATUS – EXAMPLES

These are some contrasting examples of decisions by the English courts and the Charity Commission on charitable status that illustrate the fine distinctions which sometimes have to be drawn in interpreting the law. Many textbooks have discussions about what has or has not been accepted as charitable. Perhaps the most useful tool for gaining a flavour of what is charitable is the Register of Charities in England and Wales itself. This is maintained by the Commission and is available online. The website has an efficient search engine which allows the Register to be searched by reference to key words or areas.

The examples given below are decisions made before the 2011 Act was passed:

(1) A gift for paying for holidays for low-paid employees of a particular firm was held to be charitable, even though the beneficiaries were not a section of the public (1914).

(2) A fund set up by a merchant bank to assist sick or convalescent employees was rejected by the Commission since the beneficiaries were not a section of the public and were not in financial need (circa 1980).

(3) A trust for the poor relatives of the founder was upheld as charitable (1995). This type of case is now regarded as exceptional and it is unlikely that new charities of this type will be entered on the Register of Charities.

(4) A trust under the will of Mrs Bernard Shaw for teaching the Irish the arts of conversation and self-control was held to be charitable as it was educational (1952).

(5) A trust under the will of Mr Bernard Shaw to construct a phonetic alphabet was held to be non-charitable because, although this would have increased knowledge, the will did not provide for the results to be communicated to the public and, in any case, the trust was considered to be political (1957).

(6) A gift by will to a an enclosed order of nuns was held to be non-charitable because, although this promoted a religious purpose, there could be no proven benefit to the public from private prayer (1949).

(7) A gift to a synagogue which was open only to members was held to be charitable because the worshippers would go out into the community during the rest of the week and, thereby, spread the benefits of religious activities to the public (1966).

(8) A trust under the will of Mr Strakosch to improve relations between English and Dutch-speaking South Africans was held to be non-charitable because it was considered to be political (1952).

(9) A body established in Birmingham for the promotion of racial harmony within the local community was accepted as charitable by the Commission (1982).

(10) A rifle club and a pistol club were held not to be charities (1994).

(11) A Training Enterprise Council was held not to be a charity (1996).

(12) A trust to promote the reintroduction of the wolf into Scotland was not charitable, having a purpose that was designed to influence the opinion of the public and the decisions of the relevant Government authorities (2003).

CHAPTER 2

CONSTITUTIONAL REQUIREMENTS

2.1 SETTING UP

Forming a charity involves a number of stages. First there is the general idea, then a decision to take that idea further, a series of meetings between the promoters, followed by a period of preparation and, finally, the day on which the new charity comes into formal existence. Usually, registration (or recognition) follows soon afterwards. Anything may go wrong at any stage until the formal establishment of the charity. There are numerous pitfalls and the possibility that the promoters will disagree on the proper direction and development of the charity so that their enthusiasm for the project eventually peters out.

The first task in establishing a charity is to determine its purposes, the people who will be involved and the resources which will be available to it. This process, which may take some time, should enable a decision to be taken on the form which the charity will take. Where the charity is to be founded by an individual, a group of people or an existing organisation prepared to donate money at the outset, the classic form of declaration of trust will probably be the simplest and most convenient form of establishing the charity, since it allows the founder (or founders) a considerable degree of control. Where, however, a lot of fundraising activity is necessary and a larger number of people will be involved, it may not be practicable to proceed without building in a measure of 'democracy'. In that case, an unincorporated charitable association may be the most appropriate and flexible legal form. If the charity is to undertake activities involving the employment of a substantial number of staff, or if it will necessarily encounter commercial risks in carrying out its work, a company limited by guarantee may be the best solution. Examples of these older three forms of establishing a charity can be found in Appendices A to D. These are English precedents promulgated by the Charity Commission for England and Wales but may be adapted for use elsewhere.

At Appendices E and F are constitutions for a form of incorporated charity called a charitable incorporated organisation, again being the versions promulgated by the Charity Commission for England and Wales. This type of charity enjoys its own corporate existence, like a company, but is regulated only by the Charity Commission and not by the Registrar of Companies. Regulations under the Charities Act 2011 prescribe the essential elements of the constitution of this type of organisation. The precedents reproduced in this book provide for two different structures. The first is a CIO with a wider voting membership and the second is a CIO where the charity trustees are the only voting members.

Some charities are established by will and it cannot be emphasised too strongly that, if this course is chosen, professional advice should be obtained before the will is made. Case law is strewn with disputes as to the effect of an ineptly drafted gift and the monies intended for charity are tied up until the dispute is resolved and may be eroded or exhausted by legal costs.

There are some other cases. Where the charity is to be a housing association, the best recognised legal form is a society registered under the Co-operative and Community Benefit Societies Act 2014 (once known as an 'industrial and provident society'). Where the charity is fortunate enough to have substantial patronage, a Royal Charter may be sought. Occasionally, a charity will be set up by an Act of Parliament.

A certain amount of help can be obtained from specialist organisations, but it is generally advisable to seek professional advice before finalising the form of a new charity, and essential to do so if there is anything unusual in the proposals.

2.2 CHOOSING THE LEGAL FORM

It should be clear from the outset what the effect will be of choosing one form of establishing a charity over another. Once the charity has been set up the trustees and officers will be bound to observe its terms and follow the procedures which it lays down.

Under English law, the simplest form to set up and operate is the declaration of trust. The trust is not a separate person from its trustees and there are no special formalities apart from the requirements of charity law, including registration in most cases. HMRC do not require trust instruments executed on or after 13 March 2008 to be stamped.

An unincorporated charitable association can also be simple to operate, provided that the terms of the constitution are clear and workable. Again, no separate legal person is created.

Running a charitable company limited by guarantee involves some operational technicalities and should not be undertaken lightly. First, the formalities on setting up the company necessitate registration as a company. It will, therefore, be desirable to use the services of a solicitor, accountant or company formation agent. The company is a separate legal person from those who run it. There are also a number of requirements under company law which will have to be observed in addition to the requirements of charity law. The company must have a registered office (an official address); annual returns and accounts must be submitted to Companies House; a register of members must be kept and an annual general meeting of the members held. There is an important requirement *not* to continue to operate if the company is insolvent, ie if its assets are not sufficient to enable its debts and other liabilities to be met. Company law is underpinned by statutory offences.

The situation is the much the same in Northern Ireland except that all charities must register with the Northern Irish Commission. Setting up a charity in Scotland is a little different. An organisation sends its governing document, an application form and trustee declaration forms to OSCR. OSCR will assess the application against the charity test and, if successful, the organisation will be entered on the Scottish Register of Charities. It is registration as a charity which confers charitable status.

A charitable incorporated organisation is a form of charity whose structure is intended to relieve trustees of many of the complicated company law requirements. It comes into existence as a charity when registered by the regulator.

Whatever form you choose, your constitution, whether a declaration of trust, rules of an unincorporated association or a company's articles of association, must make it clear what the purposes of the organisation are, how it is to achieve those purposes, who is to benefit and the extent of the area of benefit. Each and every purpose must be a charitable purpose. The purposes of an organisation are usually set out in its constitution in an 'objects clause'. The Charity Commission for England and Wales has a number of model objects for various types of charity and these are reproduced in Appendix G. Organisations with poorly defined objects may well find their application for registration rejected, leading to delay in getting on with the work that those involved want to do. In some cases, where an accepted model is not used, it is wise to send the Commission a draft of the proposed governing instrument and even seek to discuss the matter with them to explain exactly what is proposed.

2.3 REGISTRATION IN ENGLAND AND WALES

Most charities in England and Wales must be registered with the Charity Commission. The main exceptions are those classed as 'exempt charities', listed in Sch 3 of the Charities Act 2011. These charities will have their own 'principal regulator' and cannot be registered. Again, certain charities are 'excepted charities' which do not need to register if their annual income is under £100,000. Very small charities, which have annual gross income of under £5,000 and which are not CIOs, do not have to register and the Commission does not currently register them save in special circumstances, such as where registration is a condition of a substantial gift. This does not alter their status as a charity, which is a matter of the general law, and they are nonetheless subject to regulation by the Commission.

2.3.1 Exempt charities

Exempt charities consist of certain major charities and types of charities listed in the Charities Act 2011, Sch 3. Exempt charities cannot register and are subject to their own 'principal regulator'. Apart from institutions such as the British Museum and the British Library, they include most universities, colleges, registered friendly societies and certain providers of social housing. They also include Qualifying Academy Proprietors (operating free schools and academies), which are regulated by the Department for Education.

2.3.2 Excepted charities

Some charities do not need to register because they are 'excepted' from that requirement. These include Scout and Guide groups and churches and chapels of certain Christian denominations providing that their gross income does not exceed £100,000 a year. They do not have to register or produce annual returns, but are otherwise subject to Charity Commission regulation.

2.3.3 Registration process

The registration process is explained on the Commission web pages. There is an online application portal. You will need to provide:
- your organisation's main bank or building society details;
- its public contact details, including a postal address;
- a copy of the governing document as a PDF file;
- in the case of a company: a copy of the certificate of incorporation and memorandum;
- proof that your charity's income is over £5,000 (unless it is a CIO).

Trustee declaration forms from each trustee must also be submitted.

2.3.4 Name of charity

The Charity Commission will consider the name of the new charity. If they find that it is the same as, or similar to, the name of an existing charity, they may require it to be changed. This applies to informal names and acronyms, as well as the formal, legal title of the charity. They may also require a new name to be chosen if the proposed name is misleading or offensive.

2.3.5 Registration number

Once the Charity Commission have accepted a proposed charity for registration a registration number will be allocated to the charity. This should be recorded since it will need to be quoted in future correspondence with both the Commission and HMRC. It will usually appear on the charity's literature.

2.3.6 Significance of registration

Registration does not itself confer charitable status, except in the case of a CIO, which only comes into being when registered. Whether any other sort of trust or organisation is a charity is a matter of the general law and depends on its purposes rather than any specific formality. The significance of registration for most charities is that it provides conclusive proof that the organisation is legally a charity and has complied with the legal obligation to register. This does not mean that it is necessarily well run, although the Charity Commission's monitoring activities are designed to provide an assurance that there is a degree of supervision applicable, at least to larger charities. A charity which should be registered, but by some oversight has not been registered, can be registered late, but the trustees may be asked to send the Commission more information, including accounts, than is required for a proposed charity.

Details of the charity's purposes and finances are publicly available on the Commission's website. Registration underlines the fact that a charity is for the public benefit, for which the charity trustees are accountable.

Every registered charity with a gross income of £10,000 or more in its last financial year must state the fact that it is registered on many of its official publications, including cheques, invoices and fundraising literature.

2.4 REGISTRATION IN SCOTLAND

OSCR maintains a register of charities and, unlike in England, Wales and Northern Ireland, charitable status is dependent on registration. All bodies which represent themselves as charities in Scotland are required to register, subject to certain exceptions, and this includes charities established in England, Wales or Northern Ireland which occupy land or premises or carry on activities in a shop, office or similar premises in Scotland.

2.5 REGISTRATION IN NORTHERN IRELAND

In Northern Ireland, all charities are required to register. The Charity Commission is in the process of 'calling forward' existing charities for registration in tranches. New charities seeking to apply to HMRC for charitable tax exemptions should indicate this in the 'Special Circumstances' section of an 'Expression of Intent' form submitted to the Commission. This will enable the Commission to determine whether to add the charity to the 'special circumstances' list and fast-track its registration.

2.6 CHANGING THE CONSTITUTION

Practical experience in administering a charity, or changes in its resources, in the relevant law or in the circumstances of the beneficiaries, or more general changes in society, may convince the trustees that the governing instrument needs to be altered or updated. In extreme cases, the purpose of the charity may no longer provide a sensible use for its assets. It is one of the principles of charity law that, if necessary, and provided that the correct procedure is carried out, the purposes or other provisions of a charity's governing instrument may be altered. In fact, it is the trustees' legal duty to take steps to introduce change, where this is necessary in order to make effective use of the charity's resources.

If it appears that an alteration is needed, it is often wise first to double check that an unduly restrictive interpretation of the existing document has not been adopted. Sometimes trustees will be advised that there already exists an implied power to use the charity's resources for the new activity which they have in mind.

If a more liberal interpretation will not assist, or would strain the language of the governing instrument, the next question is whether there is a specific power to alter the instrument.

2.6.1 Alteration to the constitution of a charitable company

There is a power contained in the Companies Act 2006 for a company to alter its articles of association. In the case of a charitable company in England and Wales, if it is proposed to change the objects clause, or to any provision in the articles which governs the use of the charity's assets or so as to authorise benefits to be conferred on directors, members or connected persons, the Charity Commission's written consent will be needed in advance and it will also be necessary to follow the procedures of company law to effect the required change. Failure to obtain the Commission's consent means the alteration is of no effect.

The Commission are unlikely to give their consent without good reason and will normally expect the new purposes to be akin to the original purposes. A fundamental change, for example to assist old people instead of children or vice versa, or to benefit the inhabitants of a completely different geographical area, is not likely to be accepted by the Commission, without at least negotiating some special arrangement to keep any existing assets available for the old purposes. The amendment must be registered at Companies House in the usual way and notice of the change given to the Commission.

The position is the same in Northern Ireland. In Scotland, the charity must give at least 42 days' advanced notice of certain proposed changes or actions to OSCR and cannot proceed without its consent. These are:
(a) amending its constitution so far as it relates to its purposes,
(b) amalgamating with another body,
(c) winding itself up or dissolving itself,
(d) applying to the court in relation to any action set out in paragraphs (a)–(c).

Except in the case of a change which alters the charity's purposes, which requires express consent, consent is deemed to have been given if a refusal or a direction not to effect the change for a period up to 6 months is not given within 28 days of the giving of notice. Other changes to the constitution must be notified to OSCR within 3 months.

2.6.2 Alteration to the constitution of a CIO

Part 11 of the Charities Act 2011 allows the members of a CIO to amend its constitution. A 75% majority of members voting is required at a general meeting and unanimity of members if the decision is made otherwise than at a general meeting. The power is not exercisable in such a way as to cause the CIO to cease to be a charity. The prior written consent of the Commission is required for any proposed amendment which would change the purposes of the CIO, alter the application of its property on dissolution or allow benefits to be obtained by the charity trustees, members of the CIO or connected persons. The amendment is ineffective without such consent. The copy of the resolution containing the amendment, the amended constitution and any other documents or information required by the Commission must be sent to the Commission within 15 days and the amendment only takes effect when registered.

Scottish Charitable Incorporated Organisations also have power to amend their constitutions but a two-thirds majority of the members voting is required if the resolution is passed at a general meeting or there must be unanimity of members generally if the resolution is not passed at a general meeting. The prior consent of OSCR is required to the alteration of purposes. The provisions as to CIOs in Northern Ireland are not yet in force.

2.6.3 Express power of alteration of the constitution of unincorporated charities

There is often an express power of alteration in the constitution of an unincorporated charitable association. If such a power exists the procedures must be followed meticulously. This generally means notifying the members in advance and calling a general meeting. If a change in the purposes is envisaged, it is wise to consult the relevant regulator well in advance, even where the constitution does not specifically require this. The same applies in the case of a declaration of trust which contains an express power of alteration. In England, Wales and Northern Ireland such changes will need to be notified to the relevant Commission. In Scotland, the prior consent of OSCR will be required in the case of any of the actions referred to in **2.6.1** above.

2.6.4 Alternative procedures

If there is no power of alteration, or if the power in question does not extend to the sort of alteration envisaged (for example, where it specifically excludes a change in the purposes of the charity) and the trustees are convinced that the purposes should be altered, there are two alternative procedures, depending on the size of the charity and the jurisdiction in which it is governed.

2.6.4.1 Statutory power in England, Wales and Northern Ireland

Part 13 of the Charities Act 2011 confers powers on the trustees of unincorporated charities in England and Wales to alter the purposes or administrative provisions of the charity. If the income of the charity did not exceed £10,000 in its last financial year and it does not hold 'designated land' (land required by the governing document to be used for the purposes of the charity) the trustees have a statutory power to pass a resolution (by a two-thirds majority) to alter the charity's purposes. They must be satisfied that it is expedient in the interests of the charity and any new purposes must be akin to the original purposes. The terms of the resolution must then be sent to the Charity Commission together with a statement of the reasons for the alteration. The alteration does not take effect until 60 days after notice has been received by the Commission and will not do so if the Commission objects to the alteration either on procedural grounds or on the merits of the proposal. There are rather wider powers to change administrative provisions which apply even where the income of the unincorporated charity exceeds £10,000. Similar provisions apply in Northern Ireland under Part 12 of the 2008 Act, but the power is not available in Scotland. A Scottish charity without a power to amend its constitution will need to apply to OSCR for a reorganisation scheme.

2.6.4.2 Scheme in England, Wales and Northern Ireland

Where an alteration is outside the power of the charity, it will be necessary to apply to the Charity Commission for a 'scheme'. A scheme is a legal document, equivalent to a court order, which modifies or replaces the existing governing instrument. Many older charities are now governed entirely by a scheme or series of schemes. The Commission for England and Wales have considerable experience of making schemes and have developed an extensive body of precedents. The Northern Irish Commission has recently been created but will no doubt draw on the experience of its English and Welsh cousin. The procedure in England and Wales is set out below.

2.6.4.2.1 Procedure

The trustees should first write to the Charity Commission, or seek an interview, to explain the difficulties in administering the charity under its present governing instrument, identifying every difficulty. They should be ready with their ideas for a more workable arrangement but be prepared to consider alternatives which the Commission, from their experience of similar situations, may suggest. Once the Commission are satisfied of the need for a scheme and have agreed on what it is broadly to achieve, it will invite the trustees to make a formal application.

The Commission will then prepare a draft scheme for the trustees to consider. Uncontroversial schemes may then be made without the need for publicity, but in more controversial cases the trustees will be expected to have carried out consultations and the Commission might direct further publicity for the proposals. It will then consider any further representations received. In very complex or controversial cases, it may decide that the matter would be better determined by the court and decline to exercise its own powers to make a scheme.

Assuming that there are no objections (which is usually the case) or that the objections can be overcome, the Commission will seal the new scheme, thus bringing it into effect. The remaining step is the publication of final notices to the effect that the scheme has been established.

There is a right of appeal to the First-tier Tribunal (Charity) from the decision of the Commission to make a scheme, which may be brought by the Attorney General or a person interested in the charity. Ordinarily, appeals must be brought within 3 months. Such appeals are quite rare but trustees should remember in the immediate aftermath of the making of a scheme that there is a risk that it might be set aside or modified. Where possible, trustees should avoid entering into major expenditure or commitments in reliance upon the scheme until it is clear that an appeal will not be pursued.

The trustees will not need professional advice concerning the establishment of a scheme unless the Commission require them to obtain it or, in some cases, the trustees have specific proposals of their own and wish to formulate them in detail, rather than simply relying on the Commission's recommendations.

2.6.4.2.2 Cy-près doctrine

A scheme may either alter the administrative arrangements of the charity, for example by changing the composition of the body of trustees, or it may alter the purposes of the charity, or both. Where the purposes are to be altered the Commission are bound by the cy-près (pronounced 'see pray') doctrine, a Norman-French expression which goes back to the fourteenth century and means (probably) 'close to' or 'akin to'. The existence of this doctrine is one of the reasons why some charities have survived for hundreds of years and still perform a useful and relevant function. Statute provides when a cy-près occasion has arisen. In summary property may be applied cy-près:

- where the original purposes, in whole or in part have been fulfilled, or cannot be carried out, or cannot be carried out according to the directions given and to the spirit of the gift;
- where the original purposes provide a use for part only of the property available;
- where the property available and other property applicable for similar purposes can be more effectively and suitably used in conjunction and applied to common purposes, having regard to the spirit of the gift on the

one hand and current social and economic circumstances on the other, which are referred to in the 2011 Act as 'the appropriate considerations';

- where the original purposes were laid down by reference to an area which then was but has since ceased to be a unit for some other purpose, or a class of persons or an area which has for any reason since ceased to be suitable, again having regard to the appropriate considerations, or to be practical in administering the gift; or
- where the original purposes have been adequately provided for by other means;
- where the original purposes have ceased, as being useless or harmful to the community or for other reasons, to be in law charitable, or ceased in any other way to provide a suitable and effective method of using the property available by virtue of the gift, regard again being had to the appropriate considerations.

A good cy-près scheme will enlarge the discretion of the trustees by not being too specific about the method of fulfilling the charity's purpose, thus enabling the charity to adapt to future changes in the surrounding circumstances.

There are also schemes available for the application of moneys raised by an appeal that has failed, for example where a charity has run an appeal for a specific purpose and the sums raised are insufficient to allow that purpose to be carried out. The reason that a scheme is required in such circumstances is that where money has been given by donors for a particular charitable purpose, it would be a breach of trust to apply them to another purpose.

The provisions as to schemes in Northern Ireland are substantively the same.

2.6.4.3 Scheme in Scotland

In Scotland, there is an analogous regime allowing OSCR to make a 'reorganisation scheme' altering the purposes or administrative provisions of the charity. Trustees of Scottish charities should contact OSCR.

2.6.5 Reviewing aims and procedures

As a general rule, it is a good idea for trustees to give serious consideration to a charity's purposes, administrative provisions and general direction on a regular basis, possibly quite frequently when the charity is operating in a rapidly changing field. In addition, changes in local government or health service administration or in recommended methods of treatment, changes in local or central government provision or grant-making policies, or the establishment of other organisations operating in the same field, can all provide specific reasons to consider change.

2.6.6 The new governing instrument

The original of the new document should be kept in a safe place, with the earlier documents, and a copy should be supplied to each of the trustees and senior officers.

2.7 MERGER

It may be desirable to merge two or more charities which have compatible purposes, in order to achieve economies of scale, avoid duplication of effort and make more effective use of the combined assets. There are various practical questions which must be resolved, for example who will be trustees, whether all existing staff will continue to be employed, what the name of the new charity will be and where it will have its headquarters, etc. Serious consideration of these matters must be undertaken and adequate time and discussion should be allowed to find the best available solution. It is also important that one body which is taking on the functions of another should carry out careful checks to ensure that there are no hidden problems – either financial or legal – in its past administration.

2.7.1 Transfer of assets

There are several possible legal methods of merging charities, depending on the original governing instruments. The simplest method is for one charity to wind up under a power contained in its constitution and transfer its assets over to another charity, which may, or may not, effect some alteration in its name or governing instrument as a consequence.

Another method of achieving amalgamation is to set up a new charity incorporating elements from the original charities, which then wind up and transfer their assets to the new charity.

Where this is done, problems can arise where a charity which has been wound up has been left a legacy or is entitled to payments under covenant. One way of dealing with this in the past was to maintain the charity which would otherwise cease to exist as a 'shell' to receive further legacies. However, statute now provides a more satisfactory solution. Part 16 of the 2011 Act provides for a register of charity mergers. Where a 'relevant charity merger' – achieved by the transfer of the assets to a charity of another charity which is then to cease to exist – is registered in the register of charity mergers, then, with some exceptions, a gift to the transferring charity will be treated as a gift to the recipient. The situation is the same in Northern Ireland under Part 14 of the 2008 Act.

Sometimes, however, a charity will not have a power in its constitution allowing it to transfer its assets and wind itself up. In this case there are two methods of achieving the result depending on the size of the charity.

2.7.1.1 *Statutory power*

If the income of an unincorporated charity in England and Wales did not exceed £10,000 in its last financial year and the charity does not hold designated land, the trustees are permitted by statute to pass a resolution (by a two-thirds majority) to transfer all its assets to another charity having similar objectives. The restriction on the power to charities with an income of no more than £10,000 does not apply if the proposal is to transfer the assets to a CIO. There are additional considerations where the charity has a permanent endowment.

Notice of the resolution and the reasons for it must be given to the Commission, which can direct public notice of the resolution to be given. The resolution takes effect 60 days after the Commission has received notice of the resolution, during which time it may object on procedural grounds or on the merits of the decision, in which case the resolution will not take effect.

When transferred, the assets are held by the recipient charity subject to any restrictions on expenditure to which it was subject as property of the transferor charity and the trustees of the recipient charity must secure, so far as is reasonably practicable, that the property is applied for such of its purposes as are substantially similar to those of the transferor.

Similar provisions apply in Northern Ireland although they allow a transfer to be effected by a charity holding designated land where the value of the land does not exceed £90,000. There is, however, no dispensation from the requirement that the charity has a gross income of no more than £10,000.

2.7.1.2 *Scheme*

In other cases the appropriate procedure will be to apply to the Charity Commission (or in Scotland, OSCR) for a scheme, which may either simply authorise the transfer of assets or, if the situation requires more elaborate arrangements, take the form of a cy-près or reorganisation scheme formally providing for the charities concerned to be administered as one charity. The cy-près procedure enables the original charities to continue to exist in a technical sense, so that the new combined charity is thus entitled to any covenanted payments or legacies to which the original charities are, or may become, entitled.

2.7.1.3 *Amalgamation of CIOs*

CIOs may apply to the Commission to amalgamate. It must be supplied with the proposed constitution of the merged CIO and copies of resolutions by each of the amalgamating CIOs approving the amalgamation and adopting the proposed new constitution. The resolutions must be passed by a 75% majority of those voting at a general meeting, or unanimously by the members if not passed at a general meeting. On amalgamation, the property, rights and liabilities of the old CIOs are transferred to the new amalgamated CIO, the old bodies are dissolved and a subsequent gift to any of the old CIOs is treated as a gift to the amalgamated CIO.

Similarly, the members of a CIO may resolve to transfer its assets to another CIO. The resolution must again be passed by a 75% majority of those voting at a general meeting, or unanimously by the members if not passed at a general meeting, but the resolution will not be effective until approved by the Commission. There must also be a resolution by the transferee CIO, with the same requirements as to majority, accepting the transfer.

The Commission must refuse to confirm the resolution of the transferor CIO if it considers that there is a serious risk that the transferee CIO would be unable properly to pursue the purposes of the transferor CIO and may do so if the transferor and transferee are not sufficiently matched with regard to their purposes, the disposition of property on disposition and the extent to which a benefit may be conferred on the trustees, members or connected persons.

SCIOs may also apply to OSCR to amalgamate or resolve (subject to OSCR confirmation) to transfer its property to another SCIO. The requisite majority for the relevant resolutions is two-thirds of the members voting at a general meeting, or unanimity if not passed at a meeting).

2.8 WINDING UP

Some charities continue indefinitely while others, such as appeal funds, have a limited lifespan from the outset and cease to exist once their purposes have been achieved and their assets have been used. In other cases a charity may be brought to an end deliberately, either in the course of a de facto amalgamation, or to replace an existing, unincorporated association with a charitable company. A charity may also be brought to an end because it has ceased to be financially viable or to perform a useful function.

A charitable company may be wound up under the general law. It ought to be wound up (or at least should cease to operate) if it becomes insolvent, ie if its assets will not cover its liabilities. Its constitution should state that any assets remaining after all liabilities have been met should be transferred to another charity having similar objectives or, failing that, should be applied for some other charitable purpose. It is wise to attempt to find a recipient charity which is carrying on work which the defunct charity would have supported if it had been able to do so, and to ensure that the recipient charity is registered (if it is liable to be registered) and is up to date with its accounts. If the remaining assets are sufficient, or if the purposes to be supported are being carried on by different charities, there may be more than one recipient.

There is no reason why a recipient charity should not be a charity which is administered by one or more of the charity trustees of the defunct charity, provided, of course, that the purpose of the recipient charity is similar. That should not, however, be the only reason for choosing that recipient. The trustees retain, to the end, their fiduciary duty to apply the charitable funds conscientiously for the purpose for which they were contributed, and must be prepared to justify their decisions on objective grounds.

In Scotland, the consent of OSCR is required to the winding up or dissolution of a charity other than a SCIO (which is achieved by application to OSCR in any event).

2.8.1 Express power to wind up

In the case of a charitable unincorporated association or a modern trust, it is usual to find an express power to wind up and a direction to apply the remaining assets (if any) for similar charitable purposes. If there is no power of dissolution, but there is a power of amendment which is not expressly restricted, it may be possible to adopt an amendment to the constitution which confers a power of dissolution. It is advisable to consult the Charity Commission, OSCR or an independent legal adviser before doing so, to ensure that the power is properly exercised and cannot be challenged at a later date. Books and records should be kept for at least 6 years.

Once a charity in England and Wales has been dissolved and its remaining assets transferred, the last trustees should write to the Commission with a copy of the final statement of account, showing that no assets remain, and ask the Commission to remove the charity from the register. The Commission are bound to remove any charity which has ceased to exist or to operate and will not re-allocate the registration number but keep a record of it. Books and records should be kept for at least 3 years thereafter in the case of companies and CIOs and 6 years in the case of other forms.

2.8.2 Statutory power

Sometimes there will be no express power permitting the dissolution of an unincorporated charity. If, particularly in the case of an older trust or a charity governed by a scheme, there is any permanent capital (technically called 'permanent endowment', meaning that the charity has the use of the income but must preserve the capital) there will generally be no power to wind up the charity because the endowment simply cannot be spent. Statute provides mechanisms to get around this problem. Where the gross income of the charity does not exceed £1,000 and the value of the endowment does not exceed £10,000, the trustees may resolve to free the endowment from restrictions on the expenditure of capital. The charity trustees must be satisfied that the purposes set out in the trusts to which the fund is subject could be carried out more effectively if the capital of the fund, or the relevant portion of the capital, could be expended as well as income accruing to it, rather than just such income. This will allow the fund to be spent. There is a similar power for larger unincorporated charities, but the concurrence of the Charity Commission is required. Substantively identical provisions apply in Northern Ireland.

2.8.3 Winding up of CIOs

If the requisite 75% majority has been achieved at a general meeting (or there is a unanimous vote otherwise than at a general meeting) on a resolution to wind up a CIO in England and Wales, an application can be made to the Commission for the dissolution of the CIO by removing it from the register. This cannot be done if:

(a) the CIO has any debts or other liabilities that have not been settled or otherwise provided for in full; or

(b) any decision which must be taken for the purpose of giving effect to the constitutional directions has not been taken.

There are various other restrictions where the CIO is subject to insolvency procedures. Criminal sanctions apply. Insolvent CIOs may be wound up under the Insolvency Act 1986. Specialist advice should be obtained. In Scotland both solvent and insolvent SCIOs may apply to OSCR for dissolution.

2.9 CY-PRÈS SCHEMES – EXAMPLES

The following examples illustrate schemes which have been made, or on which decisions have been taken, where the original purposes of the charities were no longer viable:

(1) Roman's bequest for games which would have been illegal: memorial to testator in some other way (circa AD300).

(2) Surplus almshouse land: used for school (eighteenth century).

(3) Trust to maintain bishopric in America: trust to maintain bishopric in Canada (nineteenth century).

(4) Elizabethan charity for the redemption of captives of the Barbary pirates: trust for educational purposes (nineteenth century).

(5) Ancient charities for prisons: trust for relief of poverty (nineteenth century).

(6) Ancient charity for boys out of control: boys' public school (nineteenth century).

(7) Historic almshouse building no longer required for housing purposes: museum (1961).

(8) Charity to relieve the poor rate: trust to benefit inhabitants generally (1971).

(9) Trust to provide eleven barrels of white herrings and eight barrels of red herrings to the poor of a fishing village: trust for relief of need in the area (1973).

(10) Teetotal village hall: alcoholic drinks permitted (1975).

(11) Hospital which closed: grant-making trust to relieve the sick (1976).

(12) Appeal fund to provide village hall (never built) to commemorate the Coronation: provision of a public clock and garden to commemorate the Queen's Silver Jubilee (1977).

(13) Ancient charity to give loans to young men: trust for education and advancement in life for young people (1988).

(14) Elizabethan charity to maintain trunk road through London: trust to benefit inhabitants of relevant boroughs (1989).

(15) Old charities to provide grazing rights for freemen of borough and their widows: trust for benefit of all the inhabitants (1993)

(16) Scheme to permit the merger of two independent schools in Lytham St Annes (2012).

CHAPTER 3

MONEY AND PROPERTY

3.1 ACCOUNTING

It is clear that anyone who controls money held for public purposes should keep a careful record of it and be accountable to the public for its use. Whatever other economies are adopted, the area of financial control and accountability should not be skimped, even if this involves expenditure which does not directly further the charity's purposes.

3.2 ACCOUNTS AND RECORD-KEEPING

In England and Wales charity trustees must ensure that accounting records are kept in respect of the charity which are sufficient to show and explain all the charity's transactions, and which are such as to disclose at any time, with reasonable accuracy, the financial position of the charity at that time, and enable the trustees to ensure that accounts prepared comply with the applicable regulations. In Scotland 'proper accounting records' must be kept. The records must be kept for at least 6 years.

In Northern Ireland the equivalent provisions of the Charities Act (Northern Ireland) 2008 are not yet fully in force and there are interim reporting requirements in place. The reporting requirements in Northern Ireland will therefore not be discussed here.

3.2.1 Structure

For accounting periods starting on 1 January 2015, charitable companies and other forms of charities preparing accounts on an accruals basis must decide whether to prepare the accounts under the Financial Reporting Standard for Smaller Entities ('FRSSE') or the Financial Reporting Standard ('FRS 102'). The Charity Commission and the Scottish Charity Regulator have produced a Statement of Recommended Practice ('SORP') for those two regimes. The FRSSE regime is only applicable to charities meeting two of the following three criteria in the current and previous year:
- gross income not exceeding £6.5m;
- total assets not exceeding £3.26m;

- no more than 50 staff.

There are different thresholds for groups.

The accounts of a charity prepared under the FRSSE regime should comprise the following:

- a statement of financial activities (endearingly abbreviated to 'SoFA') that provides an analysis of a charity's income and expenditure and movement in funds in the reporting period;
- a balance sheet which sets out a charity's assets and liabilities and retained funds at the end of the reporting period;
- for charities that are companies, an income and expenditure account included either within the SoFA, or as a separate summary income and expenditure account in addition to the SoFA where necessary to meet the reporting requirements of company law;
- notes to the accounts that explain the accounting policies, provide more details of how the income and expenditure is made up, and provide extra information about particular assets and liabilities, or about particular funds or transactions; and
- an optional cash flow statement.

The cash flow statement is compulsory for charities subject to the FRS 102 regime.

In all accounts, corresponding figures for the previous accounting period should be given and the period covered by the accounts should also be shown.

3.2.2 Small charities that are not limited companies

A charity that is not a limited company and whose annual income does not exceed the threshold set by the regulations (currently £250,000) is treated as a small charity and may opt to produce accounts on a receipts and payments basis instead of the accruals basis assuming that this is not prohibited by its governing document. In Scotland, the charity must have an income of less than £250,000 to prepare accounts otherwise than on the accruals basis.

3.2.3 Formats

The financial statements must be presented in a form which follows the regulations and the applicable SORP. The notes to the accounts can be used to amplify the information in both numeric and narrative form. Further narrative information can be given in the annual report (see below).

3.2.4 The annual report

In addition to the accounts of the charity, trustees are also required to prepare a separate document known as the annual report in respect of each financial year.

For an unincorporated charity in England and Wales with an income not exceeding £500,000 and assets not exceeding £3.26 million only a simple report is required. This will include:
- objectives and activities;
- achievements and performance;
- financial review;
- structure, governance and management;
- reference and administrative details.

Unless the charity is a CIO, the annual report and relevant accounts only need to be submitted to the Commission in England and Wales if the charity's income is more than £25,000, but charities with income below that threshold must be ready to do so if required. The most recent annual report and accounts must be made available to the public.

Larger charities must submit to the Commission a fuller report in accordance with the relevant SORP. Companies must also file directors' reports and accounts with Companies House.

At Appendix H is the Commission's model annual report for an unincorporated charity preparing its accounts on the receipts and payments basis. Appendix I is a model annual report for a larger charity taking the form of a company limited by guarantee. Both precedents were prepared before the introduction of the new SORPs referred to above.

The requirement to prepare and submit an annual report does not apply to exempt charities or to unregistered excepted charities, but the Commission may require the latter to do so.

3.2.5 Branches

One area which often leads to confusion is the treatment of branches in the accounts of the charity. A branch can sometimes be known by another name such as 'supporters' group', 'friends of ...' and so on.

Branches are defined as entities or administrative bodies set up, for example, to conduct a particular aspect of the business of the main charity or to conduct the business of the main charity in a particular geographical area. They may or may not be legal entities which are separate from the main charity. It is a matter of law whether a branch is a legal entity in its own right.

It is normal for a charity to use branches in different ways, usually for fundraising, and it can be argued that any money raised in the name of the charity must belong to it. However, branches should only be included in the accounts of the charity if they are under its control. A group of friends, for example, who raise funds for the charity but are not themselves undertaking charitable activities would not constitute a branch.

A branch usually has most of the following characteristics:
(1) it uses the name of the main charity in its title;
(2) it raises funds exclusively for the charity, for use either at head office or local level;
(3) it uses the registration number of the main charity to obtain tax relief;
(4) it is perceived by the public to be a branch of the charity;
(5) the main charity supports it with material, publicity, staff funding etc.

3.3 INDEPENDENT AUDIT

In general, smaller charities are required to have their accounts examined by an independent person falling into one of the categories set out in the 2011 Act whom the trustees reasonably believe to have the requisite ability and practical experience to carry out a competent examination of the accounts. Larger charities must have a professional audit.

The question whether a particular charity must be audited is determined initially by the governing document. If that says the accounts are to be audited, then they must be – irrespective of the size of the charity.

It is common to use the word 'audit' in such documents, especially if they are of long standing. If it was not the intention to have a professional 'audit' carried out, and the size of the charity permits, then the document may be interpreted as requiring no more than an independent examination. Otherwise, an amendment may be sensible.

After looking at the document, the next question to be considered is whether the charity is a company. If it is, it must have its accounts audited if its gross income for the period exceeds £500,000, or its gross assets exceed £3.26 million and its gross income exceeds £250,000. If not, it follows the rules for other types of charity.

In England and Wales, charities with a gross income of £25,000 or less are not required to have their accounts independently examined or audited. Charities with a gross income of more than £25,000 and no more than £250,000 must have their accounts subjected to external scrutiny but can choose independent examination or audit, unless their governing document requires an audit. Charities with a gross income of more than £250,000 and no more than £500,000 and who do not have gross assets exceeding £3.26 million may also choose between independent examination and audit, subject to the requirements of their governing document. Above those thresholds, a statutory audit is required. In Scotland all charity accounts are subject to scrutiny and regulations set out the circumstances in which independent examination or audit will be required.

3.4 TAX AND RATES

Charities and those people who give to charities benefit from generous and long-standing reliefs from tax. Charities also benefit from relief from business rates. It has been said that the reason for this generosity is that charities were performing public service tasks before taxation (and certainly before income tax) was introduced; taxing charities would, therefore, benefit no one. Be that as it may, the existence of tax reliefs is a strong, motivating factor for those contemplating setting up or supporting a charity and it is open to any individual taxpayer to avoid paying tax by making (larger) charitable contributions instead.

3.4.1 Income and capital gains

Relief is available on receipts from all sources except trading (other than trading in direct furtherance of the charity's main purpose or by beneficiaries of the charity), provided that the receipts are used or applied for charitable purposes. There are also exemptions for small trading and fund-raising activities.

3.4.2 Property used for charitable purposes

A charity in rateable occupation of land and buildings is entitled to 80% relief from non-domestic rates on property used wholly or mainly for charitable purposes, or for fundraising. In addition, the local authority has a discretion to grant further relief up to 100%, although this must generally be applied for, and justified, every year.

3.4.3 Gift Aid

Where a supporter gives a charity a sum, both the supporter (if a higher rate taxpayer) and charity benefit. The payment is tax-deductible and the charity is entitled to claim from HMRC an amount equivalent to the basic rate of tax on the amount of the gift. There is a scheme to allow charities to claim gift aid on small cash donations (under £20) up to a specified total amount without a gift aid declaration.

3.4.4 Payroll Giving Scheme

Under the Payroll Giving Scheme, an employee whose employer participates in the Scheme is able to make regular donations to charity and receive tax relief on the donations automatically at their top rate of tax.

3.4.5 Gifts

Gifts to charity which would otherwise attract capital gains tax or inheritance tax are exempt. This situation arises where a gift of land, chattels or investments is made to a charity by will or during the donor's lifetime.

3.4.6 HM Revenue and Customs guidance

HMRC produces some very helpful guidance, as well as official forms, for use by charities and their supporters. Reference should be made to its pages on www.gov.uk. It is recognised generally that gifts to charity should be encouraged and that charities should be encouraged to take advantage of the tax reliefs available to them. Indeed, trustees could be held liable for a breach of trust if they cause the charity an actual or notional loss by failing to take advantage of the available tax reliefs. In complex cases, where the situation is not covered by HMRC forms or guidance, advice from a lawyer or accountant will be desirable.

3.5 INSURANCE

3.5.1 Fire, other damage and theft

Charity trustees should insure property belonging to the charity against the usual risks such as fire, other damage and theft. Whilst security precautions which are consistent with the purposes of the charity are prudent and may, indeed, help to reduce the premium payable, it is only in the most exceptional cases and after full consideration of all the implications that a body of charity trustees will escape criticism if it decides not to insure the charity's property. For the great majority of charities, such insurance is essential.

3.5.2 Vandalism and terrorism

Charities with buildings in vulnerable places must now consider insurance against the risk of deliberate damage from vandalism and terrorism.

3.5.3 Legal expenses insurance

Charities may purchase insurance to cover the cost of legal expenses which may arise if the charity has to bring or defend legal proceedings and would otherwise have to pay the costs of those proceedings to the extent that they are not recoverable from the opposing party.

A charity providing services might also wish to obtain professional indemnity insurance to cover claims of negligence made against it.

3.5.4 Public and employer's liability

Insurance is also required against the risk of public liability and employer's liability. Failure to insure against these risks renders the trustees potentially liable on a personal basis, if the charity is unincorporated.

3.5.5 Fidelity insurance

A connected issue is fidelity insurance, where an agent or employee of the charity has, in practice, to be given a large measure of responsibility and cannot be supervised constantly by the trustees.

3.5.6 Particular risks

In some circumstances, it may be desirable to take out specific insurance against a particular risk on an ad hoc or short-term basis. For example, insurance might be needed if the charity has received a legacy which it plans to spend, but there is a chance that a relative or dependant of the deceased can make a successful claim under the Inheritance (Provision for Family and Dependants) Act 1975. Event insurance may cover losses from the cancellation of events as a result of bad weather and so forth

3.5.7 Liability insurance

This can provide additional protection for charity trustees in certain cases. This insurance protects a trustee against the possibility of having to personally meet a liability arising from a breach of trust, or breach of duty towards the charity (except a wilful or reckless breach of duty). Trustees may always insure themselves, at their own expense, against such liability, but the Charities Act 2011 now permits the policy to be purchased by the charity if the trustees are satisfied that it is in the best interests of the charity to do so. Trustees can be insured in respect of:

(a) any breach of trust or breach of duty committed by them in their capacity as charity trustees or trustees for the charity; or
(b) any negligence, default, breach of duty or breach of trust committed by them while acting as directors or officers of the charity (if it is a body corporate) or of any body corporate carrying on any activities on behalf of the charity.

The terms of such insurance must exclude the provision of any indemnity for a person in respect of:

(a) any liability incurred by him or her to pay:
- a fine imposed in criminal proceedings; or
- a sum payable to a regulatory authority by way of a penalty in respect of non-compliance with any requirement of a regulatory nature (however arising);

(b) any liability incurred by him or her in defending any criminal proceedings in which he or she is convicted of an offence arising out of any fraud or dishonesty, or wilful or reckless misconduct, by him or her; or

(c) any liability incurred by him or her to the charity that arises out of any conduct which he or she knew (or must reasonably be assumed to have known) was not in the interests of the charity or in the case of which he or she did not care whether it was in the best interests of the charity or not.

3.5.8 Other means of financial protection

In cases where insurance cannot be obtained by the charity there are other methods of obtaining financial protection. In some cases, a person or body other than the charity will have an insurable interest in the subject matter, for example where a painting or sculpture is lent by a charity to a museum or gallery, which itself undertakes to insure it. In other cases, such as where the risk in question is a commercial risk, it may be necessary to consider setting up a limited liability company, which may not itself be a charity, to carry out the activity which gives rise to the risk. This arrangement is common where a charity wishes to raise money through some trading activity.

3.6 INVESTMENT

Charity money which is not due to be spent in the near future should be working for the charity. Funds which will be required within a short time should be placed on deposit at a recognised bank or building society, or some other short-term arrangement should be made to preserve them safely.

Where it is known that funds will not be required for some time, and it is possible to calculate the amount which will then be needed, it is worth considering investment in a short-term investment. It is sometimes possible to achieve capital growth in this way by careful planning and timing.

In the case of permanent endowment or capital funds which are unlikely to be required for several years ahead, the trustees are able to take a longer view and consider specifically not only the charity's need for income but also the desirability of achieving capital growth.

3.6.1 Common investment funds

A sensible choice for many bodies of trustees in England and Wales is to invest in a common investment fund ('CIF'), which is itself a charity and is established exclusively for the investment of charity funds. A CIF operates in a similar way to an investment trust but is able to pay its dividends gross. Common deposit funds ('CDFs') are similarly available to charities.

A new development has been the creation of 'ethical' CIFs which are particularly designed for charities whose objects (for example the promotion of temperance) render certain types of investments (such as shares in distilleries) peculiarly unsuitable.

3.6.2 Powers of investment

Modern governing instruments nearly always contain unrestricted investment powers, enabling the trustees to choose any form of investment, whether in the UK or abroad. Normally, however, trustees should avoid the acquisition of property which does not produce any income or which is in any way speculative, including an unsecured loan, since such a choice is not compatible with the trustees' role of obtaining income to use for the charity's purposes, while protecting the charity's assets.

3.6.2.1 *Statutory powers (unincorporated charities)*

Where there is no express power of investment in the governing instrument, the trustees have statutory powers of investment in England and Wales arising from the Trustee Act 2000. Similarly wide powers have been introduced in Scotland. In addition there are specific statutory duties for trustees.

3.6.3 Advice on investments

Trustees should bear in mind the desirability of spreading their funds between a number of investments, rather than keeping all their eggs in one basket. It is essential that the trustees should obtain advice from a reputable financial adviser who has substantial experience and is registered under the financial services legislation. It is desirable to obtain such advice and to instruct the adviser to keep the charity's investments under review, even where the trustees themselves include someone with relevant experience.

3.6.3.1 *Investment advisers*

In some cases, particularly larger charities, the trustees will not be in a position personally to manage the charity's investment portfolio. It may, therefore, be wise to appoint either an investment advisor or some other expert to undertake this task and delegate the power to acquire and dispose of investments to that person or firm. There must be a written contract between the charity and the investment manager and a written investment policy and it must be reviewed regularly. The trustees should have regular meetings with the experts, confine the expert strictly to the charity's legal powers of investment, receive prompt and regular reports of all transactions, reserve the power to cancel the arrangement at any time.

3.6.4 Holding of investments

The normal rule is that the investments should be held in the name of the charity or the trustee body, if incorporated, or in the names of the individual trustees. It is not, of course, convenient for the investments to be held by a number of individual trustees in the long term, since trustees change and records, therefore, have to be updated in order to avoid difficulties later.

In some cases, the use of a nominee may be considered. Where there is scope for a two-tier governing body, it is often convenient to appoint a trust corporation or other more or less permanent body to hold the investments safely for the charity whilst the day-to-day investment and other management decisions are taken by the more rapidly changing body of charity trustees. Where this system has been set up formally, the holding body, if it is a trust corporation, may be designated the custodian trustee and the charity trustees designated the managing trustees.

3.6.4.1 Incorporation

A two-tier structure is not always desirable, particularly if there is likely to be a good deal of movement in the funds. In England and Wales, if the charity is not itself incorporated it may be wise to consider incorporation of the trustee body under the Charities Act 2011. By this procedure, which involves an application to the Charity Commission for a certificate of incorporation, the trustee body is given a name and legal personality of its own. This can bring considerable administrative benefits, not least in the holding of investments.

3.7 LAND AND BUILDINGS

Buildings (except caravans and other removable structures) legally form part of the land on which they are built. Therefore, for convenience, wherever 'land' is referred to in this book, any buildings on the land are included in that expression.

Charities own land for two main purposes: as an income-producing investment or for their own use. It is worth noting that, judging by past history, land has performed as a better long-term investment for charities than any other investment. The endowments of very old, established charities which are well-endowed today all consisted of land, some of which was of very little value at the outset. Functional land includes almshouses, village halls, recreation grounds, art galleries, museums, places of worship, church halls, schools, hospitals, hostels, swimming pools, historic monuments, archaeological sites, community centres, leisure centres, libraries, women's refuges and the administrative offices of charities.

Land may be owned outright, leased, rented or hired. Where the charity is the owner of land, the trustees are subject to a number of responsibilities as property-owners. They are obliged to make arrangements for repairs and insurance to the extent that these duties are not undertaken by anyone else. In addition, where they occupy land they are liable for business rates and water bills.

In the case of leasehold or rented land, charities will be responsible for paying the rent and observing the covenants in the lease. In Scotland there may be feu duties or other incidents.

3.7.1 Holding of land

Title to land is normally held in the name of the charity or the trustee body, if incorporated, or in the name of a custodian trustee, or in the names of the individual trustees, where neither the charity nor the trustee body is incorporated and there is no custodian or corporate holding trustee.

If individual trustees hold the land there must be at least two individual trustees in order to give a valid receipt for capital money, ie to be able to sell, mortgage or exchange the land or grant a lease at a premium. This immediately gives rise to the problem that unless every new trustee is appointed by deed and amendments are made to the particulars kept at the Land Registry (if the land is registered), the title will be vested in a dwindling number of individuals, some of whom may cease to be trustees, and technical problems may arise when it is necessary, at some future date, to prove the charity's ownership.

This problem can be overcome by one of two methods, outlined below.

3.7.1.1 Certificate of incorporation

When the land is held on a short lease, or it is expected that there will be frequent transactions, as where land is held as an investment and leases will need to be granted or enforced from time to time, or where the land is likely to be sold, it is appropriate to consider applying to the Charity Commission for a certificate of incorporation under the Charities Act 2011 or the equivalent legislation in Northern Ireland, once brought into force. Alternatively, and in Scotland (where incorporation of the trustees by certificate is not available), it may be considered wise to set up a limited liability company to be appointed as the trustee, or holding trustee, of the charity.

3.7.1.2 Land vested in the Official Custodian

In cases where the land is likely to be held for many years to come, for example where it constitutes a permanent endowment of the charity and is used for its charitable purposes, the ideal solution is to apply to the Charity Commission for an order vesting title to the land in the Official Custodian for Charities. In some cases, assistance from the charity's legal adviser may be necessary. The Official Custodian then, technically, holds the title and in the case of registered land is recorded as the proprietor at the Land Registry, but has no personal responsibilities and powers of management. All powers and responsibilities remain with the charity trustees, who are entitled to enter into agreements or take proceedings relating to the land in the name of the Official Custodian. The position will be the same in Northern Ireland when the relevant provisions are brought into force.

3.7.2 Sale, exchange or leasing of land in England and Wales

Before 31 December 1992, charities were frequently required to obtain the Charity Commission's consent, or an order excepting the charity from the requirement to obtain consent, to the sale, exchange or leasing of land. Under the system which has operated since then, the transaction can in most cases go ahead without any involvement by the Commission.

Consent is not required where the charity disposes of land to another charity, or leases it to a beneficiary otherwise for the best rent reasonably obtainable and for the purposes of the charity, in accordance with the express provisions in the trusts. There is also no need for consent where the transaction is authorised by an Act of Parliament or a scheme made by the Commission (or the court).

In all other cases, consent is always required where the other party to the transaction is one of the trustees; or a donor to the charity; or other connected person within the meaning of the 2011 Act; or where the charity will not get the best price or rent obtainable; or where the procedures laid down in the legislation cannot, for some reason, be carried out. In those cases, consent must be obtained *before* the trustees commit themselves to the deal and the Commission, who will need to be satisfied that the transaction is in the charity's interests, will inform the trustees of their detailed requirements.

3.7.2.1 *Proceeding without consent*

In the majority of cases, the trustees will have to follow the required procedures which are designed to safeguard both the charity and the trustees personally. Before committing themselves to any transaction (ie in the case of a sale, before exchanging contracts), the trustees must instruct an independent, qualified surveyor to make a written report on the proposed transaction, which covers all the items listed in the regulations including the measurements of the land, any planning permission, and the value of the land, and to advise on the best method of marketing and disposing of the land. The trustees must then carry out any marketing recommended by the surveyor, for example by placing notices at the site or in the local newspaper and reach a positive decision that the proposed terms are the best that the charity can obtain. Only then may the trustees commit themselves to the transaction.

In the case of functional land required by the governing document to be held for the purposes of the charity, a sale, exchange or long lease should not normally take place unless the trust contains a power of sale (or leasing), since this is inconsistent with a straightforward trust to use the land for a specified purpose. If there is no power of sale, it may be possible to find that it is implied in the particular circumstances, such as where the sale will *not* mean that the charity ceases to hold and use land for a charitable purpose. Otherwise, the Charity Commission may be willing to make a scheme to confer an express power. If there is a power of sale and the purpose of the sale is not simply to buy a replacement property, additional steps must be carried out before the land is sold. Whatever marketing arrangements are made the trustees must advertise the proposed sale and invite comments from the public. They must then consider any objections or suggestions received from the public before proceeding.

Simpler arrangements are permitted for short leases without a premium. A lease for up to seven years may be granted without a written report from a surveyor as long as the trustees obtain and consider the advice on the proposed disposition of a person who is reasonably believed by them to have the requisite ability and practical experience to provide them with competent advice and they are satisfied that the terms are the best that can reasonably be obtained for the charity. A lease for up to 2 years of land held on trust for functional purposes need not be specifically advertised.

3.7.2.2 Formalities

Specific formalities must be followed in the actual contract, agreement, lease, conveyance, deed of gift or transfer, whenever land is acquired or disposed of by a charity, including an exempt charity. These are designed to make it clear whether the land is subject to the restrictions imposed by law and, in the case of dispositions, whether the procedures have been followed. This is not, therefore, an area of conveyancing which the lay person can expect to be able to undertake without legal advice.

3.7.3 Mortgage of land

Apart from being an investment or a charitable facility, charity land can be a valuable financial resource in the sense that it can be mortgaged in order to secure a loan (for example to fund a project). The Charities Act 2011 lays down a procedure for borrowing on the security of charity land without the need for the Charity Commission's consent. This involves obtaining advice from a financial expert (who must be entirely unconnected with the lender but may be an employee of the charity) concerning the charity's need to borrow, whether the rate of interest is reasonable and whether the charity can afford the loan charges.

3.8 MAKING GRANTS

Some charities operate entirely by giving grants of money or other forms of financial assistance to individuals or to other charities for furtherance of the charitable purposes of those charities. Some of the smallest and some of the largest charities in the UK operate in this way. Others make occasional grants or loans. If charity money is to be used effectively, sensible methods of selecting recipients, fixing the level and period of support, and following up the way in which the grant has been used should be adopted.

3.8.1 Objective of grant

First, consideration must be given to the objective of the assistance proposed. This will depend on the purpose of the awarding charity, which may be very specific, for example relieving need in a particular area, or very general, such as furthering any charitable purpose at the discretion of the trustees. The purpose of the charity sets the limits for grant making but, in most cases, since funds are never unlimited, the trustees must take a policy decision on the kinds of grant they will normally consider. Policy decisions are not fixed, and policy decisions are often modified from time to time in the light of experience, the needs of potential recipients and the resources available.

3.8.2 Applications for assistance

Secondly, the trustees must decide whether they will invite applications or find other ways of identifying recipients. This depends largely on the breadth of the purpose and area of benefit and on how close the charity, or its trustees, are to the proposed beneficiaries. In the case of a local charity, it may be preferable for the trustees or their staff to find individual beneficiaries through local schools, churches or other organisations, or the local authority, rather than to seek applications. This is important particularly where there may be some doubt about whether those most in need of help will come forward by themselves. In a large area, and where grants are normally given to charities rather than individuals, postal applications are usual. In those cases, care is needed in targeting potentially successful applicants and designing the application form (if any) to enable the applications to be considered efficiently.

3.8.3 Policy guidelines

When a charity has numerous applications to consider, policy guidelines assist in reducing the number to manageable proportions and it may be sensible to divide the task of giving detailed consideration and carrying out any further investigations between different members of the trustee body. It is the trustees as a whole, however, who are responsible for the allocation of funds.

It is always wise to check out various issues, such as the other sources of funds available to an applicant; the effect (if any) which the proposed assistance will have, in the case of individuals, on any statutory benefits to which they are entitled; and, in the case of grants to charities, whether they have complied with their obligations to register and submit accounts. It is also prudent to find out exactly what the money will be used for and, in cases of grants to charities, to check that the proposals are within the objects of the recipient charities. These precautions help to ensure that the grant will be effective.

Not every recipient will be well enough organised to manage the grant if it is paid in one lump sum and, in any case, the grant-making charity may not have the whole amount available at once. In such cases, the payments may be made by instalment and the grant-making charity may wish to impose conditions, such as receiving an account or a school report, and checking that the grant is being used effectively before paying out future instalments. It is not uncommon for grants to be paid over 3 years or longer.

Monitoring the use made of grants, by means of spot checks, questionnaires and follow-up correspondence, is generally worthwhile, since it enables the trustees to keep a check on the effectiveness of the grant and modify their policy and procedures for the future. Provided that the amount is not excessive, the additional time and money will be well spent.

Effectiveness is not everything, however. Unlike statutory bodies spending taxpayers' money under bureaucratic controls, charities are in the fortunate position of being speedy, imaginative and able to conduct small-scale experiments from time to time. They do not exist to ape the provision made by central or local government, but have their own agenda in which they can give help or take initiatives which the statutory system cannot attempt. Independence is a boon, which should be valued. Charities can be originators, experts and leaders in their own fields.

3.9 RAISING FUNDS

Most new charities are not endowed by their founders but must raise funds in order to survive and grow. Some charities need to raise funds for particular projects from time to time. Fortunately, people are often generous when they are convinced that their gifts will be put to good use, or they may merely be attracted by enthusiastic, heart-warming or heart-touching advertisements.

In addition, the National Lottery has provided a means of collecting money for good causes on a vast scale. Charities may apply for grants from the Big Lottery Fund, the Heritage Lottery Fund or UK Sport to name but three. Further information is available at www.lotterygoodcauses.org.uk.

Fundraising is not in itself a charitable purpose, so an organisation set up purely to raise funds is not a charity. However, moderate fundraising, including expenditure for that purpose, is allowable as part of the administration of a charity. If fundraising is likely to involve a substantial amount of cost and effort, and certainly where it will dominate the activities of the charity, it is wise to set up a separate organisation to carry it out.

3.9.1 Managing fundraising

Managing the raising of funds has its own expertise, and trustees should not assume that they can be successful fundraisers without taking advice from someone who knows about the problems involved. On the other hand, trustees should be wary of committing themselves to a commercial fundraiser without checking his or her credentials. So many charities have had disastrous experiences with cynical or incompetent 'professionals' that enhanced controls have been introduced to regulate the sort of agreement which is allowed and require disclosure of fundraisers' remuneration. A charity (or its trustees) cannot be held to an agreement which does not comply with the law. It is hoped that the revised régime will increase public confidence as well as the confidence of the charities themselves.

The Institute of Fundraising has developed a voluntary Code of Fundraising Practice. Trustees should consider this guidance to determine current best practice. Trustees should also refer to the Charity Commission's guidance entitled 'Charities and Fundraising' (CC20).

3.9.2 Methods of fundraising

There are as many ways of raising funds as human ingenuity can devise and, as with so many other activities, there are fashions which change from time to time. Generally, it is easier to raise money for a cause which appeals to the emotions of prospective donors, and for a specific project rather than for basic running costs. Additional incentives may be provided if the beneficiaries and/or donors are involved in some specific activity, which can be entertaining or instructive in itself, or by the provision of prizes or rewards. Occasionally, two or more charities may combine their efforts in a creative way which helps to place their work in a different perspective.

3.9.3 Restrictions on fundraising

The law impinges on particular types of fundraising activities in England and Wales in different ways:

(1) The regular buying and selling of goods or services is considered 'trading' and, unless it is carried out in actually furthering the objects of the charity or by the beneficiaries it will be taxable. Small-scale trading is acceptable, however.

(2) If a professional fundraiser or commercial organisation solicits funds for a charity by means of a broadcast or over the telephone, it is obligatory to provide an opportunity for someone who contributes £100 or more (in the case of a broadcast only if by credit or debit card) to cancel the payment within 7 days, and, where goods have been purchased, when they have been returned.

(3) It is unlawful for a professional fund-raiser to solicit money or other property for the benefit of a charity unless he does so in accordance with a

written and signed agreement with the charity satisfying the requirements of the Charitable Institutions (Fund-Raising) Regulations 1994.

(4) Lotteries are subject to extensive regulation, overseen by the Gambling Commission. Small and large society lotteries and local authority lotteries require either a licence from the Gambling Commission or registration with a licensing authority, while private or incidental non-commercial lotteries do not.

(5) Advertising and broadcasting is subject to the law of libel and the advertising and broadcasting Codes of Practice, which reflect public opinion on what is fair and decent. As with all advertising, exaggerated claims tend to be counter-productive.

(6) It is wise for charities to beware of political controversy; although views may be strongly held within the organisation itself, it is not the purpose of any charity to campaign for a change in the law, either in the UK or elsewhere. In addition, the expression of seemingly political views is likely to be off-putting to potential supporters.

(7) Local and road safety regulations may need to be checked where an outdoor activity, such as a bicycle ride, is planned, and permission from landowners affected will be required.

(8) Health and safety regulations, food regulations and licensing laws, as well as the detailed terms of hiring and insuring premises will be relevant where premises are to be used for a sale, a dance or other event which is likely to attract large numbers.

(9) If funds are to be collected from the public by door-to-door collections or in a public place such as the street, a shopping precinct or other place to which the public have access without payment, the charity will need to obtain a permit from the local authority or the police or, if the appeal or flag day is to be nationwide, a door-to-door collection can be authorised by an exemption order from the Cabinet Office. Various conditions are likely to be imposed, including, possibly, conditions to protect public order and traffic control, and collectors will be required to have badges and certificates (sometimes combined in one) to prove that they are genuine.

3.9.4 Fundraising records

It is vitally important to keep careful records of money raised by fundraising efforts and the cost of raising it, so as to be able to judge whether a similar effort should be made another time and to report back quickly to supporters on the immediate result, and also to report later on the use to which the funds have been put. It is questionable whether charities are right to suggest to supporters that by giving a stated amount they will enable the charity to do something specific and individual (such as feed a starving child for a month) but it is useful and valuable to be able to point to a particular project or initiative which, through money contributed by the public, has become a reality, and it is arguable that a greater public response will be encouraged if the donors can share the charity's feeling of achievement.

Several of the larger national charities capitalise on this by setting up or encouraging the formation of local or regional 'branches' or groups of 'friends' whose main practical function is to raise funds for the central organisation. It is usual for these groups to be given permission to quote the national charity's registration number while raising funds. This may be sensible and effective in many cases, but it is worth pointing out that the national body must then take responsibility for whatever is said or done in its name. It should also ensure that it has approved the constitution of the local group (and can control any amendments to it) and that it receives the local group's accounts, which should be incorporated into the national body's own accounts.

3.9.5 Fundraising agreements

Part II of the Charities Act 1992 and the regulations made under it introduced controls on 'professional fundraisers' and 'commercial participators'. A professional fundraiser is a person or firm which carries on business as a fundraiser or is engaged to raise funds for a fee amounting to at least £1,000 per year or per project, or at least £10 per day. It does not include an employee of the charity concerned or certain other persons or institutions.

A commercial participator is any person or organisation (except a professional fundraiser) which carries on any kind of business, and uses a charity connection in an advertising or sales campaign, or other promotional venture, for example a business which advertises that part of the price of its goods will be given to charity. This does not include a charity's trading subsidiary.

The legislation is enacted to protect the public by ensuring that when they are asked to give to a charity, or support a charity, by a professional fundraiser or commercial participator, they will know how much of what they contribute will go to the charity, and how much to the professional or commercial organisation. When soliciting funds or promoting goods or services, the professional fundraiser or commercial participator is obliged by law to state the basis of his remuneration, and must specify what charity or charities will benefit. In addition, agreements with charities by professional fundraisers and commercial participators must contain certain provisions, or they will not be enforceable against the charity.

Before entering into a fundraising agreement, therefore, it is wise for a charity to seek professional advice from someone other than the fundraiser concerned.

Broadly analogous provisions have been enacted by the Charities and Benevolent Fundraising (Scotland) Regulations 2009, which also cover collections for benevolent bodies. Reference should be made to those provisions. Again, the fundraising provisions of the Charities Act (Northern Ireland) 2008 are not yet in force.

3.10 ACCEPTING GIFTS AND LEGACIES

It might be supposed that there are no problems for a charity in accepting gifts and legacies. However, it is sometimes necessary to give the matter careful thought.

There may be technical problems connected with gifts and legacies. A gift of anything other than money must be made in the correct manner and in favour of the correct person. There can be serious difficulties in the case of gifts by will if the recipient charity is incorrectly described, and in such cases there may even be competition between charities for the gift.

Sometimes, it is not clear whether a specific charity is referred to in a will. In England and Wales, the procedure depends on whether or not the gift takes the form of a trust (including a trust to administer the residue of an estate). If there is a trust, the Charity Commission will deal with the matter and a scheme may be required. They should be approached direct.

If there is a simple gift (for example to 'cancer research') without any trust, the executors should apply in the first instance to the Treasury Solicitor. The Treasury Solicitor acts for the Attorney-General, who can then use a procedure under the Royal Sign Manual (which he operates for the Queen) to direct the gift to a suitable charity or purpose.

In most cases, there will be some indication of the charity, or the sort of charity, which the testator wished to benefit. It is helpful to the Commission or the Treasury Solicitor to know which charity or charities the testator supported during his or her lifetime.

It is rare for such problems to be referred to the court and, of course, it is desirable that they should not be in view of the costs inevitably incurred, which reduce the amount available for charity.

3.10.1 Refusal to accept gifts

Occasionally, the trustees of a charity, for some good reason, decide that they do not wish the charity to accept a gift. The trustees must only decide not to accept a gift where the refusal is in the best interests of the charity. They must act reasonably and prudently in all matters relating to the charity and need always to bear in mind that their prime concern is its interests. They must not let any personal views or prejudices affect their conduct as trustees. There may be circumstances in which the acceptance of the gift is impractical or it would entail a liability which outweighs its value, or there may be reputational risk to the charity in accepting the gift. In difficult cases, the trustees should refer the matter to the Charity Commission and seek an order authorising the refusal.

3.10.2 Gifts subject to conditions

If the gift is subject to a condition or expressed to be for some particular purpose which does not enable the trustees to pool it with the rest of the charity's resources it may be necessary to register the gift as a 'subsidiary charity' (ie one which is technically a separate charity and which is administered alongside an existing registered charity), and show it separately in the accounts. This happens frequently in the case of school charities, to which former staff and pupils often give a prize fund for particular subjects or sports.

The same principle applies in the case of funds given for a specific purpose during the lifetime of the donor or funds raised by an appeal for a specific project. The money or property which has been given to the charity is held by the trustees on a special trust for that purpose and cannot be treated as part of the charity's general funds.

3.10.2.1 *Failure of purpose*

When the funds available cannot reasonably be used for the specified purpose, for example where the cost is too great or planning permission is refused, it is not open to the trustees simply to use the funds for other purposes, unless the terms of the gift or the appeal literature specifically allow for this. In strict law, in these situations the trustees hold the funds on behalf of the donors. If there is a single, identifiable, living donor the problem may quite easily be resolved by going back to him or her, explaining the problem and requesting permission (preferably in writing) to use the funds for another purpose of the charity.

If, on the other hand, it is not possible to identify or trace all the donors, for example where the money has come from cash collections or from a fundraising concert or other event or where the donor is no longer alive, the purpose can only be altered by a scheme.

There are two procedures associated with the making of a scheme in this situation, outlined below, depending on whether the gift is made by will or otherwise.

3.10.2.2 *'General charitable intention'*

If the gift is made by will the normal procedure, which avoids an application to the court, is first to determine whether there was a 'general charitable intention' on the part of the testator. If so, it is best to reach an agreement between the charity and the residuary beneficiaries or persons who would be entitled on intestacy, then to obtain the approval of the Treasury Solicitor acting for the Attorney-General on a destination for the fund which is cy-près the testator's intention, and then to ask the Charity Commission to make a scheme to direct the funds for that purpose. The executors will be in charge of the funds and will normally carry out the correspondence until the scheme is made.

3.10.2.3 *Identifiable donors*

If the funds have been raised by an appeal, a scheme will not be made until all identifiable donors who can be found are contracted and asked either to sign a written disclaimer or ask for their money back. There is a procedure for advertising for donors to come forward. Moneys obtained by cash collections using collection boxes or similar means, and the proceeds of any lottery, competition, entertainment, sale or similar money-raising activities are conclusively presumed to have been given by unidentifiable donors. When the scheme has been established the trustees will have to put any funds given by donors who could not be contacted aside for 6 months.

3.10.3 Avoiding failure

In view of the potential difficulties, which can be time-consuming and expensive for the charity, it is prudent to offer advice and guidance to would-be donors, informing them of the purposes for which gifts would be welcome and, above all, making the proper name and address of the charity quite clear to them. It may also help to identify a charity by its registered number in addition to its name. Most problems arise where a charity changes its name (or address) or where its publicity material is vague or inaccurate on technical details. In the case of appeals, it is sensible to state an alternative purpose in case the appeal fails to reach or overshoots its target or if the project in question cannot be carried out at the end of the day, and to ask donors to state, when making their contributions, whether they wish to have their money returned in such an event.

3.11 PATRONS AND SPONSORS

Artists, composers and architects have all relied on the patronage, ie material support and protection, of wealthy and well-placed individuals. From the Enlightenment onwards, charities of all kinds have often had patrons. Today, the patronage of a member of the Royal Family, a media star or a representative of excellence in the charity's field of work is regarded by many charities as a valuable asset which can ensure that the charity is taken seriously, adds dignity to formal occasions and helps in fundraising.

The role of the patron, however, does not now involve the direct provision of cash or commissions. This function has been taken over by the sponsor.

A sponsor is more likely to be a commercial organisation than an individual and is more often limited to a specific project, such as the publication of the charity's newsletter, the provision of equipment to be used by the charity or the support of a particular fundraising event, and is also limited in terms of the amount of support provided. In addition, the sponsor expects to receive a tangible benefit for itself, such as increased public awareness of its goods or services, from its association with the charity.

All kinds of odd combinations, some witty, result from sponsorship agreements by charities, which can be very beneficial to both parties. Care is needed, however, in the initial choice of sponsor, since its own reputation will be linked with the charity's and it could, for example, be embarrassing if an environmental charity was sponsored by an industrial concern which turned out to be a polluter, or a temperance charity was sponsored by a multi-purpose company which diversified into alcoholic drinks. Charities should also be wary of being so grateful for the sponsorship that they allow the sponsor's name to dominate the charity's publicity. If charitable funds are used to any substantial extent to promote a non-charitable body, the trustees could be liable for a breach of trust and the charity could be taxed on the amount spent.

3.12 TRADING

Some charities pursue trading activities in their charitable work. For instance, a charity which runs workshops for disabled people as a method of relieving their disability is carrying out a trade if the goods produced are sold. Similarly, a charity for educational purposes may operate through a fee-paying school or other institution, and it is also common to find the league of friends of a hospital providing extra comforts for the patients by means of a hospital shop or flower stall. However, there are unlikely to be any tax or legal difficulties in these cases.

3.12.1 Trading activities as an adjunct to charitable purpose

Where, for example, a university contracts to carry out research for a commercial organisation, a cathedral sells art books or souvenirs or a bar is established in a community centre, the trading activity may enhance, as well as help to finance, the charitable purpose but is an adjunct to, rather than a method of carrying out, the charitable purpose. Caution must be exercised if a trading activity of this kind becomes successful or begins to assume importance as an element in the charity's finances. If the trend continues, it will be necessary to consider hiving off the trading activity to a separate, non-charitable body – usually, but not necessarily, a limited company.

3.12.2 Trading for the purpose of raising funds

Trading which is carried out purely for the purpose of raising funds need have nothing to do with the work or purpose of the charity, although it will often promote its name. For example, the sale of T-shirts and other promotional goods, the issue of gift catalogues, a dining club, a second-hand clothes shop or even a specific business, such as publishing or estate agency, may be conducted exclusively in support of a charity. This does not make the trade a charitable purpose, nor can an organisation devoted to that trade be a charity, even if all the profits are used for wholly charitable purposes. The trading company will not, however, be a 'commercial participator' for the purposes of the Charities Act 1992, if it is controlled by the charity, for example if the charity owns the majority of the shares.

It follows that a charity is not in a position to use its funds to support the trading activity since this would normally be an application of funds for a non-charitable purpose and a breach of trust. There are rare exceptions. The purchase of shares in a trading company or the making of a loan at a market rate of interest to a trading body can, in some circumstances, be regarded as a proper investment for the funds of the charity, assuming that its powers of investment are wide enough to permit this and satisfactory financial advice is obtained. In most cases, however, the fact that the charity is asked to provide financial support is an indication of economic weakness on the trading company's part and should sound a clear warning to the trustees that the charity should not allow itself to become too dependent on the trading company or too closely connected with its problems. It is better for the trading body to obtain its finance from an independent source.

When the arrangements are working satisfactorily, they can prove very beneficial. The preferred system is for the trading body, which may be a company or, for example, a social club, to covenant the whole or part of its taxable profits to the charity. As a result, the trading body is relieved from tax on the amount paid each year and the charity is entitled to recover the amount in question from HMRC.

In addition, the charitable relief from business rates is available for charity shops and commercial outlets within charity premises, and VAT reliefs may be available.

CHAPTER 4

MANAGEMENT

4.1 CHOOSING TRUSTEES

Although the trustees themselves may not consider the personality of trustees to be important (and charity employees may have a sneaking preference for the kind of trustee who remains in the background), the character of the governing body of a charity is a key to the character and reputation of the charity and may be vital to its success or failure.

People become trustees for a variety of reasons, often subjective. In some cases they are elected by the members or appointed by outside bodies, such as the local authority, or from the beneficiary class, such as people suffering from a specific disease or their families or the users of facilities provided by the charity for the community. In such cases, there may be an opportunity for the continuing trustees to influence the appointment or even suggest a particular person. In other cases, the trustees are appointed by the continuing trustees directly.

Generally, it is helpful if the trustees have something in common with each other, since this eases communication between them and tends to minimise the scope for sterile arguments about peripheral issues. The most important common interest should, of course, be a sincere desire to carry out the charity's purposes effectively, but successful teamwork can be built up if the trustees also have a specific geographical or religious link, even where the charity is not confined to a particular locality or a particular religious denomination.

There are dangers for the well-being of the charity, however, if the trustees are too closely identified with each other, and especially if two or more of them are related (unless, of course, the charity is a family charity). There are also serious risks of stagnation if the same people remain in office as trustees for years on end, especially where they are all of a similar age. There is always a danger that long-standing trustees come to regard the charity as their own fiefdom and become fiercely resistant to innovation.

Ideally, a body of trustees should not be a monoculture but should contain representatives of different skills, age groups, sexes and social backgrounds, with a regular turnover so that no one becomes indispensable, and new ideas are constantly being brought into the discussions. Arrangements vary, but 3 years is a reasonable term of office and it is wise to adopt a system under which trustees are required to have a break from their duties after two consecutive terms of office. It should also be possible for trustees to resign when their own circumstances change, without feeling that they are placing an unfair burden on their co-trustees.

The risk of taking on an unknown colleague can be avoided if, in advance of any formal appointment, a prospective trustee is invited to attend a few meetings as an observer. A similar compromise may provide a sympathetic solution to the problem of an elderly trustee, who can no longer be expected to take an active part in the administration of the charity but for whom complete retirement would cause a serious sense of loss.

The qualities which a charity trustee should ideally possess are: attention to detail, reliability and judgment, since other people will be affected by the trustees' decisions; a willingness to listen and learn, since in the charity world new developments are taking place constantly; and a measure of toughness in order to safeguard the charity's interests. To the extent that such paragons are not always available, these qualities can be provided in combination by the whole trustee body.

It will also be appropriate to look for specific qualities required by the purposes, organisation and needs of the particular charity. Thus, it might be useful to have a medical practitioner on the body of trustees of a charity which promotes medical research or care for the sick, a landowner or property expert where the charity's assets include land and buildings; a parent or teacher where the charity is concerned with young children; and so forth. Any charity can benefit from the contribution of a sympathetic accountant, lawyer or company secretary. Apart from the direct contribution to the trustees' own decision-making, a trustee's expertise can also be useful to the work of any member of the staff of the charity who has the same or a relevant profession or function.

4.2 TRUSTEE MEETINGS

The essence of the decision-making process within a charity is the meeting of the trustees. The conduct of meetings may be laid down in detail in the governing instrument, in which case the requirements must be strictly followed but, in addition, charities tend to develop their own traditions, which differ widely. In all cases, the essentials of an effective meeting are adequate preparation, fair and efficient chairmanship and accurate, readable minutes. This applies whether the meeting is held in person or (as the constitution may permit) by means of a telephone conference or electronic means.

4.2.1 Preparation

Before the meeting, the clerk or secretary, or the director of the charity (who in many cases performs the secretarial function at trustee meetings) should discuss with the chairman the proposed agenda, the order in which items should appear and the timing of the meeting. It is as well to have a proposed time for the end of the meeting as well as the beginning. The notice of the date and time of the meeting, the agenda and any supporting papers should normally be sent to each of the trustees in ample time for them to arrange their diaries and study the papers. The governing document may specify how meetings are to be called and its requirements must be followed.

Trustees should be encouraged to give their apologies in advance if they are unable to attend, since this may affect the quorum. In some cases, a meeting may need to be arranged to suit the timetable of a particular trustee who has some special contribution to make to an item on the agenda.

There is no reason why those who cannot attend should not be invited to give their views in advance, but it must always be remembered that they will not have heard the discussion and cannot veto a decision by that means.

Meetings should be held in a quiet environment, with adequate space and where the trustees will not be interrupted.

4.2.2 Quorum

There must be a quorum if the meeting is to take any decisions. Where a meeting is unexpectedly inquorate, it is often worthwhile to continue with the discussion, with a view to ratification of any provisional decisions at the next meeting.

Some trustee bodies do not find it necessary to put a matter to the vote, whilst other bodies vote on every point; it is a matter of style and tradition. Voting should normally be by a show of hands or other tangible indication of preference, given only after full discussion has taken place.

4.2.3 Chairmanship

The chairman's role is to conduct the meeting and see that it gets through its business. The purpose of the casting vote is not to give the chairman extra powers but to enable him or her to end the discussion on a particular item. For this reason, the convention is that the chairman should not use the casting vote to alter an existing policy or to impose a controversial decision on the trustees. This does not mean that the chairman should be passive. In many cases, the chairman exercises leadership which is appreciated by his or her fellow trustees and helps the charity to operate in a dynamic way. On the other hand, the chairman must be fair and try to encourage all the trustees (even recently appointed trustees) to participate.

There will be occasions when it is desirable to invite a person other than the trustees and their secretary to attend a meeting. For example, the meeting may provide a suitable occasion to hear, at first hand, the advice of a professional adviser, or a particular employee may have a report to make or explain. Whatever the trustees' normal habits at meetings, it is worth bearing in mind that the person who has been invited is the trustees' guest for the occasion and should be shown courtesy; he or she should not, for example, be kept waiting and should not be expected to sit through irrelevant agenda items. He or she does not, of course, have a vote.

4.2.4 Minutes

Minutes should always be taken, since they will constitute the record of what was decided and may have to be referred to at a later date. They may be taken by the secretary, clerk or director or by a trustee or employee chosen for the purpose. They should not be taken by the chairman.

The arrangements should ensure that, within reason, the trustees feel free to speak their minds at the meeting. It is important that the minutes record only what is likely to be useful for the charity's records. Therefore, it is preferable that the minutes are taken by a person, rather than a mindless tape-recorder, transcription from which would, in any case, be an chore.

It is normal practice for the minutes to be circulated in draft to all those who attended the meeting and either approved or corrected at the next meeting, when they should be signed by the chairman. The minutes should then be kept in a safe place and must be available for any trustee to consult.

4.2.5 Frequency of trustee meetings

There should always be at least two meetings of the trustees each year and, in many cases, it will be necessary or desirable to hold considerably more. The governing document might specify the minimum number of meetings that must be held and again its requirements must be followed.

The precise arrangements will depend on the nature of the charity's work and the extent to which it is carried out by employees, rather than directly by the trustees. There should, in any case, be a procedure for calling a special meeting at short notice to deal with emergencies. There is no excuse for not dealing with a serious problem merely because the next scheduled meeting of the trustees is some months ahead.

In addition, there may be meetings of committees (who must report to the next full meeting if not before) and the occasional social gathering will help to keep trustees (and others) in touch.

4.3 DEALING WITH PROFESSIONALS

There are numerous occasions in the running of a charity when professional advice is desirable or essential. A charity's needs are different from those of an individual, and trustees, because they are not dealing with their own assets, are more often in the position of requiring professional advice. Obtaining and acting on professional advice can also safeguard the trustees personally from any claim that they have failed in their duties. Trustees should be able to recognise when professional advice should be obtained for the charity and be able, in practice, to obtain it.

4.3.1 Choosing a professional

The correct choice of a professional adviser is vitally important and not always easy. The quality and style of professional people varies considerably and the best recommendation is always one from a similar organisation based on personal experience. In addition to being satisfied of the competence of the adviser and, where appropriate, of professional qualifications and other credentials, trustees must consider two particular factors: fees, and the chemistry of the relationship.

4.3.1.1 Fees

Professional services cost money and it is a mistake to assume that being a charity is a passport to free advice of adequate quality. A trustee would not expect to employ, for example, a builder, to work for nothing. Fees are almost always likely to be higher than the trustees think, but they are a proper administrative expense which can and should be budgeted for. It is, therefore, essential to accept that there will be a financial cost and to make sure, at the outset, that the amount involved is known (in broad terms) and that the charity can afford that cost. Nor should trustees suppose that just because their meetings are not frequent the professional will be happy to wait for payment until the next meeting is held.

4.3.1.2 Relationship between adviser and trustees

It is essential that the individual who advises the trustees commands their respect and trust. All professional relationships require confidence on both sides and in order to be effective the trustees and senior staff must be able to work with their adviser, discuss the charity's affairs frankly and openly with him or her and take seriously the advice provided.

4.3.2 Effectiveness

Having chosen a professional adviser, it is in the charity's interests that the most effective use should be made of his or her services, both to obtain the best advice for the charity and to avoid wasted costs. For day-to-day contact it is most efficient if there is a single representative of the charity who normally deals directly with the adviser. There will be occasions when a meeting with a group of the trustees (or even with the whole trustee body) is desirable, but this is more useful for general information gathering and background than for more specific points.

A professional should not be presumed to have any more knowledge of the charity and its problems or priorities than the trustees provide. It may, therefore, be sensible to start the relationship with a written summary of the background and, in many cases, a copy of the charity's governing instrument(s) and latest report and statement of accounts. A meeting at an early stage will be helpful to clarify any points which remain in doubt and to consider the precise problem in more detail. There is no reason to assume that an initial consultation should be free of charge. Very often, the first meeting with an experienced professional will direct the charity towards the solution.

Communications thereafter will remain of prime importance. The professional will need information from time to time and this should be readily available. Letters and telephone messages should be answered promptly. The professional should also be notified of any relevant changes in the situation and kept informed generally of the charity's progress.

A good working relationship with the charity's professional advisers can be an enormous asset to the charity, but like any other relationship it needs to be nurtured and developed.

4.3.3 Problems with advisers

If there are any problems in the trustees' relationship with the adviser, he or she, or the senior partner in the adviser's firm, should be told at once and action taken to resolve the problems. There is often a simple remedy and there is, of course, no excuse for complaining of poor service only when the invoice arrives.

If, as sometimes happens for a variety of reasons, the trustees reach the conclusion that they will not stay with a particular professional adviser, they should take action to terminate the relationship at once rather than allow the relationship to deteriorate. They should remember, however, that it is unlikely that their papers will be returned until they have paid any outstanding fees.

If the worst comes to the worst, the trustees may have to consider taking legal action against a professional for loss caused to the charity through negligence. They will require prompt advice from an independent solicitor on any such move.

4.3.4 Mistakes to avoid

It is up to the trustees to consult a professional, where appropriate, as soon as a problem or potential problem appears. It is not wise to leave the consultation until the trustees have tried, and failed, to solve it themselves, thereby making the situation more complex and difficult to solve. Neither must the trustees simply ignore the problem, hoping that it will go away. Even if a particular difficulty does not materialise, it will be useful to have obtained advice for a future occasion, and the trustees may learn something beneficial to the charity in the course of obtaining the advice.

Trustees should avoid the error of thinking that they know the answer before they have asked the question. Sometimes they will find that they have asked the wrong question and that the answer is not what they had expected. In order to make the most of advice received they should keep an open mind and be prepared to listen as well as to speak.

There are few outcomes more frustrating for a professional person than to give careful, reasoned advice only for it to be ignored for some subjective reason. The occasions on which professional advice should not be followed are rare: such an outcome will usually be a waste of time for all concerned as well as a waste of the charity's money. If the reasons for the advice are not understood, the trustees should request a further, written, explanation.

On the other hand, trustees should not go to the extreme of passing on to a professional adviser the responsibility for deciding an issue of policy which is properly within their discretion. A professional will be an expert in his or her field, but the trustees remain the experts in their charity, and the decision-makers for it.

4.3.5 Particular specialists

Particular types of profession or business have their own requirements and charities should be aware that there may be special considerations or limitations.

Banking, for example, has been going through a period of rapid change with increased use of new technology. It is prudent to discuss how the charity can make the most effective use of the available services, as well as keeping costs to a minimum, and trustees should be willing to consider modifications to the charity's practices (for example by paying in all donations at a single point) to achieve these ends.

Solicitors vary enormously from the general 'High Street' practitioners to the highly specialised City firm. An increasing number are becoming familiar with charity matters but it is wise to ask.

Barristers are usually instructed via another professional person, ie a solicitor or by 'direct professional access' through an accountant, surveyor or other professional. An increasing number of barristers are authorised to accept instructions directly from the public, particularly those with expertise in charity law and associated areas.

There are two prominent 'legal directories' – The Legal 500 and Chambers and Partners – which list the leading solicitors and barristers in various areas of law, including charity law. Both are free to access on the internet.

There is a proliferation of para-legal services which may appear more attractive on cost grounds than consulting a solicitor. However, it is worth bearing in mind that charity law is a specialist area which the average licensed conveyancer, for example, may not readily be able to research. Indeed, when considering property transactions it is important for advice to be sought from a lawyer with experience of charity law. Similarly, a design consultant does not have the same training as an architect.

Charity consultants, including fundraising consultants, of whom there are a great number, do not necessarily have any professional qualification or supervision. The National Council for Voluntary Organisations ('NCVO') maintains a list of consultants covering a variety of fields, and the Institute of Fundraising has a register of members. Particular care is required when choosing an appropriate consultant and entering into an agreement. It may be sensible to contact other charities who have used consultants on similar projects, and to obtain advice on the form of agreement, or at least check for hidden 'extras'. It is usually unwise to commit the charity to a long-term contract. It should also be remembered that consultants should not normally be paid a retainer as opposed to an hourly or daily rate.

Investment advisers must be informed of the charity's investment powers and of the investment policy which the trustees propose to follow. Trustees should not assume that the charity will obtain a better deal by agreeing to pay commission rather than fees and should also be wary of hidden 'extra' charges.

4.3.6 Beauty parades

The expression 'beauty parade' is commonly used in the commercial world to describe a method of choosing between competing professionals by asking them to present what they offer. All professionals are in competition to an extent, but it will not be sensible to use this method of choosing between them unless the charity is able to provide a very clear brief of what it requires. It should also be recognised that, unless the charity is looking for the qualities of a good salesman, a beauty parade may not disclose the relevant strengths and weaknesses of the competitors. Other methods are simply to inquire carefully and to compare several estimates.

4.4 EMPLOYEES AND VOLUNTEERS

For all but the smallest charities, the effort of the trustees alone is not enough. Workers, paid or unpaid, must be recruited. In fact, many of the most prominent and influential people in the charity world today are employees rather than trustees.

Unfortunately, charities in general do not have a good track record in this sphere – there is a relatively fast turnover among charity employees. One of the reasons for this is simple lack of thought; it need not be so.

In order to attract good people to work for a charity, the charity needs to demonstrate that it can provide a satisfactory working environment, something it cannot easily do until it has discovered its own management style.

As usual, the responsibility falls on the trustees. They set the pace, indicate the expectations, decide on the rewards and, as the charity grows, choose the leaders who, in due course, will be doing much of this on their own initiative, and building up the charity's corporate culture and traditions.

It is worth using a little imagination on this topic. From the charity's point of view, the work must be done as effectively and efficiently as possible. No one should suppose that working for a charity is an easy option or that competition or its equivalent does not apply. If, however, the workers are looked upon as mere human resources, it is easy to make the mistake of demoralising them by over-work or unrealistic targets, which is likely to result in the opposite of the intended outcome.

A discussion of employment law is outside of the scope of this book; reference should be made to specialist texts and professional advice should be taken.

4.4.1 Interviewing candidates

Interviewing candidates for positions is a skill which can be learned or which can be bought in especially for the occasion. Some charities have found the specialist recruitment consultancies helpful, but it is as well if the trustees have given thought to the sorts of qualities, qualifications or skills which they are looking for to carry out the job in hand. In formal terms this is called a 'person specification'.

What, then, do workers need in order to give their best for the optimum length of time? In many cases, working for a charity brings its own reward, in the sense that the job is in itself worthwhile. That indicates a need to involve workers in the charity's goals and achievements.

Fair recruitment training is now widely available, which can help organisations avoid unintentionally excluding able candidates as a result of a flawed recruitment process.

4.4.2 Security

Security is provided, in the case of employees, by their contract of employment, which is required by law, and, in the case of both employees and volunteers, by coherent and predictable management arrangements. This can be achieved through consultation, discussion, the employee or volunteer knowing the extent of his or her responsibilities, a sense of belonging and no sudden surprises.

4.4.3 Annoyance

In this category can be included all the nagging distractions, from bullying and undue bureaucracy to machinery which does not work. A procedure for airing grievances, a method for improving procedures and a bullying and harassment policy is essential.

4.4.4 Encouragement or praise when deserved

Employees need to be reassured that their efforts are appreciated. Equally, employees need to be told if their work is not up to standard.

4.4.5 Support for weaknesses

Not everyone is good at everything, and people do not always neatly fit the job. A constructive approach enables the jobs to be modified to fit the people. The experience of volunteering shows that this can work with unpaid jobs too.

4.4.6 Training

The possibility of training or of gaining experience to allow for career development, for example specialist courses, secondments, temporary promotions and special assignments, may all be considered, but simply allowing a junior member of staff or volunteer to exercise some initiative can prove unexpectedly fruitful.

4.4.7 Fairness

It is not, in fact, a simple matter to achieve fairness. Goodwill is essential, but there must also be proper job descriptions, systems for appraising jobs and staff, annual reports with built-in checks and balances, an allowance for the differences between people (so that, for example, the loudest voice does not determine priorities) and compliance with equality legislation.

4.4.8 Remuneration (including pension rights)

Remuneration for employees, should be at, or as near, the going rate for the job as the charity can decently afford and, of course, charities are obliged to pay their eligible workers the minimum wage. Working for a charity does not remove the material concerns which affect other mortals or diminish family or other responsibilities. Providing housing for employees can be extremely helpful, but it must be borne in mind that the employee will retire in due course and may then wish to have his or her own home.

New pension arrangements came into force in October 2012. Eligible workers must be enrolled into a pension scheme and the charity must make a contribution towards it. Charities with fewer than 50 staff can do this between 1 August 2015 and 1 April 2017.

4.4.9 Remuneration of trustees

Trustees are not generally paid for acting as trustees. There is no general power to pay charity trustees for acting as trustees. To do this the charity must have authority either in its governing document, or from the Commission or the court. Charity trustees will need to note that payment for trusteeship will be a breach of trust if the appropriate authority is not in place. Similarly, it is only in rare cases that a trustee may be employed. They can, however, be reimbursed for legitimate expenses.

Payment of charity trustees (or people connected to trustees) for the provision of services to the charity may be authorised by the charity's governing document. In the absence of such an express power the Charities Act 2011 permits payment in certain circumstances. In summary, the conditions are:

- The amount or maximum amount of remuneration is agreed in writing between the charity (or charity trustees) and the person providing the service and is reasonable in the circumstances.
- The charity trustees decide that the payment to that particular person is in the best interests of the charity.
- If there is more than one trustee who is to receive remuneration from the charity (or is connected to a person who is to receive remuneration) they must nonetheless remain in the minority of trustees.
- The governing document of the charity does not contain an express prohibition on charity trustees receiving remuneration.

The trustee who stands to be remunerated (or who is connected to a person who stands to be remunerated) should not participate in the decision-making process or vote on the proposal.

4.4.10 Health and safety legislation

Health and safety legislation must, of course, be observed, whether the staff are paid or unpaid.

4.4.11 Relationship between director and trustees

The director or chief executive of a substantial charity is in a special position since his or her responsibilities towards the charity mirror those of the trustees themselves, whilst the position affords actual power and control which may exceed that of the trustees in matters of day-to-day-operation. The relationship between the trustees and the director is vitally important. Confidence on both sides is of the first importance, but the director should never be placed in the position of feeling the full weight of responsibility for the charity. He or she must be able to seek guidance, if necessary as a matter of urgency, from the trustees and must be able to look to the trustees to make decisions, particularly decisions on policy. The best ideas and suggestions do not necessarily spring from those who will have to implement them.

4.5 GOOD MANAGEMENT

From the management point of view, charities are not very different from other businesses. It is true that charities do not make money for their own sake, but there will always be some way of measuring their success, or lack of it, and their activities have very specific financial implications.

It is wise, as a charity approaches medium size, to take positive steps to plan its management by looking at its resources, actual and potential, its immediate aims and longer-term plans (and the means which are available or which will need to be developed or acquired to achieve them), its philosophy, values and style and how it presents itself.

Planning is by no means enough. Regular reviews and assessments are required and proposals must be placed in an order of priority – and followed up. From time to time, a 'SWOT' analysis is helpful, identifying Strengths, Weaknesses, Opportunities and Threats, in order to decide how best to use or cope with them. Sometimes it may be worth examining a perceived weakness to see whether it has any hidden advantages and vice versa. Another strategy is to take a particular activity within the charity, for example information systems, and undertake a thorough review.

4.5.1 Time

Time is generally in short supply: if it is not (and sometimes, of course, if it is) the charity may not be making the best use of it. An annual timetable, or workplan, setting out priorities with published target dates, can help in giving the organisation a sense of direction and coherence, and encourage commitment. Its uses are many, for besides helping the charity to avoid last-minute rushes to meet deadlines for such matters as producing the accounts, it can provide a basis for forward planning, obtaining funds, measuring performance and reorganising working practices. A single policy decision on the time in which letters or applications are answered or whether the unsuccessful applications are to be answered at all, will help to create norms of working and reasonable expectations on the part of applicants and correspondents.

Special care is needed when the charity has outlying groups or branches, or where some of the activities, for example trading or campaigning, have been hived off to separate bodies, which may not themselves be charities.

4.5.2 Contract culture

Additional monitoring systems may well be required where the branches of a national body are involved in the 'contract culture', ie competing with institutions in the private sector in tendering for tasks which would previously have been carried out by local authorities, health authorities or other public bodies. Charities sometimes forget that they do not have a monopoly of care and concern and that private, for-profit organisations may deliver equally good services in the social field. A charity may, indeed, have to resolve difficult problems where its own objects and traditions conflict with the demands of the other contracting party.

4.5.3 Coherence

Coherence, in the sense that the organisation should have an inner logic, is necessary to avoid confusion about what people are supposed to be doing. Communication, reporting back and accountability within the whole set-up are essential to avoid misunderstanding. Whilst there may be good reasons for the same people to be involved in different aspects of activities, care is needed to ensure that the structures are not allowed to become obscure, or unduly complex.

4.5.4 Charity consultants

If trustees find that they have inherited a management structure which seems obscure or difficult, or have any reason to be dissatisfied with the arrangement and cannot readily find a solution, it may be worthwhile to engage the services of a charity consultant or management consultant to investigate, advise and, perhaps, put into place a new system.

Management should not be seen as an end in itself, but always as a means to furthering the charity's purposes in the most effective way. Nor is it something which is 'done' by one group of people to another. It should involve everyone, including the trustees.

4.6 STATIONERY

It may be thought that stationery is unimportant and that the content of what is communicated is the charity's only concern. This is not the attitude of the law.

Every registered charity in England and Wales (with an annual gross income of £10,000 or more) is obliged to state the fact that it is a registered charity on all its official documents, including cheques, invoices, receipts and written or printed appeals for funds. It is an offence for a trustee or employee of a charity to authorise the issue of a document which does not comply with this requirement (unless there is a reasonable excuse).

Every limited liability company, charitable or not, is obliged, by company law, to give its full name on all its outgoing documents and, in the case of a charitable company, must state that it is a charity. Non-compliance is an offence. Some communications must also contain the company number. Similar requirements as to disclosure of name and status apply to CIOs.

A body which is registered for VAT should quote its VAT registration number on all invoices and receipts.

These legal requirements can be observed in any reasonable way which the trustees decide, as long as relevant statements are legible and given in English (or in Wales, in Welsh). There is, thus, scope for incorporating them in the design of the stationery and using it to announce or present the charity in a suitable way.

Stationery, which many people will receive, provides the first direct impression about the charity and its style and values. It will be useful to consider particular points, such as whether the paper should be recycled (reflecting concern with environmental issues), whether there should be a logo or script which will give some idea of the charity's purpose or philosophy in encapsulated form, and how much information, for example about patrons, staff or trustees, should be provided on the notepaper (bearing in mind that such details can change).

If the charity provides a service which is of financial value, or even if it merely wishes its work to be identifiable, it is worth considering registration of the design or logo as a service mark at the Intellectual Property Office. A solicitor, patent attorney or trade mark attorney can be engaged to advise on and make the application, but it is also possible to apply direct, and official guidance is provided.

4.6.1 Cost

The cost of stationery is a major constraint and, again, can be used positively to indicate the charity's concern for economy. It is, in any case, an inexcusable extravagance to use expensive, printed or high quality stationery for internal paperwork. Many organisations now use electronic letter templates and print them using office printers, rather than ordering letter paper from a commercial printer. This is fine as long as staff or volunteers do not create their own versions omitting the required information referred to above.

The paperwork used for seeking funds needs special attention, and may differ according to the person or body to whom it is addressed. Commercially popular, 'glossy' brochures will not necessarily convey the message that the charity needs (as opposed to spends) money. Unduly long and detailed submissions or those which are very closely typed, are not likely to be read in full. A naïvely organised piece of writing will risk conveying the message that funds will also be organised naïvely.

4.7 COMPUTERS

Computer technology is capable of transforming a charity's efficiency, by cutting out labour-intensive routines. It aids presentation immeasurably, and enables management information of high quality to be provided promptly to decision-makers, thus adding to the charity's professionalism. Just as easily, however, it can lead to obstacles, frustrations and consequential expense. No one is immune from making mistakes, particularly in a rapidly developing field. It is well worth seeking advice, not only from suppliers but also from other organisations performing comparable tasks, before acquiring the equipment or software, and arranging for appropriate training. There are numerous organisations which offer training.

Increasingly, charities are using modern forms of communication such as e-mail and the internet. Information provided by such methods may appear authoritative, but it is not subject to independent checks and should be treated with caution. In addition, copyright in material put out over the internet is difficult to protect in view of the ease with which it can be downloaded.

4.7.1 Websites and social media

Information technology not only makes running your charity easier, it is likely to provide your public face. An attractive website with information about a charity's aims and work can help increase your profile and attract donors and volunteers. Many charity websites allow visitors to sign up to email newsletters to keep them informed about the charity's activities.

Social media can be daunting to those unfamiliar with information technology but it is not difficult to pick up and it can be a valuable tool in getting your message across. Blogs, or 'micro-blogs' such as Twitter, can provide real-time details of your activities, as well as allowing you to keep up-to-date with news in your sector by 'following' other organisations. Facebook and LinkedIn will let you set up pages with information about your charity. The power of social media was recently illustrated by the 'Ice Bucket Challenge' which raised awareness of amyotrophic lateral sclerosis and motor neurone disease and encouraged donations to research.

4.8 PREMISES

A charity which is a limited company or registered under the Co-operative and Community Benefit Societies Act 2014 must have a registered office, clearly marked as such. However, there is no requirement for a charity to have its own actual office or premises and, in fact, many small charities, and some larger, grant-making charities, are administered from the homes of the trustees or the director or from the place of work of a part-time clerk or secretary.

Charities whose work involves the use of land or buildings, or who employ a number of employees (or volunteers) all working together, however, need their own premises. These may be owned, or leased or, in some cases, held on a contractual licence which does not amount to a tenancy. They may be used exclusively by the charity or shared with other organisations, including, sometimes, other charities.

4.8.1 Appearance of premises

Where the premises are used for the functional purposes of the charity, for example as a college or hospital or church or veterinary clinic, the functional use will determine the way the accommodation is arranged and will influence the appearance of the building. There can be no better (and no worse) advertisement for the charity than the outside of its functional property (and the interior too, if it is open to the public). It may become a landmark in the district, and it is to be hoped that it will not be an eye-sore. It should also be considered whether the site and building are suitable for the practical requirements of the charity.

Where the premises are the charity's headquarters or office, rather than being directly used to deliver a service to beneficiaries in person, their external appearance and internal functioning are equally important. Like stationery, they give a message to the world at large about the charity's values and approach to its work. In this case, however, the message tends to be a continuing and often permanent one which would be difficult or expensive to alter drastically.

The right sort of message will be conveyed if the approach to the premises is clearly signposted, the entrance accessible (to the disabled as well as the able-bodied) and is neither scruffy nor too imposing. If there are reception arrangements these should put visitors at their ease and, perhaps, include posters, leaflets or other materials which illustrate the charity's work and priorities.

4.8.2 Regulations

Trustees and officers should take care to ensure that they are aware of and comply with all the various regulations regarding the use of office and other buildings and any proposed alterations to them, for example fire regulations, health and safety regulations, building regulations and planning permissions.

Problems foreseen are often avoided, and one of the essentials is to provide staff with clear instructions about what to do in the event of fire or other emergencies. Policy decisions on eating and drinking in the building are helpful and smoking is, of course, now prohibited in the workplace.

4.8.3 Listed buildings

Many charities work from listed buildings, which may provide a pleasant general environment but prove difficult to adapt as the charity expands (in view of the conflict between modern safety standards and the conservation interest). Security from theft or damage is also increasingly necessary, and may be difficult to reconcile with other considerations. Adaptations or special arrangements may be required where sensitive equipment is installed.

4.8.4 Moving premises

Moving premises, for example when a charity acquires its own premises for the first time, or when it decides to move to a different or cheaper location, brings its own opportunities and risks. Simple precautions, such as notifying regular contacts of the proposed change of address, should be planned well in advance and may provide a good occasion for a wider and more general mailshot.

Budgeting for the new premises is essential and in this process the longer-term, as well as the shorter-term, should be considered. For example, questions to be raised could be as follows: Should a reserve fund for future repairs and decorations be set up from the start? Will the existing equipment be sufficient? Will the new location enable savings to be made on incidental costs, for example: can staff be recruited locally, saving on season ticket loans?

4.8.5 Neighbours

It is also useful to research the local services and facilities and to consider whether savings could be achieved or efficiency increased by co-operating with neighbours. It is most important that a charity should have good relations with its neighbours. Like any other business or resident, a charity is part of the local community and will be noticed and talked about. Good relations are vital where the activity of the charity is likely to cause concern to those living or working close by and who are not well-informed about how the charity operates. People who take the 'not in my backyard' approach and who object to activities they fear can often be pacified by a patient explanation of the purpose of the work, whether it is rehabilitation of drug users or the keeping of donkeys, and of the safeguards which the planners (presumably) have thought sufficient.

4.9 TRAINING

For some groups of people, regular training courses are taken for granted as a normal part of working life. For others, training does not seem relevant. For the latter group, training of the type given on a formal course may not be appropriate. However, there will undoubtedly be other forms of learning which they would welcome and enjoy. Included under the heading of 'training' for the purposes of this book are methods of learning connected directly or indirectly with the work of a charity.

Many trustees, employees and advisers of charities will have undergone professional or vocational training as part of their education. Most professions now require active members to undergo 'continuing professional development' to keep themselves up to date in a wide choice of subjects, some of which are very specialised. As a matter of interest, such formal courses include charity law for solicitors.

4.9.1 Self-help

In addition, individuals may gain access to further training opportunities by joining a professional association. For example, a lawyer who is interested may join the Charity Law Association or the Society of Trust and Estate Practitioners, and attend sociable meetings at which talks will be given. A chartered secretary may join the Charity Secretaries Group of the Institute of Chartered Secretaries and Administrators, which provides much the same benefits. A charity accountant may join the influential Charity Finance Group. Management training, as already noted, is widely available, whether at vast expense and prestige or through local authority courses for the voluntary sector or at some intermediate level or cost. Some so-called management courses are, unfortunately, eccentric or experimental and are best avoided. It is often better to start by joining an association of people performing similar work functions and decide, after discussion of the experiences of others, what course would be most suitable for an individual.

4.9.2 Academic institutions

Academic institutions are increasingly moving into the area of training for work with charities. For example, St Mary's University, Twickenham offers an MA in charity management and South Bank University in London offers courses in charity finance and management.

4.9.3 Technical skills training

Training in technical skills is readily available at all levels of computing and other uses of information technology. In such a rapidly changing field, it is difficult for people to honestly claim that they know it all already.

4.9.4 Special courses

There are also courses designed with very particular types of students in mind, for example self-assertiveness.

4.9.5 Opportunities for staff

A good employer will encourage staff to undertake training courses whether by offering study leave or providing in-house training, but to make this worthwhile it is essential that the employee is given credit for the training undertaken and asked to make use of it. Charities need to have a policy on training.

One of the problems faced by junior staff or certain specialists is that they are categorised when they enter the charity's service and, in reality, have no opportunity of career development or diversification, except by leaving to go to another job. This is extremely wasteful of the very people whom a charity should be retaining and developing. It accords with the flexible spirit of most charities that such employees should be given better opportunities.

4.9.6 Informal training

Apart from formal training courses and organised professional activities there is a great deal of activity, within the charity world, in the sphere of informal learning through meetings and discussions. These can be of inestimable benefit not only to the participants themselves, whose problems at work will fall into perspective when compared with the experience of other people in similar posts, but also to the charity itself. Often at minimal cost, and during a lunch hour or in the early evening, those involved in running a charity can imbibe new ideas, gain in morale and bring back to the charity a sense of being part of a larger movement and of being near the forefront of the thinking within it.

Most of these meetings and discussions are advertised regularly by the NCVO or elsewhere in the charity press, and are attended not only by charity workers but also by trustees. There are many reasons why trustees should make more efforts to attend such meetings, both to learn and to contribute.

In-house training may sound more mundane, but there is certainly a place for a period of induction for new trustees, staff and volunteers, and there is no reason why these should not be combined to give the newcomers a chance to meet one another. There is also an advantage in getting staff and trustees together for conferences or meetings, or merely for social events, from time to time. It may also prove a useful and relatively painless method of bringing to light potential areas of conflict, and enable preventative or remedial action to be taken promptly. In addition, there may be scope for specialist training where the charity runs an institution, performs an unusual function, or has particular traditions which involve special ways of doing things.

For some charities, it may be economical, and provide additional interest for participants, to arrange a combined training activity with another charity, or another branch of the same charity, or with another organisation in the locality.

Learning and training should be an enjoyable, positive experience. It should also help to bind participants together, to facilitate co-operation and team-building and to reinforce the concept of belonging to the organisation and 'owning' its policies. It is therefore desirable to seek the best training available. On the other hand, it has cost implications and charities must be wary of extravagance. A constructive approach is to regard the cost as equivalent to an investment and to be careful both about initial selection and monitoring and utilising the service which has been provided.

4.10 TROUBLESHOOTING

No charity, however well-run, is immune from the occasional disaster or hitch. The importance lies in what is done about it and what is learned from it. Any action taken determines the degree to which the charity's credibility is damaged, and even whether or not the charity survives. Loss of credibility does not only mean loss of potential for fundraising; it can also make it difficult to recruit good staff or trustees or to be taken seriously by the authorities and others whom the charity wishes to reach.

It should be remembered that serious incidents affecting charities should be reported to the relevant regulator. This includes significant loss to the charity's money or other assets, or harm to reputation, as well as the offer of a large donation from an unverified source.

4.10.1 Physical emergencies

Physical emergencies can be dealt with by practical steps, for example by having well-thought-out procedures to deal with fire or flood, and adequate insurance cover.

4.10.2 Insurance

Insurance will also go some way to assist in the case of financial loss through negligence or theft or other dishonesty on the part of members of staff, although careful selection procedures, including the taking-up of references and prudent financial management which avoids putting temptation in people's way, is preferable and usually effective.

4.10.3 Negligence

Losses caused by the negligence of advisers or other independent contractors should be recoverable from their professional indemnity insurers, if necessary through court action. This is one of the arguments in favour of appointing a surveyor or architect to supervise work on a building project.

4.10.4 Tenants' defaults

The defaults of tenants who are not beneficiaries of the charity can be guarded against by taking adequate deposits on the grant of the tenancy, making sure that there is an effective system for collecting rent and investigating every suspected breach of covenant. The strict requirements as to tenancy deposit protection schemes must of course be observed.

4.10.5 Compensation

Failures by suppliers or service-providers can be dealt with by a claim for compensation. Similarly, if a trustee wanders off the straight and narrow and commits a breach of trust, prompt action, if necessary through the courts, will often provide the best solution.

4.10.6 Problems

Troubleshooting is less straightforward in three sets of circumstances, outlined below.

4.10.6.1 Running out of money

A charity that has made plans on the strength of promises of money that do not materialise may find it impossible to continue to operate on anything like the scale it envisaged, and may be forced to make staff redundant or even to wind up the charity. In the case of a charitable company, the charity trustees will be personally at risk of having to pay the charity's debts if they allow it to continue operating while it is technically insolvent (ie cannot pay its debts from its assets). It *must*, therefore, stop operations.

It is wise to cease operating in such circumstances even where company law does not provide this incentive. This is particularly so in the case of unincorporated charities where the trustees may find themselves personally liable if the assets of the charity are insufficient to meet its liabilities. It is then up to the trustees to take urgent steps either to find the required funds or to reorganise the charity's work in a way which is practicable. It may involve a radical alteration to the constitution or functions of the charity, or amalgamation with a similar charity, or even a takeover by another body of trustees.

If a charity is vulnerable through dependence on grant aid, the staff must be made aware of this, and sufficient financial advice should be obtained in order that staff and beneficiaries may be protected as far as possible. This is also another very good reason for maintaining co-operative relationships with other bodies.

4.10.6.2 *Charity Commission inquiry*

Anyone may make a complaint about a particular charity to the Charity Commissions in England Wales or Northern Ireland, who have the staff and resources to investigate any complaint which is well-founded and does not refer to an exempt charity or a charity outside of their respective jurisdictions. There are other bodies which will investigate complaints against specific types of exempt charity.

The Commissions have a number of wide-ranging powers to protect the assets of a charity. They may decide to remove one or more of the trustees or officers, appoint new trustees, appoint a receiver and manager to run the charity or even cause the transfer of the assets to another charity. Further, the relevant Commission or Attorney-General may decide to bring legal proceedings against one or more of the trustees for their misconduct.

Although a large proportion of the complaints investigated ultimately prove unfounded, the fact that a charity is being investigated, which is frequently of interest to the press, grant-makers and others, tends to indicate that something is wrong with the charity or its administration and this, in itself, can be very damaging.

To avoid uncalled for complaints, charity trustees should, first, take care not to do anything which would allow staff, tenants, advisers or beneficiaries to feel that they have been unfairly treated, and internal complaints procedures should be established to deal with such problems. Regrettably, there are occasions when the director or other senior staff member has become alienated from the trustees and, despite the risk to his or her job, will take a perceived problem to the Commission instead of consulting the trustees. Secondly, it is prudent to establish good relationships with the press, by providing ample information and responding helpfully when asked.

If a serious complaint is made or a formal investigation is proposed, one of the most constructive responses, which will generally be welcomed by the Commission, is for the charity to set up its own inquiry to establish the facts and correct and learn from any mistakes which have been made. This is not only very helpful and positive in itself, but enables any press reports to sound positive, and underlines the fact that the trustees, not the disaster, are in charge.

4.10.6.3 OSCR *inquiries*

Similar powers can be exercised in relation to Scottish charities by the OSCR. It has extensive powers which it may exercise following an inquiry, including directing a person acting on behalf of the charity to cease to so act, or to suspend them from doing so.

4.10.7 Mediation

It is a regrettable fact that many charities suffer, from time to time, from internal disputes, either within the workforce or the trustee body or between one and the other. There is no reasonable excuse for such self-defeating and destructive behaviour, which fits no one's idea of charity.

Publicity is extremely damaging in this situation, both because it encourages attitudes to harden and because of its effect on the charity's public image.

Good management, open communications, the careful selection of trustees and staff, a strong sense of commitment and agreed priorities will all help to guard against this kind of calamity. If it does arise, however, feelings are likely to run high, righteous indignation flourishes and intemperate words may appear in print.

The use of alternative dispute resolution ('ADR') is now accepted as a preferred course to litigation and involves a series of techniques aimed at finding solutions without recourse to the courts. Arbitration is one method, but tends to be costly. Another, less expensive and, in many ways, more satisfactory, technique is mediation. A mediator, preferably someone who has been specially trained in the method and who may be nominated by an independent outside agency, is appointed to assist the parties to reach a solution by agreement. The mediator's fees are paid equally by both sides to ensure impartiality. The process is not binding unless and until an agreement is reached. The mediator will not impose the solution but try to bring out the underlying common ground between the parties and discover in what ways the matters which they regard as most important can be incorporated into the solution. Most mediations result in a final, binding agreement, and those which do not often make the remaining stages in the dispute simpler and easier to deal with.

CHAPTER 5

EUROPE

5.1 HOW CHARITIES FIT IN

There are equivalents of charities in European countries other than the UK and the Republic of Ireland, but since their legal systems are predominantly based on Roman law, which did not have the need to develop the trust concept or the concept of charitable purposes, English law stands out as having the most developed legal concept of charity and the most refined methods of supervision and accountability. In relation to what we recognise as charities, the technical form of the organisation is far more important in Europe than in this country. In Europe, two main categories are prevalent: *foundations*, which are similar to UK charitable trusts but have a corporate form; and *associations*, which are similar to what would be called voluntary organisations in the UK. In addition, churches in Europe carry out a good deal of charitable work directly.

5.1.1 Social economy

The social economy covers much more than charitable purposes or organisations. It includes non-charitable friendly societies, agricultural co-operatives and other mutual trading bodies, housing associations and what is known as 'social tourism', ie the provision of holidays for workers or for the poor. Such organisations may operate in commercial ways, except that their aim is not profit but the benefit of members or a section of the public. They are sometimes designated, in French, organisations 'sans but lucratif', a phrase which is closer in meaning to 'non-profit-distributing', or the American phrase 'not-for-profit' than to the usually inexact 'non-profit-making'.

It may be many years before decisions are taken and implemented to harmonise the rules (including supervision and tax reliefs) between Member States, but there are some signs of convergence. For example, the European Court of Justice has declared that the practice of applying charity tax reliefs only to donors to domestic charities to be in breach of EU principles. The law relating to Gift Aid was thus amended to include donations to organisations in the EU that meet the UK definition of charities. Regulations designed to prevent money laundering and funds being used for terrorist purposes are in place.

5.2 EUROPEAN LAW

As a result of being a signatory to the European treaties, the UK is subject to EU law, which must be applied by UK courts. There are, however, different kinds of EU legislation which affect us in different ways.

5.2.1 Treaties

The treaties, which may be amended and supplemented from time to time, are the primary legislation and directly applicable to governments and commercial (and other) entities. They define the areas of policy for which the Community is responsible and set out general principles, for example on competition, which can have a direct effect on the way economic activities operate. The Maastricht Treaty (which came into force on 1 November 1993) established the European Union. This has since been amended by later treaties.

5.2.2 Regulations

Regulations are binding, unavoidable and directly applicable in the courts of all Member States.

5.2.3 Directives

Directives are addressed to national governments and require them to introduce domestic legislation to achieve a stated result. The method of achieving that stated result is for the individual Member State to decide. Directives are, naturally, less detailed than regulations and deal with policy. However, they are binding on the Member States, who must report what steps have been taken to implement them and do so by a specified date.

5.2.4 Decisions

Decisions are addressed to particular Member States, institutions or individuals, on whom they are binding.

5.2.5 Recommendations and Opinions

Recommendations and Opinions are not binding but, nevertheless, carry considerable weight, and may be referred to in decisions of the European Court of Justice.

5.3 EUROPEAN INSTITUTIONS

There is an interlocking (and confusing) series of institutions which carry out the functions of the EU in ways which are still being refined and developed.

The following summary of the European institutions explains in outline the various bodies involved in the development and implementation of EU policy.

5.3.1 Council of the European Union

The Council of the European Union (formerly the Council of Ministers) is the principal legislative assembly and, whilst it was originally intended to legislate only on proposals from the European Commission, it has taken on the role of initiating policy. The configuration of the Council depends on the question at issue. Thus, at the General Affairs Council meetings the European affairs Ministers of Member States will be present, whereas more specialised ministers will attend meetings of other configurations, dealing with such matters as agriculture. The Presidency of the Council of the European Union is a post which is held by Member States, in turn, for 6 months at a time, and enables the holder to set the agenda.

5.3.2 Committees of Permanent Representatives

Preparatory work for meetings of the Council of the European Union is carried out by one of the Committees of Permanent Representatives ('COREPERS 1 and 2') and, below them, by a number of committees and working parties which advise the Council and Commission and analyse Commission proposals. There is also an informal group of committees advising on policy areas which are not covered by the treaties.

5.3.3 European Council

The European Council existed informally for some time but was placed on a formal footing by the Treaty of Lisbon, which also created the role of President of the European Council. It consists of the heads of government of the Member States and the heads of the Commission, who aim to set goals and make policy decisions (sometimes on specific issues), consider the admission of new members to the Community, resolve internal problems and deal with challenges which face the Community from outside. Meetings are held at least every 6 months.

5.3.4 European Commission

The Commission is often described as the Civil Service of the EU but, whilst it has equivalent functions, it has greater influence and power to initiate policy than a government department in the UK. It is headed by 28 Commissioners, each with responsibility for a particular area of policy allocated by the President of the Commission, who is nominated by the European Council and approved by the European Parliament. Each Commissioner is supported by a 'cabinet' of officials. There are various grants available from the Commission to support projects which further the interests of the EU.

5.3.5 Directorates General

Below the Commissioners are the Directorates General, whose responsibilities are concerned with different areas of policy and several of them may involve some engagement with the charitable sector. These include the Directorates General for Education and Culture; Employment, Social Affairs and Inclusion; Environment; General Enterprise and Industry; and Humanitarian Aid and Civil Protection.

5.3.6 European Parliament

The European Parliament is a directly elected assembly whose members sit for terms of 5 years. At present there are 751 MEPs. Members gravitate to various groups, according to their national party, the most prominent of which are the European People's Party and the Progressive Alliance of Socialists and Democrats. There is also the European Reformists and Conservatives Group, the Alliance of Liberals and Democrats for Europe, the Greens/European Free Alliance and Europe of Freedom and Direct Democracy, amongst others. The procedural arrangements make provision for representation of the various groupings, both in plenary sessions and in committees.

The plenary sessions take place in Strasbourg or Brussels and the committees meet in Brussels. Researchers and parliamentary staff make use of the library for information on social issues, to which charities may usefully contribute material.

The main functions of the European Parliament are the consideration of proposed legislation via the committees (see below) and, most importantly, the setting of the budget. The European Parliament is able to suggest amendments to legislative proposals and to add new areas of expenditure to the budget, but the power to propose legislation primarily rests with the Commission.

5.3.7 Committees

The committees carry out most of the work of the Parliament. There are 20 standing committees. The concerns of charities are not covered by any one committee but are distributed between several, including the standing committees for Culture and Education, Foreign Affairs (which has a human rights sub-committee), and Employment and Social Affairs. The committees examine proposals from the Commission on which the opinion of Parliament is sought, and each is led by a 'rapporteur'.

5.3.8 European Economic and Social Committee

The European Economic and Social Committee ('EESC') consists of 353 members chosen by the governments of Member States and representing three main groups – employers, workers and others (including environmental protection agencies, the professions, small businesses, consumers and local authorities). This committee was established because it was considered that the European Parliament did not provide enough scope for the discussion of these specific interests. The Committee is divided into six sections, dealing with Agriculture, Rural Development and the Environment;. Economic and Monetary Union and Economic and Social Cohesion; Employment, Social Affairs and Citizenship; External Relations; the Single Market, Production and Consumption; and Transport, Energy, Infrastructure and the Information Society. There is a plenary session in Brussels nine times a year, and the sections give influential Opinions, prepared by rapporteurs after careful consultation, on EU affairs.

Referral of a question to the Committee for its Opinion is sometimes mandatory, in cases where it concerns social policy or the European Social Fund, but is otherwise optional. The Committee may also give an Opinion on its own initiative.

5.3.9 Committee of the Regions

The Committee of the Regions was established in 1994 by the Maastricht Treaty. It represents regional interests and is composed of 353 representatives of local and regional authorities.

5.3.10 European Foundation

The European Foundation for the Improvement of Living and Working Conditions, usually referred to as just the European Foundation or 'Eurofound', is based in Dublin. Its members represent employers, trade unions and governments. The Foundation produces detailed reports on major issues, including, for example, housing projects for the young and counselling for the long-term unemployed, and also holds conferences on particular themes.

5.3.11 The Structural Funds

There are two 'structural funds' of relevance to charities: the European Regional Development Fund and the European Social Fund. The former supports regional development, economic change and enhanced competitiveness, while the latter embraces adaptability of workers and enterprises, access to employment and participation in the employment market, social inclusion and employment of disadvantaged people. Both make grants, including to charitable organisations, principally administered in member states. In addition, there are 'Community Initiatives' and various other programmes of relevance to charities which aim to promote a more balanced economic and social development.

5.3.12 Council of Europe

The Council of Europe is not an institution of the European Community but was set up after the Second World War to safeguard the cultural heritage of the European peoples, especially respect for human rights and the rule of law by democratic institutions, and to encourage social and economic progress.

It consists of a Committee of Ministers and a Parliamentary Assembly, both drawn from the democratic institutions in European countries, and a Congress of Local and Regional Authorities.

5.4 INTERACTION

Making positive use of the European institutions and obtaining grants from them is an art in itself. The following may help to indicate areas which are worth exploring.

5.4.1 European Commission

To influence Community legislation and the adoption of new policies the best approach may be via the Commission, which, in formulating legislative and policy proposals, has a healthy tradition of consulting people and organisations which have expertise in the subject, and setting up committees for this purpose. Social Economy Europe provides a forum for discussion with the Commission of general matters affecting bodies within the social economy and gives these organisations better visibility at a political level.

The Commission also monitors Community policy and supervises its implementation, by making decisions, regulations and directives, ensuring consistency and collecting (and spending) revenue (for example VAT). The Commission shares with the European Court of Justice the role of ensuring compliance with Community legislation, for example failures on the part of national governments to implement directives.

5.4.2 European Parliament

As indicated above, the European Parliament does not initiate legislation, although it can ask the Commission to submit legislative proposals to it. Indirect influence through the library has already been mentioned.

It is also possible to influence ultimate decision-making by persuading an MEP to suggest amendments to proposed legislation which comes to the Parliament for its opinion before being laid before the Council of the European Union.

5.4.3 European Economic and Social Committee

The EESC is not a decision-making body, but it does exercise influence on policy and may be persuaded to recruit expert advisers from charities operating in the field which it is considering, or to incorporate, in its reports, information or materials produced by relevant charities.

5.4.4 European Foundation

Similar influences may be possible in relation to Eurofound reports. Attendance at a conference may also prove very helpful in establishing contacts for the charity with others concerned with similar problems.

5.4.5 International non-governmental organisations

The work of the Council of Europe with International Non-Governmental Organsations (INGOs) has led to increased influence for these bodies. They can apply for 'participatory status' as a member of the Conference of INGOs in a number of fields. Such status is granted to organisations which are particularly representative of their fields at European level. A charity which is not itself an international body can gain influence indirectly through one which is.

5.5 NETWORKS AND UMBRELLA BODIES

There is an enormous proliferation of networking bodies which operate throughout Europe and, for most charities, they provide the ideal way to examine ways of both operating directly and gaining useful knowledge from other European countries. Some are listed below:

(1) The National Council for Voluntary Organisations ('NCVO') in the UK provides very practical guidance to member organisations on how and with whom to make contact, on networking and how to apply for grant aid. It aims to act as spokesman, in Europe and in Westminster and Whitehall, for the voluntary sector generally.

(2) The European Council of Associations of General Interest ('CEDAG') is a network emanating originally from the Council of Europe, which is leading moves for more formal arrangements within the Community for consultation with charities and other voluntary bodies.

(3) In addition, CEDAG uses its influence to press for funding for charitable work and has helped to establish an interest group for the sector (known as the Social Economy Intergroup) within the European Parliament. This is likely to provide an effective means of enabling charities, and the voluntary sector generally, to make members of the European Parliament aware of the issues which affect the sector.

(4) The European Foundation Centre ('EFC') represents grant-making bodies across Europe.

(5) The International Society for Third Sector Research ('ISTR') promotes education and research concerning 'civil society, philanthropy, and the nonprofit sectors' on an international basis.

APPENDIX A

CHARITABLE TRUSTS: MODEL TRUST DEED

Reproduced with the kind permission of the Charity Commission https://www.gov.uk/government/publications/setting-up-a-charity-model-governing-documents

A trust is likely to be appropriate where the charity:
- will not have a membership; and
- is unlikely to employ a significant number of staff or carry on any kind of business.

Guidance to consider before you begin

You may find it helpful to begin by reading the following guidance on our website:
- The comprehensive information under *Start up a charity*
- *Registering as a Charity* (CC21). Its checklist of questions will help you to decide how best to set up the charity.
- *Choosing and Preparing a Governing Document* (CC22). This gives advice on the practicalities of completing the charity's governing document and on the different provisions which may be needed.
- Our guidance *The Essential Trustee – What you need to know* (CC3), which sets out the basics that all charity trustees need to know.

Next steps

1. Completing the trust deed

Once you have decided to apply to register a charitable trust, please read the trust deed and its accompanying guidance notes carefully.

Some clauses contain blank spaces that you will need to fill in.

The model is intended to be sufficiently flexible to deal with most eventualities. If you want to include special or complex provisions which are not contained in it you should consider asking a solicitor to help you. Please make clear any changes you make and why they are necessary. This will help us to consider your application as quickly as possible. We cannot guarantee to accept every organisation which uses the model trust deed as charitable. We must consider each case separately.

2. After you have completed the model trust deed, please:
   - execute the deed – this involves signing and dating it in the presence of a witness – the notes give more detail about this; and
   - check whether the deed needs to be stamped by HM Revenue & Customs (see next page under 'Does the deed need to be stamped?')

3. Applying to register

To register a new charity, apply online. (The online application material includes *Application for registration – guidance notes*.)

Please attach a copy of your final executed trust deed and your signed Trustee Declaration to your application. If you cannot attach these documents to your application please proceed to apply online and we will email you instructions about how to send them to us.

If you cannot apply online, please contact us using the link from our website homepage.

4. How long will it take?

We can normally make a decision in 15 working days if an organisation:
   - uses our model wording for its objects (as set out in the *Example charitable objects* on our website);
   - shows that its activities are consistent with the objects;
   - shows that any private benefit is incidental and is properly managed; and
   - uses our model governing document,

Other applications will need closer consideration and so will take longer (especially where the charity's purposes are novel and/or at the boundaries of what is charitable).

Does the deed need to be stamped?

Deeds executed before 1 December 2003 require stamping.

Deeds executed on or after 1 December 2003 but before 13 March 2008 only require stamping if the deed declares trusts over stocks and shares.

Deeds executed on or after 13 March 2008 do not require stamping.

If your Deed needs to be stamped then you should send it (or a certified copy of it) to:

HM Revenue & Customs
Birmingham Stamp Office
City Centre House
30 Union Street
Birmingham
B2 4AR

Further information can be found on the HM Revenue & Customs website (www.hmrc.gov.uk) or by ringing the Stamp Duty helpline: 0845 603 0135.

THIS DECLARATION OF TRUST IS MADE

the .... day of .... 20 .... by ....

....

....

....

....

....

('the first trustees')[1]

The first trustees hold the sum[2] of

£ ....

....

....

on the trusts declared in this deed and they expect that more money or assets will be acquired by them on the same trusts.

NOW THIS DEED WITNESSES AS FOLLOWS:

1. **Administration**
   The charitable trust created by this deed ('the charity') shall be administered by the trustees. (In this deed, the expression 'the trustees' refers to the individuals who are the trustees of the charity at any given time. It includes the first trustees and their successors. The word 'trustee' is used to refer to any one of the trustees.)

2. **Name**[3]
   The charity shall be called

---

[1] Insert full names and addresses. (Clause 9 specifies the minimum number of trustees.) The first trustees should be the same people whose signatures are witnessed at the end of this declaration of trust and whose names appear on the Application for charity registration Trustee Declaration. The charity trustees will be subject to a number of legal duties which are set out in our guidance *The Essential Trustee: What you need to know* (CC3). All prospective charity trustees should read that guidance before taking up office.

[2] Insert a description of the money or other property held. A trust cannot exist unless there is some money or property that is subject to it. A token sum of money is sufficient to create a charitable trust, but may not be enough to enable the trust to qualify for registration: see *Registering as a Charity* (CC21).

[3] The power in this clause can be exercised whenever the trustees think that the charity's interests will be served by changing its name. In general, the Commission will object to a new name only

3. **Objects**[4]
    The objects of the charity ('the objects') are:

    ....

    ....

    ....

    ....

    ....

    ....

    ....

    ....

    ....

    ....

    ....

[Nothing in this deed shall authorise an application of the property of the charity for purposes which are not charitable in accordance with section 7 of the Charities and Trustee Investment (Scotland) Act 2005 and/or section 2 of the Charities Act (Northern Ireland) 2008.]

---

if it infringes the principles set out in section 42 of the Charities Act 2011 (briefly, if the name is too similar to that of another charity, or is in some other way misleading or misrepresentative, or is offensive).

[4] Describe here clearly what it is that you intend that your charity should set out to achieve. A charity's object must be expressed in exclusively charitable terms and this can be quite difficult. Guidance is available in our guidance *Choosing and Preparing a Governing Document* (CC22) and on our website where we have provided some basic model objects. The key elements to include are: the purpose itself (eg establishing and running a school); the people who can benefit (in our example, school age children); and, if appropriate any geographic limits which may be needed to define the area of benefit. This will not always be necessary. If you do include an area of benefit, it is common to define it by reference to a local government area; this has the advantage of clarity and simplicity, but can create problems if the area is subsequently altered or abolished.

If the charity will operate in Scotland and/or Northern Ireland you should include the wording in square brackets to meet the requirements of charity law in that / those countries, deleting as required if the charity works in one of those two countries.

4. **Application of income and capital**[5]

   The trustees must apply the income and, at their discretion all or part of the capital, of the charity in furthering the objects.

5. **Powers**[6]

   In addition to any other powers they have, the trustees may exercise any of the following powers in order to further the objects (but not for any other purpose):

   (1) to raise funds. In exercising this power, the trustees must not undertake any taxable permanent trading activity and must comply with any relevant statutory regulations;[7]

   (2) to buy, take on lease or in exchange, hire or otherwise acquire property and to maintain and equip it for use;[8]

   (3) to sell, lease or otherwise dispose of all or any part of the property belonging to the charity. In exercising this power, the trustees must comply as appropriate with sections 117-122 of the Charities Act 2011;[9]

   (4) to borrow money and to charge the whole or any part of the property belonging to the charity as security for repayment of the money

---

[5] This provision enables the trustees to spend the charity's capital, but doesn't oblige them to do so (it is only the charity's income that must be applied). This makes clear that the charity's capital is not 'permanent endowment' and can be spent as income if required.

[6] Include any of the powers from the following sub-clauses which you consider necessary, numbered in sequence. Some powers are implicit in a charity's objects (for example, if the object is to provide a school, the trustees have an implicit power to acquire premises). Other powers are given by statute, often only if specific conditions are met. For example, the Trustee Act 2000 gives trustees power to acquire and dispose of land, to borrow money in many circumstances, to delegate much of the running of the charity and to invest. However, there are some things that can be done only if the charity's governing document provides express power to do them. It is sensible to set out all the powers that the charity is likely to need, for the avoidance of doubt and to remind trustees of the conditions that have to be met when they exercise those powers.

[7] This sub-clause provides a general power to raise funds through a wide variety of methods including inviting and receiving donations and legacies. The only restriction here is that it does not allow the charity to engage in taxable permanent trading for the purpose of raising funds. Although trading on a small scale is allowed: HM Revenue & Customs provides guidance on the tax treatment of different sorts of trading. If your charity is likely to raise funds from trading, our guidance *Charities and Trading* (CC35) provides detailed advice. This sub-clause does not prevent trading in order to carry out the charity's object – for example, an educational charity can charge fees for the educational services it provides.

[8] This power is helpful if the trustees wish to acquire property either for use as office premises or functionally (such as a playground or school site). Our guidance *Acquiring Land* (CC33) contains further guidance on the issue. When the trustees acquire land for the charity, the ownership of the land cannot rest with the charity directly as it has no separate legal identity. The trustees will therefore need to ensure that title to the charity's land is held in the name of individuals, or a company, in trust on behalf of the charity. Typically this can be some or all of the trustees, the Official Custodian for Charities (see *The Official Custodian for Charities' Land Holding Service* – CC13) or a nominee – see clause 6 notes.

[9] This power enables the charity to dispose of its property. Sections 117-122 of the Charities Act 2011 apply to most charities and require trustees to comply with certain conditions to ensure that they dispose of the property for the best price reasonably obtainable. Our guidance *Disposing of Charity Land* (CC28) provides more information about this.

borrowed. The trustees must comply as appropriate with sections 124 – 126 of the Charities Act 2011 if they wish to mortgage land owned by the charity;[10]

(5) to co-operate with other charities, voluntary bodies and statutory authorities and to exchange information and advice with them;

(6) to establish or support any charitable trusts, associations or institutions formed for any of the charitable purposes included in the objects;

(7) to acquire, merge with or enter into any partnership or joint venture arrangement with any other charity formed for any of the objects;

(8) to create such advisory committees as the trustees think fit;

(9) to employ and remunerate such staff as are necessary for carrying out the work of the charity;[11]

(10) to do any other lawful thing that is necessary or desirable for the achievement of the objects.

6. **Statutory powers**[12]

Nothing in this deed restricts or excludes the exercise by the trustees of the powers given by the Trustee Act 2000 as regards investment, the acquisition or disposal of land and the employment of agents, nominees and custodians.

7. **Delegation**[13]

(1) In addition to their statutory powers, the trustees may delegate any of their powers or functions to a committee of two or more trustees. A committee must act in accordance with any directions given by the trustees. It must report its decisions and activities fully and promptly to the trustees. It must not incur expenditure on behalf of the charity except in accordance with a budget previously agreed by the trustees.

(2) The trustees must exercise their powers jointly at properly convened meetings except where they have:

(a) delegated the exercise of the powers (either under this provision or under any statutory provision), or

(b) made some other arrangements, by regulations under clause 22.

(3) The trustees must consider from time to time whether the powers or functions which they have delegated should continue to be delegated.

---

[10] This provides the trustees with an explicit power to borrow. It also makes clear that if this power to borrow involves securing the loan on assets of the charity the trustees must comply with the requirements of the Charities Act 2011. Briefly, the Act requires that the trustees take advice and provide certain certificates/statements when they are borrowing money by way of mortgage. Our Operational Guidance *Borrowing and mortgages* on our website provides detailed information on this.

[11] This power cannot be used to employ trustees as staff. See clause 28.

[12] The trustees will have the wide powers conferred by the Trustee Act 2000, whether or not they are expressly included in this document. The statutory power of investment requires the trustees to take advice and to consider the need to invest in a range of different investments. Our guidance Investment of Charitable Funds: Basic Principles (CC14) provides more information about charity investments. The powers to employ agents, nominees and custodians is of particular use where a charity wishes to use an investment manager or where it owns land and needs a nominee to hold land on its behalf – see note to clause 5(2).

[13] The trustees are responsible for supervising the activities of their delegates.

8. **Duty of care and extent of liability**
   (1) When exercising any power (whether given to them by this deed, or by statute, or by any rule of law) in administering or managing the charity, each of the trustees must use the level of care and skill that is reasonable in the circumstances, taking into account any special knowledge or experience that he or she has or claims to have ('the duty of care').
   (2) No trustee, and no one exercising powers or responsibilities that have been delegated by the trustees, shall be liable for any act or failure to act unless, in acting or in failing to act, he or she has failed to discharge the duty of care.

9. **Appointment of trustees**[14]
   (1) There must be at least [ ] trustees. Apart from the first trustees, every trustee must be appointed [for a term of .... years] by a resolution of the trustees passed at a special meeting called under clause 15 of this deed.
   (2) In selecting individuals for appointment as trustees, the trustees must have regard to the skills, knowledge and experience needed for the effective administration of the charity.
   (3) The trustees must keep a record of the name and address and the dates of appointment, re-appointment and retirement of each trustee.
   (4) The trustees must make available to each new trustee, on his or her first appointment:
      (a) a copy of this deed and any amendments made to it;
      (b) a copy of the charity's latest report and statement of accounts.[15]
   (5) The first trustees shall hold office for the following periods respectively:[16]

....

....

---

[14] Insert the number of trustees in the square brackets. Unless the charity is to be administered by a company, we recommend that there are at least three trustees. This will help with the quality of decision making and the sharing of the responsibilities and duties that attach to trusteeship. (There must be at least two trustees to give a receipt for capital.) Refer also to clause 12 of the deed about trustee numbers. We would recommend that trustees are appointed for a fixed term and if you choose this option, delete the square brackets and complete the number for the term of years. If the appointment is not to be for a fixed term, delete the text in the square brackets.

[15] Our guidance *Finding New Trustees – What charities need to know* (CC30) provides guidance on effective methods of recruiting new trustees. This includes advice on what information to provide new trustees with – in addition to (a) and (b) here, the trustees might wish to provide a copy of the minutes covering the previous year's meetings.

[16] The first trustees are those individuals named at the beginning of this deed. There is no need to include sub-clause (5) if the trustees will continue in post until they retire. There are, however, benefits in including fixed periods of appointment, not least by ensuring that the appointments are regularly reviewed. If this sub-clause is included, we recommend that you 'stagger' the terms of office of the first trustees to ensure that they do not all go out of office at the same time. For example, if there are three trustees, one might be appointed for five years, one for four years and one for three years.

10. **Eligibility for trusteeship**
    (1) No one shall be appointed as a trustee:
        (a) if he or she is under the age of 18 years; or
        (b) if he or she would at once be disqualified from office under the provisions of clause 11 of this deed.
    (2) No one shall be entitled to act as a trustee whether on appointment or on any re-appointment as trustee until he or she has expressly acknowledged, in whatever way the trustees decide, his or her acceptance of the office of trustee of the charity.

11. **Termination of trusteeship**
    A trustee shall cease to hold office if he or she:
    (1) is disqualified for acting as a trustee by virtue of sections 178 and 179 of the Charities Act 2011 or any statutory re-enactment or modification of that provision;[17]
    (2) in the written opinion, given to the charity, of a registered medical practitioner treating that person, has become physically or mentally incapable of acting as a trustee and may remain so for more than three months;
    (3) is absent without the permission of the trustees from all their meetings held within a period of six months and the trustees resolve that his or her office be vacated; or
    (4) notifies to the trustees a wish to resign (but only if enough trustees will remain in office when the notice of resignation takes effect to form a quorum for meetings).

12. **Vacancies**
    If a vacancy occurs the trustees must note the fact in the minutes of their next meeting. Any eligible trustee may be re-appointed. If the number of trustees falls below the quorum in Clause 17(1), none of the powers or discretions conferred by this deed or by law on the trustees shall be exercisable by the remaining trustees except the power to appoint new trustees.

13. **Ordinary meetings**[18]
    The trustees must hold at least two ordinary meetings each year. One such meeting in each year must involve the physical presence of those trustees who attend the meeting. Other meetings may take such form, including video conferencing, as the trustees decide provided that the form chosen enables the trustees both to see and to hear each other.

14. **Calling meetings**[19]

---

[17] Our guidance *Finding New Trustees – What charities need to know* (CC30) explains what sections 178 and 179 of this Act covers. In very broad terms, someone who has been convicted of offences involving deception or fraud, or who is an undischarged bankrupt or who has been removed from office as a trustee by us will be disqualified for acting as a trustee.

[18] We provide guidance on meetings in our guidance *Charities and Meetings* (CC48).

[19] Insert the name of one of the first trustees who will call the first meeting. 'Clear days' does not include the day on which the notice would be received by the trustee or the day on which the meeting is held. Section 332 of the Charities Act 2011 sets out how notice may be given by post. In broad terms, the charity may send notice to each trustee at the UK address held in the

The trustees must arrange at each of their meetings the date, time and place of their next meeting, unless such arrangements have already been made. Ordinary meetings may also be called at any time by the person elected to chair meetings of the trustees or by any two trustees. In that case not less than ten days' clear notice must be given to the other trustees. The first meeting of the trustees must be called by . or, if no meeting has been called within three months after the date of this deed, by any two of the trustees.

15. Special meetings

A special meeting may be called at any time by the person elected to chair meetings of the trustees or by any two trustees. Not less than four days' clear notice must be given to the other trustees of the matters to be discussed at the meeting. However, if those matters include the appointment of a trustee or a proposal to amend any of the trusts of this deed, not less than 21 days' notice must be given. A special meeting may be called to take place immediately after or before an ordinary meeting.

16. Chairing of meetings

The trustees at their first ordinary meeting in each year must elect one of their number to chair their meetings. The person elected shall always be eligible for re-election. If that person is not present within ten minutes after the time appointed for holding a meeting, or if no one has been elected, or if the person elected has ceased to be a trustee, the trustees present must choose one of their number to chair the meeting.

The person elected to chair meetings of the trustees shall have no other additional functions or powers except those conferred by this deed or delegated to him or her by the trustees.

17. Quorum

(1) Subject to the following provision of this clause, no business shall be conducted at a meeting of the trustees unless at least one-third of the total number of trustees at the time, or two trustees (whichever is the greater) are present throughout the meeting.

(2) The trustees may make regulations specifying different quorums for meetings dealing with different types of business.

18. Voting

At meetings, decisions must be made by a majority of the trustees present and voting on the question. The person chairing the meeting shall have a casting vote whether or not he or she has voted previously on the same question but no Trustee in any other circumstances shall have more than one vote.

19. Conflicts of interests and conflicts of loyalties[20]

A charity trustee must:

---

charity's records: no notice is required for trustees living outside the UK. The notice would be regarded as being received on the day when 'in the ordinary course of post' it is expected to arrive: so a first class letter should be expected to arrive 1 day after posting and that is the day on which the notice would be regarded as being received.

[20] This reflects good practice on managing conflicts of interests and loyalties.

(1) declare the nature and extent of any interest, direct or indirect, which he or she has in a proposed transaction or arrangement with the charity or in any transaction or arrangement entered into by the charity which has not been previously declared; and

(2) absent himself or herself from any discussions of the charity trustees in which it is possible that a conflict will arise between his or her duty to act solely in the interests of the charity and any personal interest (including but not limited to any personal financial interest).

Any charity trustee absenting himself or herself from any discussions in accordance with this clause must not vote or be counted as part of the quorum in any decision of the charity trustees on the matter.

20. **Saving provisions**[21]

    (1) Subject to sub-clause (2) of this clause, all decisions of the charity trustees, or of a committee of the charity trustees, shall be valid notwithstanding the participation in any vote of a charity trustee:

    (a) who is disqualified from holding office;

    (b) who had previously retired or who had been obliged by this deed to vacate office;

    (c) who was not entitled to vote on the matter, whether by reason of a conflict of interests or otherwise

    if without the vote of that charity trustee and that charity trustee being counted in the quorum, the decision has been made by a majority of the charity trustees at a quorate meeting.

    (2) Sub-clause (1) of this clause does not permit a charity trustee to keep any benefit that may be conferred upon him or her by a resolution of the charity trustees or of a committee of charity trustees if, but for sub-clause (1), the resolution would have been void, or if the charity trustee has not complied with clause 19 (Conflicts of interests and conflicts of loyalties).

21. **Minutes**

    The trustees must keep minutes, in books kept for the purpose or by such other means as the trustees decide, of the proceedings at their meetings. In the minutes the trustees must record their decisions and, where appropriate, the reasons for those decisions. The trustees must approve the minutes in accordance with the procedures, laid down in regulations made under clause 22 of this deed.

22. **General power to make regulations**

    (1) The trustees may from time to time make regulations for the management of the charity and for the conduct of their business, including

    (a) the calling of meetings;

    (b) methods of making decisions in order to deal with cases or urgency when a meeting is impractical;

    (c) the deposit of money at a bank;

    (d) the custody of documents; and

---

[21] This reduces the risk of trustees' decisions being declared invalid for purely technical reasons.

(e) the keeping and authenticating of records. (If regulations made under this clause permit records of the charity to be kept in electronic form and requires a trustee to sign the record, the regulations must specify a method of recording the signature that enables it to be properly authenticated.)[22]

(2) The trustees must not make regulations which are inconsistent with anything in this deed.

23. **Disputes**[23]

If a dispute arises between the trustees about the validity or propriety of anything done by the charity trustees under this deed, and the dispute cannot be resolved by agreement, the trustees' party to the dispute must first try in good faith to settle the dispute by mediation before resorting to litigation.

24. **Accounts, Annual Report and Annual Return**[24]

The trustees must comply with their obligations under the Charities Act 2011 with regard to:

(1) the keeping of accounting records for the charity;
(2) the preparation of annual statements of account for the charity;
(3) the auditing or independent examination of the statements of account of the charity;
(4) the transmission of the statements of account of the charity to the Commission;
(5) the preparation of an Annual Report and its transmission to the Commission;[25]
(6) the preparation of an Annual Return and its transmission to the Commission.[26]

25. **Registered particulars**[27]

---

[22] The Electronic Communications Act 2000 and the Electronic Signatures Regulations 2002 permit electronic signatures to be accepted as evidence, subject to certain conditions. This sub-clause summarises those conditions. Regulations are effectively the internal procedures adopted by the trustees for the effective administration of the charity. They cannot be used to change any of the provisions in this deed – clause 31 of this deed sets out the procedure for amending the provisions of this deed.

[23] Disputes: It is good practice to include provisions for dealing with any disputes that arise between trustees. Litigation can be expensive, and litigation about the internal affairs of a charity would almost certainly constitute 'charity proceedings', which can be taken only with the Commission's authority. We would usually require the parties to a dispute to have tried mediation first.

[24] Guidance on our website sets out the key accounting requirements for charities. All charities with incomes over £10,000 must send accounts to the Charity Commission within 10 months of the end of the financial year to which the accounts relate.

[25] All charities with annual incomes of over £10,000 must send us their Annual Report within 10 months of the end of their financial year.

[26] All charities with annual incomes of over £10,000 must complete an Annual Return and send it to us within 10 months of the end of their financial year: the return provides a summary of key financial data and is used by us for monitoring purposes to detect issues which might require our attention or guidance.

[27] A charity's entry includes its name, correspondence address, objects and governing document. The Commission issues to every charity once a year an Annual Update form on which these details can conveniently be supplied. Trustees must provide details of any change in the entry although they do not have to use this form.

The trustees must notify the Commission promptly of any changes to the charity's entry on the Central Register of Charities.

26. **Bank account**[28]

   Any bank or building society account in which any of the funds of the charity are deposited must be operated by the trustees and held in the name of the charity. Unless the regulations of the trustees make other provision, all cheques and orders for the payment of money from such an account shall be signed by at least two trustees.

27. **Application of income and property**[29]
   (1) The income and property of the charity must be applied solely towards the promotion of the objects.
      (a) A charity trustee is entitled to be reimbursed out of the property of the charity or may pay out of such property reasonable expenses properly incurred by him or her when acting on behalf of the charity.
      (b) A charity trustee may benefit from trustee indemnity insurance cover purchased at the charity's expense in accordance with, and subject to the conditions in, section 189 of the Charities Act 2011.
   (2) Subject to clause 28, none of the income or property of the charity may be paid or transferred directly or indirectly by way of dividend, bonus, or otherwise by way of profit to any charity trustee.

28. **Benefits and payments to charity trustees and connected persons**[30]
   (1) General provisions

---

[28] The trustees can make regulations (under clause 22) to allow others associated with the operation of the charity such as employees or volunteers to sign cheques and other orders in relation to the charity's bank accounts so long as these activities are properly managed so as to reduce the risk of fraud. For example, the trustees might allow two senior employees or volunteers to sign cheques up to a defined face value, with a limit on the total value of cheques which they are authorised to sign in any one month. For charities which operate electronic bank accounts, there is guidance on trustee duties and operational best practice in *Internal Controls for Charities* (CC8) on our website.

[29] This clause sets out a trustees' entitlement to reasonable expenses and reflects the provisions in the 1993 Act about a charity trustee's entitlement to benefit from trustee indemnity insurance. It is included in the deed to inform people involved with the charity. It further reflects charity law requirements that the income and property of a charity must be applied solely to further its objects and not to benefit the charity trustees (except as permitted by the governing document – see clause 28 – or other express power). The trustees have a duty to ensure that the funds are correctly applied in accordance with this principle.

[30] Charity trustees may only benefit from their charity if they have express legal authorisation to do so (such as a clause in the trust deed). This restriction extends to people closely connected to a trustee ('connected persons' – this term is defined in Interpretation clause 33). This clause clarifies the restrictions that apply to the charity trustees. Even where trustees are allowed to benefit from the charity, this must only happen where the benefit is in the interests of the charity. Our guidance Trustee expenses and payments (CC11) provides more information about trustee benefits.

This clause permits a minority of the charity trustees or connected persons to receive payments and other benefits in certain instances (such as for goods and services they supply to the charity), subject to the stated controls. The option also allows other types of trustee benefit, subject to the Commission's prior consent.

These powers cannot be adopted by existing charities without the authority of the Charity

No charity trustee or connected person may:
(a) buy or receive any goods or services from the charity on terms preferential to those applicable to members of the public;
(b) sell goods, services or any interest in land to the charity;
(c) be employed by, or receive any remuneration from, the charity;
(d) receive any other financial benefit from the charity;
unless the payment or benefit is permitted by sub-clause (2) of this clause or authorised by the court or the Charity Commission ('the Commission'). In this clause a 'financial benefit' means a benefit, direct or indirect, which is either money or has a monetary value.

(2) Scope and powers permitting trustees' or connected persons' benefits
(a) A charity trustee or connected person may receive a benefit from the charity in the capacity of a beneficiary of the charity provided that a majority of the trustees do not benefit in this way.[31]
(b) A charity trustee or connected person may enter into a contract for the supply of services, or of goods that are supplied in connection with the provision of services, to the charity where that is permitted in accordance with, and subject to, the conditions in, section 185 of the Charities Act 2011.
(c) Subject to sub-clause (3) of this clause a charity trustee or connected person may provide the charity with goods that are not supplied in connection with services provided to the charity by charity trustee or connected person.
(d) A charity trustee or connected person may receive interest on money lent to the charity at a reasonable and proper rate which must be not more than the Bank of England bank rate (also known as the base rate).[32]
(e) A charity trustee or connected person may receive rent for premises let by the trustee or connected person to the charity. The amount of the rent and the other terms of the lease must be reasonable and proper. The charity trustee concerned must withdraw from any meeting at which such a proposal or the rent or other terms of the lease are under discussion.
(f) A charity trustee or connected person may take part in the normal trading and fundraising activities of the charity on the same terms as members of the public.

(3) Payment for the supply of goods only – controls
The charity and its charity trustees may only rely upon the authority provided by sub-clause (2)(c) of this clause if each of the following conditions is satisfied:

Commission.
No part of the clause allows trustees to receive payment for acting as a trustee.

[31] If your charity will benefit all local inhabitants in a specific geographical area (eg as a community trust) you may wish to substitute the following wording: 'A trustee or connected person may receive a benefit from the charity as a beneficiary provided that it is available generally to the beneficiaries of the charity.'

[32] The charity should document the amount of, and the terms of, the trustee's or connected person's loan.

(a) The amount or maximum amount of the payment for the goods is set out in an agreement in writing between the charity and the charity trustee or connected person supplying the goods ('the supplier') under which the supplier is to supply the goods in question to or on behalf of the charity.

(b) The amount or maximum of the payment for the goods in question does not exceed what is reasonable in the circumstances for the supply of the goods in question.

(c) The other charity trustees are satisfied that it is in the best interests of the charity to contract with the supplier rather than someone who is not a charity trustee or connected person. In reaching that decision the charity trustees must balance the advantage of contracting with a charity trustee or connected person against the disadvantages of doing so.

(d) The supplier is absent from the part of the meeting at which there is discussion of the proposal to enter into a contract or arrangement with him or her or it with regard to the supply of goods to the charity.

(e) The supplier does not vote on any such matter and is not to be counted when calculating whether a quorum of trustees is present at the meeting.

(f) The reason for their decision is recorded by the charity trustees in the minute book.

(g) A majority of the charity trustees then in office are not in receipt of remuneration or payments authorised by clause 28.

(4) In sub-clauses (2)-(3) of this clause:
  (a) 'charity' shall include any company in which the charity:
    (i) holds more than 50% of the shares; or
    (ii) controls more than 50% of the voting rights attached to the shares; or
    (iii) has the right to appoint one or more trustees to the board of the company.
  (b) In sub-clauses (2) and (3) of this clause 'connected person' includes any person within the definition set out in clause 33 (Interpretation).

29. Repair and insurance[33]

The trustees must keep in repair and insure to their full value against fire and other usual risks all the buildings of the charity (except those buildings that are required to be kept in repair and insured by a tenant). They must also insure suitably in respect of public liability and employer's liability.

30. Expenses

The trustees may use the charity's funds to meet any necessary and reasonable expenses which they incur in the course of carrying out their responsibilities as trustees of the charity.

---

[33] These are the minimum requirements and trustees should consider if any other forms of insurance are needed.

31. **Amendment of trust deed**
    (1) The trustees may amend the provisions of this deed, provided that:
        (a) no amendment may be made to clause 3 (Objects), clause 8 (Duty of care and extent of liability), clause 27 (Application of income and property) and clause 28 (Benefits and payments to charity trustees and connected persons), clause 32 (Dissolution) or this clause without the prior consent in writing of the Commission; and
        (b) no amendment may be made that would have the effect of making the charity cease to be a charity at law.
        (c) no amendment may be made to alter the objects if the change would undermine or work against the previous objects of the charity.
    (2) Any amendment of this deed must be made by deed following a decision of the trustees made at a special meeting.[34]
    (3) The trustees must send to the Commission a copy of the deed effecting any amendment made under this clause within three months of it being made.

32. **Dissolution**
    (1) The trustees may dissolve the charity if they decide that it is necessary or desirable to do so. To be effective, a proposal to dissolve the charity must be passed at a special meeting by a two-thirds' majority of the trustees. Any assets of the charity that are left after the charity's debts have been paid ('the net assets') must be given:
        (a) to another charity (or other charities) with objects that are the same or similar to the charity's own, for the general purposes of the recipient charity (or charities); or
        (b) to any charity for use for particular purposes which fall within the charity's objects.
    (2) The Commission must be notified promptly that the charity has been dissolved and, if the trustees were obliged to send the charity's accounts to the Commission for the accounting period which ended before its dissolution, they must send the Commission the charity's final accounts.

33. **Interpretation**
    (1) In this deed:
        all references to particular legislation are to be understood as references to legislation in force at the date of this deed and also to any subsequent legislation that adds to, modifies or replaces that legislation
    (2) 'connected person' means:
        (a) a child, parent, grandchild, grandparent, brother or sister of the trustee;
        (b) the spouse or civil partner of the trustee or of any person falling within sub-clause (a) above;

---

[34] Note that a change of name under clause 2 need only be made by resolution; it does not require to be confirmed by deed.

(c) a person carrying on business in partnership with the trustee or with any person falling within sub-clause (a) or (b) above;
  (d) an institution which is controlled –
      (i) by the trustee or any connected person falling within sub-clause (a), (b), or (c) above; or
      (ii) by two or more persons falling within sub-clause (d)(i), when taken together
  (e) a body corporate in which –
      (i) the charity trustee or any connected person falling within sub-clauses (a) to (c) has a substantial interest; or
      (ii) two or more persons falling within sub-clause (e)(i) who, when taken together, have a substantial interest.
(3) Sections 350 – 352 of the Charities Act 2011 apply for the purposes of interpreting the terms used in sub-clause (2) above.

IN WITNESS of this deed the parties to it have signed below[35]

1. **Signed as a deed by:**

1(a) ....

on this .... (day) of ....(month) .... (year)

in the presence of:

1(b) ....

Witness's name:

....

Witness's address:

....

....

....

2. **Signed as a deed by:**

2(a) ....

---

[35] This is set out to enable up to six trustees to sign and for these signatures to be witnessed so that the document has the formality of a deed. The first trustees named at the beginning of the document should sign. The witness(es) should be independent and not, for example, a close family relation of any of the first trustees. The first trustee should sign at 1(a) and the witness should sign at 1(b) and put his or her name and address where indicated; the next trustee should sign at 2(a) and the witness to that signature should complete 2(b) and so on until all the trustees have signed. If there are more than six trustees, please add further space following the pattern adopted for the first six sets of details.

on this .... (day) of ....(month) .... (year)

in the presence of:

2(b)...

Witness's name:

....

Witness's address:

....

....

....

3. Signed as a deed by:

3(a)...

on this .... (day) of ....(month) .... (year)

in the presence of:

3(b)...

Witness's name:

....

Witness's address:

....

....

....

4. Signed as a deed by:

4(a)...

on this .... (day) of ....(month) .... (year)

in the presence of:

4(b)...

Witness's name:

....

Witness's address:

....

....

....

5. **Signed as a deed by:**

5(a) ....

on this .... (day) of ....(month) .... (year)

in the presence of:

5(b) ....

Witness's name:

....

Witness's address:

....

....

....

6. **Signed as a deed by:**

6(a) ....

on this .... (day) of ....(month) .... (year)

in the presence of:

6(b) ....

Witness's name:

....

Witness's address:

....
....
....

APPENDIX B

COMPANY NOT HAVING A SHARE CAPITAL[1]

Reproduced with the kind permission of the Charity Commission
https://www.gov.uk/government/publications/setting-up-a-charity-model-governing-documents

ARTICLES OF ASSOCIATION FOR A CHARITABLE COMPANY

Articles of Association of

....

....

....

1   The company's name is[2]

....

....

....

(and in this document it is called the 'charity').

2   **Interpretation**[3]
In the articles:

---

[1] Details about the requirements of the Companies Act 2006 are available from Companies House www.companieshouse.gov.uk and our website www.charitycommission.gov.uk.

[2] Insert company name. In general, the Commission can accept any name but has the power to direct registered charity names to be changed in the circumstances set out in section 42(2) of the Charities Act 2011, which are explained in our guidance *Registering as a Charity* (CC21) and in our Operational Guidance *Names of charities* available on our website. In very broad terms, the name should not be offensive, or identical to (or too like) the name of any other charity, or likely to mislead the public about its purposes, activities, status, or connections.

[3] The articles include reference to a company secretary. Having a company secretary is no longer a legal requirement. Accordingly, the references to the company secretary are such that the charity can operate without one if it wishes to do so. Apart from the definition of 'secretary' and 'officers' in this interpretation article, there are also references to the secretary in articles, 41(3) and article 48.

'address' means a postal address or, for the purposes of electronic communication, a fax number, an e-mail or postal address or a telephone number for receiving text messages in each case registered with the charity;

'the articles' means the charity's articles of association;

'the charity' means the company intended to be regulated by the articles;

'clear days' in relation to the period of a notice means a period excluding:
- the day when the notice is given or deemed to be given; and
- the day for which it is given or on which it is to take effect; 'the Commission' means the Charity Commission for England and Wales; 'Companies Acts' means the Companies Acts (as defined in section 2 of the Companies Act 2006) insofar as they apply to the charity;

'the directors' means the directors of the charity. The directors are charity trustees as defined by section 177 of the Charities Act 2011;

'document' includes, unless otherwise specified, any document sent or supplied in electronic form;

'electronic form' has the meaning given in section 1168 of the Companies Act 2006;

'the memorandum' means the charity's memorandum of association;

'officers' includes the directors and the secretary (if any);

'the seal' means the common seal of the charity if it has one;

'secretary' means any person appointed to perform the duties of the secretary of the charity;

'the United Kingdom' means Great Britain and Northern Ireland; and

words importing one gender shall include all genders, and the singular includes the plural and vice versa.

Unless the context otherwise requires words or expressions contained in the articles have the same meaning as in the Companies Acts but excluding any statutory modification not in force when this constitution becomes binding on the charity.

Apart from the exception mentioned in the previous paragraph a reference to an Act of Parliament includes any statutory modification or re-enactment of it for the time being in force.

3 **Liability of members**

The liability of the members is limited to a sum not exceeding £10, being the amount that each member undertakes to contribute to the assets of the charity in the event of its being wound up while he, she or it is a member or within one year after he, she or it ceases to be a member, for:
(1) payment of the charity's debts and liabilities incurred before he, she or it ceases to be a member;
(2) payment of the costs, charges and expenses of winding up; and
(3) adjustment of the rights of the contributories among themselves.

4 **Objects**[4]

The charity's objects ('Objects') are specifically restricted to the following:

---

[4] The articles of a non-charitable company are not required to have objects. However, a charitable company's articles must specifically restrict the company to only furthering

....
....
....
....
....
....
....
....
....

[Nothing in the articles shall authorise an application of the property of the charity for purposes which are not charitable in accordance with section 7 of the Charities and Trustee Investment (Scotland) Act 2005 and/or section 2 of the Charities Act (Northern Ireland) 2008.]

5   **Powers**[5]

The charity has power to do anything which is calculated to further its Object(s) or is conducive or incidental to doing so. In particular, the charity has power:

(1) to raise funds. In doing so, the charity must not undertake any taxable permanent trading activity and must comply with any relevant statutory regulations;[6]

---

charitable objects.
Insert the purpose(s) for which the company has been formed. A charity's objects must be expressed in exclusively charitable terms. Guidance is available in *Choosing and Preparing a Governing Document* (CC22). The key elements to include are:
• The purpose itself (eg establishing and running a school)
• the people who can benefit; and if appropriate
• any geographic limits which may be needed to define the area of benefit. This will not always be necessary. If you do include an area of benefit, it is common to define it by reference to a local government area: this has the advantage of clarity and simplicity, but can create problems if the area is subsequently altered or abolished.
If the charity will operate in Scotland and/ or Northern Ireland you should include the wording in square brackets to meet the requirements of charity law in that / those countries, deleting as required if the charity works in one of those two countries.

[5] It is useful to include these powers to avoid any misunderstanding of the nature of the key powers available to the charity and the conditions that have to be met when exercising the powers. Examples of powers that companies already have include a power to insure and a power to amend the articles of association: note however that this power of amendment may in certain circumstances only be exercised with our prior consent under s 198 of the Charities Act 2011 (see our Operational Guidance *Alterations to governing documents: charitable companies* on our website).

[6] This provides a general power to raise funds through a wide variety of methods including inviting and receiving donations and legacies. The only restriction here is that it does not allow

(2) to buy, take on lease or in exchange, hire or otherwise acquire any property and to maintain and equip it for use;[7]

(3) to sell, lease or otherwise dispose of all or any part of the property belonging to the charity. In exercising this power, the charity must comply as appropriate with sections 117 and 122 of the Charities Act 2011.[8]

(4) to borrow money and to charge the whole or any part of the property belonging to the charity as security for repayment of the money borrowed or as security for a grant or the discharge of an obligation. The charity must comply as appropriate with sections 124 – 126 of the Charities Act 2011 if it wishes to mortgage land;[9]

(5) to co-operate with other charities, voluntary bodies and statutory authorities and to exchange information and advice with them;

(6) to establish or support any charitable trusts, associations or institutions formed for any of the charitable purposes included in the Objects;

(7) to acquire, merge with or to enter into any partnership or joint venture arrangement with any other charity;

(8) to set aside income as a reserve against future expenditure but only in accordance with a written policy about reserves;

(9) to employ and remunerate such staff as are necessary for carrying out the work of the charity. The charity may employ or remunerate a director only to the extent it is permitted to do so by article 7 and provided it complies with the conditions in that article;[10]

(10) to:
  (a) deposit or invest funds;
  (b) employ a professional fund-manager; and
  (c) arrange for the investments or other property of the charity to be held in the name of a nominee;

---

the charity to engage in taxable permanent trading for the purpose of raising funds. (Trading on a small scale is allowed. HM Revenue & Customs provides guidance on the tax treatment of different sorts of trading.) If your charity is likely to raise funds from trading, our guidance *Trustees, trading and tax* (CC35) provides detailed advice. The terms of this power do not prevent trading in order to carry out the charity's objects – for example, an educational charity can charge fees for the educational services it provides.

[7] This power is helpful if the charity is to acquire property either for use as office premises or functionally (such as a playground or school site). Our guidance *Acquiring Land* (CC33) contains further guidance on the issue.

[8] This power enables the charity to dispose of its property. Sections 117 – 122 of the Charities Act 2011, apply to most charities and require compliance with certain conditions to ensure that charity property is disposed of for the best terms reasonably obtainable. Our guidance *Sales, leases, transfers or mortgages: What trustees need to know about disposing of charity land* (CC28) provides more information about this.

[9] This provides the company with an explicit power to borrow. It also makes clear that if this power involves securing the loan on land of the charity, it must comply with the requirements of the Charities Act 2011. Briefly, the directors are required to take advice and provide certain certificates/statements when they are borrowing money by way of mortgage. Our Operational Guidance *Borrowing and mortgages* on our website provides detailed information on this.

[10] This power cannot be used to employ directors as staff. See article 7.

in the same manner and subject to the same conditions as the trustees of a trust are permitted to do by the Trustee Act 2000;[11]

(11) to provide indemnity insurance for the directors in accordance with, and subject to the conditions in, section 189 of the Charities Act 2011;

(12) to pay out of the funds of the charity the costs of forming and registering the charity both as a company and as a charity.

6   **Application of income and property**

(1) The income and property of the charity shall be applied solely towards the promotion of the Objects.[12]

(2)

(a) A director is entitled to be reimbursed from the property of the charity or may pay out of such property reasonable expenses properly incurred by him or her when acting on behalf of the charity.

(b) A director may benefit from trustee indemnity insurance cover purchased at the charity's expense in accordance with, and subject to the conditions in, section 189 of the Charities Act 2011.

(c) A director may receive an indemnity from the charity in the circumstances specified in article 57.

(d) A director may not receive any other benefit or payment unless it is authorised by article 7.[13]

(3) Subject to article 7, none of the income or property of the charity may be paid or transferred directly or indirectly by way of dividend bonus or otherwise by way of profit to any member of the charity. This does not prevent a member who is not also a director receiving:

(a) a benefit from the charity in the capacity of a beneficiary of the charity;

(b) reasonable and proper remuneration for any goods or services supplied to the charity.

7   **Benefits and payments to charity directors and connected persons**[14]

---

[11] The Trustee Act 2000 provides wide powers of investment and requires the charity to take advice and to consider the need to invest in a range of different investments. Our guidance *Investment of Charitable Funds: Basic Principles* (CC14) provides more information about charity investments. We strongly recommend that the directors record any investment policy in writing; they are legally required to do so if they delegate their investment function to an investment manager. The powers to employ agents, nominees and custodians are of particular use where the charity wishes to use an investment manager.

[12] Reflects charity law requirements that the income and property of a charity must be applied solely to further its objects and not to benefit the charity directors (except as permitted by the governing document – see article 7 – or other express power). The directors have a duty to ensurethat the funds are correctly applied in accordance with this principle.

[13] Sets out a director's entitlement to reasonable expenses and reflects the provisions in the Charities Act 2011 about a charity director's entitlement to benefit from trustee indemnity insurance. It is included in the articles of association to inform people involved with the charity.

[14] Directors are under a specific duty to avoid a situation in which they have, or can have, a direct or indirect interest that conflicts, or possibly may conflict, with the interests of the company (section 175(1) of the Companies Act 2006). This duty can be modified as regards a conflict of interests arising in relation to a transaction or arrangement with the company if it is permitted

(1) **General provisions**
No director or connected person may:
(a) buy any goods or services from the charity on terms preferential to those applicable to members of the public;[15]
(b) sell goods, services, or any interest in land to the charity;
(c) be employed by, or receive any remuneration from, the charity;
(d) receive any other financial benefit from the charity;
unless the payment is permitted by sub-clause (2) of this article, or authorised by the court or the Charity Commission.
In this article a 'financial benefit' means a benefit, direct or indirect, which is either money or has a monetary value.

(2) **Scope and powers permitting directors' or connected persons' benefits**
(a) A director or connected person may receive a benefit from the charity in the capacity of a beneficiary of the charity provided that a majority of the directors do not benefit in this way.[16]
(b) A director or connected person may enter into a contract for the supply of services, or of goods that are supplied in connection with the provision of services, to the charity where that is

---

by the company's articles of association (section 175(3) of the Companies Act 2006).
Where a benefit is authorised by an order of the Court or of the Charity Commission, the duty to avoid a conflict of interests does not arise (section 105(9) of the Charities Act 2011).
In addition, authorisation may be given by the unconflicted directors to a conflict of interests where the company's constitution includes a provision enabling them to provide such authorisation (section 175(5) of the Companies Act 2006).
Article 7 provides the necessary structure for all the benefits either to be specifically authorised by the articles within the terms of section 175(3) of the Companies Act 2006 (as modified by section 181 for charitable companies) or to be authorised by the Commission so that the duty in section 175(1) of the Companies Act 2006 does not apply. In addition, because of the specific duty of section 175 of the Companies Act 2006, some provision has been made for conflicts of duties where a director owes a duty of loyalty to another organisation but the unconflicted directors consider it is in the best interests of the charity for that director to continue as a director. This provision can be found at article 9.
Benefits and payments to charity directors and connected persons – Charity directors may only benefit from their charity if they have express legal authorisation to do so (such as a clause in the articles of association). This restriction extends to people closely connected to a director ('connected persons' – this term is defined in Interpretation article 61). This article clarifies the restrictions that apply to the charity directors. Even where directors are allowed to benefit from the charity, this must only happen where the benefit is in the interests of the charity. Our guidance *Trustee expenses and payments* (CC11) provides more information about directors' benefits.
This article permits a minority of the charity directors or connected persons to receive payments and other benefits in certain instances (such as for goods and services they supply to the charity), subject to the stated controls. The option also allows other types of director benefit, subject to the Commission's prior consent.

[15] This does not prevent a director from buying or leasing land from the charity: such transactions will however require the Commission's consent under section 117 of the Charities Act 2011. Any financial benefit authorised by this article must be within the stated definition.

[16] If your charity will benefit all local inhabitants in a specific geographical area you may wish to substitute the following wording: 'A director or connected person may receive a benefit from the charity as a beneficiary provided that it is available generally to the beneficiaries of the charity.'

permitted in accordance with, and subject to the conditions in, sections 185 and 186 of the Charities Act 2011.

(c) Subject to sub-clause (3) of this article a director or connected person may provide the charity with goods that are not supplied in connection with services provided to the charity by the director or connected person.

(d) A director or connected person may receive interest on money lent to the charity at a reasonable and proper rate which must be not more than the Bank of England bank rate (also known as the base rate).[17]

(e) A director or connected person may receive rent for premises let by the director or connected person to the charity. The amount of the rent and the other terms of the lease must be reasonable and proper. The director concerned must withdraw from any meeting at which such a proposal or the rent or other terms of the lease are under discussion.

(f) A director or connected person may take part in the normal trading and fundraising activities of the charity on the same terms as members of the public.

(3) Payment for supply of goods only – controls

The charity and its directors may only rely upon the authority provided by sub-clause (2)(c) of this article if each of the following conditions is satisfied:

(a) The amount or maximum amount of the payment for the goods is set out in an agreement in writing between the charity or its directors (as the case may be) and the director or connected person supplying the goods ('the supplier') under which the supplier is to supply the goods in question to or on behalf of the charity.

(b) The amount or maximum amount of the payment for the goods does not exceed what is reasonable in the circumstances for the supply of the goods in question.

(c) The other directors are satisfied that it is in the best interests of the charity to contract with the supplier rather than with someone who is not a director or connected person. In reaching that decision the directors must balance the advantage of contracting with a director or connected person against the disadvantages of doing so.

(d) The supplier is absent from the part of any meeting at which there is discussion of the proposal to enter into a contract or arrangement with him or her or it with regard to the supply of goods to the charity.

---

[17] The charity should document the amount of, and the terms of, the director's or connected person's loan.
These powers cannot be adopted by existing charities without the authority of the Charity Commission. None of these provisions allow directors to receive payment for acting as a director.

(e) The supplier does not vote on any such matter and is not to be counted when calculating whether a quorum of directors is present at the meeting.
(f) The reason for their decision is recorded by the directors in the minute book.
(g) A majority of the directors then in office are not in receipt of remuneration or payments authorised by article 7.

(4) In sub-clauses (2) and (3) of this article:
   (a) 'charity' includes any company in which the charity:
      (i) holds more than 50% of the shares; or
      (ii) controls more than 50% of the voting rights attached to the shares; or
      (iii) has the right to appoint one or more directors to the board of the company.
   (b) 'connected person' includes any person within the definition in article 61 'Interpretation'.

8 **Declaration of directors' interests**[18]

A director must declare the nature and extent of any interest, direct or indirect, which he or she has in a proposed transaction or arrangement with the charity or in any transaction or arrangement entered into by the charity which has not previously been declared. A director must absent himself or herself from any discussions of the charity directors in which it is possible that a conflict will arise between his or her duty to act solely in the interests of the charity and any personal interest (including but not limited to any personal financial interest).

9 **Conflicts of interests and conflicts of loyalties**[19]

(1) If a conflict of interests arises for a director because of a duty of loyalty owed to another organisation or person and the conflict is not authorised by virtue of any other provision in the articles, the unconflicted directors may authorise such a conflict of interests where the following conditions apply:

---

[18] This article imposes a duty on the directors to declare an interest in any transaction of the charity and to absent themselves from any discussion where there may be a conflict between their personal interests and those of the charity. This would include, for example, discussions about the need for the provision of a particular service which one of the directors might have an interest in supplying (although in this example the terms of section 185 of the Charities Act 2011 would already make it necessary for the director to absent him/herself). Statutory duties to declare any interests came into force on 1 October 2008 (sections 177 and 182 of the Companies Act 2006).

[19] This article permits unconflicted directors to authorise a conflict of interests arising from a duty of loyalty owed by a director to another organisation or person provided that there is no direct or indirect benefit of any nature received by the director in question or by a connected person. Such a procedure is permitted by section 175(4) and (5) of the Companies Act 2006 (as modified for charitable companies by section 181) where provision is made for it in the articles. The Commission considers that such a procedure should be limited to conflicts arising from a duty of loyalty to another organisation or person where there is no direct or indirect benefit of whatever nature to the director or to a connected person. In other circumstances involving a situation leading to a conflict of interests on the part of a director, the Commission is able to authorise the director to act notwithstanding the conflict where it is satisfied that this would be expedient in the interests of the charity (section 105 of the Charities Act 2011).

(a) the conflicted director is absent from the part of the meeting at which there is discussion of any arrangement or transaction affecting that other organisation or person;
(b) the conflicted director does not vote on any such matter and is not to be counted when considering whether a quorum of directors is present at the meeting; and
(c) the unconflicted directors consider it is in the interests of the charity to authorise the conflict of interests in the circumstances applying.
(2) In this article a conflict of interests arising because of a duty of loyalty owed to another organisation or person only refers to such a conflict which does not involve a direct or indirect benefit of any nature to a director or to a connected person.

10 Members
(1) The subscribers to the memorandum are the first members of the charity.
(2) Membership is open to other individuals or organisations who:
   (a) apply to the charity in the form required by the directors; and
   (b) are approved by the directors.
(3)
   (a) The directors may only refuse an application for membership if, acting reasonably and properly, they consider it to be in the best interests of the charity to refuse the application.
   (b) The directors must inform the applicant in writing of the reasons for the refusal within twenty-one days of the decision.
   (c) The directors must consider any written representations the applicant may make about the decision. The directors' decision following any written representations must be notified to the applicant in writing but shall be final.
(4) Membership is not transferable.
(5) The directors must keep a register of names and addresses of the members.[20]

11 Classes of membership
(1) The directors may establish classes of membership with different rights and obligations and shall record the rights and obligations in the register of members.
(2) The directors may not directly or indirectly alter the rights or obligations attached to a class of membership.
(3) The rights attached to a class of membership may only be varied if:
   (a) three-quarters of the members of that class consent in writing to the variation; or
   (b) a special resolution is passed at a separate general meeting of the members of that class agreeing to the variation.

---

[20] It is very important for the good administration of the charity to keep the register of members up to date: failure to do so can result in a number of problems, including serious difficulties with the calling of annual or general meetings. It should also be remembered that section 116 of the Companies Act 2006 sets out certain requirements for making the register available to members of the charity and to the public.

(4) The provisions in the articles about general meetings shall apply to any meeting relating to the variation of the rights of any class of members.

12 Termination of membership

Membership is terminated if:
(1) the member dies or, if it is an organisation, ceases to exist;
(2) the member resigns by written notice to the charity unless, after the resignation, there would be less than two members;
(3) any sum due from the member to the charity is not paid in full within six months of it falling due;
(4) the member is removed from membership by a resolution of the directors that it is in the best interests of the charity that his or her or its membership is terminated. A resolution to remove a member from membership may only be passed if:
    (a) the member has been given at least twenty-one days' notice in writing of the meeting of the directors at which the resolution will be proposed and the reasons why it is to be proposed;
    (b) the member or, at the option of the member, the member's representative (who need not be a member of the charity) has been allowed to make representations to the meeting.

13 General meetings

(1) The charity must hold its first annual general meeting within eighteen months after the date of its incorporation.
(2) An annual general meeting must be held in each subsequent year and not more than fifteen months may elapse between successive annual general meetings.[21]

14 The directors may call a general meeting at any time.

15 Notice of general meetings

(1) The minimum periods of notice required to hold a general meeting of the charity are:
    (a) twenty-one clear days for an annual general meeting or a general meeting called for the passing of a special resolution;
    (b) fourteen clear days for all other general meetings.
(2) A general meeting may be called by shorter notice if it is so agreed by a majority in number of members having a right to attend and vote at the meeting, being a majority who together hold not less than 90 percent of the total voting rights.
(3) The notice must specify the date time and place of the meeting and the general nature of the business to be transacted. If the meeting is to be an annual general meeting, the notice must say so. The notice

---

[21] We provide guidance on meetings in *Charities and Meetings* (CC48), produced in association with The Institute of Chartered Secretaries and Administrators (ICSA). This article makes provision for an annual general meeting. However, an annual general meeting is not a legal requirement and this article can be amended where this is appropriate. If no provision is to be made for an annual general meeting, consequential amendments will be required to articles 15(1)(a), 15(3), 32, 33(2) and 37(2).

must also contain a statement setting out the right of members to appoint a proxy under section 324 of the Companies Act 2006 and article 22.

(4) The notice must be given to all the members and to the directors and auditors.[22]

16 The proceedings at a meeting shall not be invalidated because a person who was entitled to receive notice of the meeting did not receive it because of an accidental omission by the charity.

17 Proceedings at general meetings
  (1) No business shall be transacted at any general meeting unless a quorum is present.
  (2) A quorum is:
    (a) [ ] members present in person or by proxy and entitled to vote upon the business to be conducted at the meeting; or
    (b) one tenth of the total membership at the time
    whichever is the greater.[23]
  (3) The authorised representative of a member organisation shall be counted in the quorum.

18
  (1) If:
    (a) a quorum is not present within half an hour from the time appointed for the meeting; or
    (b) during a meeting a quorum ceases to be present;
    the meeting shall be adjourned to such time and place as the directors shall determine.
  (2) The directors must reconvene the meeting and must give at least seven clear days' notice of the reconvened meeting stating the date, time and place of the meeting.
  (3) If no quorum is present at the reconvened meeting within fifteen minutes of the time specified for the start of the meeting the members present in person or by proxy at that time shall constitute the quorum for that meeting.[24]

19
  (1) General meetings shall be chaired by the person who has been appointed to chair meetings of the directors.

---

[22] This article provides for 21 days' notice for an annual general meeting or a general meeting called for the passing of a special resolution. The only legal requirement in respect of notice for general meetings of a private company specifies notice of at least 14 days. Accordingly, this figure can be substituted if considered appropriate.
Notice of a general meeting is required to include a statement setting out the rights of members to appoint a proxy (section 325 of the Companies Act 2006).

[23] Insert the figure for the quorum. This should be set with care. If it is too high, any absences may make it difficult to have a valid meeting. If it is too low, a small minority may be able to impose its views unreasonably. Note that article 18 sets out the procedure for dealing with situations where the meeting is inquorate.

[24] Note that this provision permits the rescheduled meeting to proceed without a quorum being present within 15 minutes of the specified start time. It also means that the number of members present in person or by proxy 15 minutes after the scheduled start of the meeting will form the quorum if the quorum required at article 17(2) is not achieved.

(2) If there is no such person or he or she is not present within fifteen minutes of the time appointed for the meeting a director nominated by the directors shall chair the meeting.
(3) If there is only one director present and willing to act, he or she shall chair the meeting.
(4) If no director is present and willing to chair the meeting within fifteen minutes after the time appointed for holding it, the members present in person or by proxy and entitled to vote must choose one of their number to chair the meeting.

20
(1) The members present in person or by proxy at a meeting may resolve by ordinary resolution that the meeting shall be adjourned.
(2) The person who is chairing the meeting must decide the date, time and place at which the meeting is to be reconvened unless those details are specified in the resolution.
(3) No business shall be conducted at a reconvened meeting unless it could properly have been conducted at the meeting had the adjournment not taken place.
(4) If a meeting is adjourned by a resolution of the members for more than seven days, at least seven clear days' notice shall be given of the reconvened meeting stating the date, time and place of the meeting.[25]

21
(1) Any vote at a meeting shall be decided by a show of hands unless before, or on the declaration of the result of, the show of hands a poll is demanded:
  (a) by the person chairing the meeting; or
  (b) by at least two members present in person or by proxy and having the right to vote at the meeting; or
  (c) by a member or members present in person or by proxy representing not less than one-tenth of the total voting rights of all the members having the right to vote at the meeting.
(2)
  (a) The declaration by the person who is chairing the meeting of the result of a vote shall be conclusive unless a poll is demanded.
  (b) The result of the vote must be recorded in the minutes of the charity but the number or proportion of votes cast need not be recorded.
(3)
  (a) A demand for a poll may be withdrawn, before the poll is taken, but only with the consent of the person who is chairing the meeting.
  (b) If the demand for a poll is withdrawn the demand shall not invalidate the result of a show of hands declared before the demand was made.

---

[25] This is a discretionary power for the members present in person or by proxy to adjourn a quorate meeting. This differs from the adjournment provisions in article 18 which are not discretionary and must be used where a general meeting is not quorate.

(4)
- (a) A poll must be taken as the person who is chairing the meeting directs, who may appoint scrutineers (who need not be members) and who may fix a time and place for declaring the results of the poll.
- (b) The result of the poll shall be deemed to be the resolution of the meeting at which the poll is demanded.

(5)
- (a) A poll demanded on the election of a person to chair a meeting or on a question of adjournment must be taken immediately.
- (b) A poll demanded on any other question must be taken either immediately or at such time and place as the person who is chairing the meeting directs.
- (c) The poll must be taken within thirty days after it has been demanded.[26]
- (d) If the poll is not taken immediately at least seven clear days' notice shall be given specifying the time and place at which the poll is to be taken.
- (e) If a poll is demanded the meeting may continue to deal with any other business that may be conducted at the meeting.[27]

22 Content of proxy notices

(1) Proxies may only validly be appointed by a notice in writing (a 'proxy notice') which –
- (a) states the name and address of the member appointing the proxy;
- (b) identifies the person appointed to be that member's proxy and the general meeting in relation to which that person is appointed;
- (c) is signed by or on behalf of the member appointing the proxy, or is authenticated in such manner as the directors may determine; and
- (d) is delivered to the charity in accordance with the articles and any instructions contained in the notice of the general meeting to which they relate.

(2) The charity may require proxy notices to be delivered in a particular form, and may specify different forms for different purposes.

(3) Proxy notices may specify how the proxy appointed under them is to vote (or that the proxy is to abstain from voting) on one or more resolutions.

(4) Unless a proxy notice indicates otherwise, it must be treated as -

---

[26] Where it is decided that a poll is to take place in these circumstances after a general meeting, all the members of the charity are entitled to vote.

[27] Article 21 sets out how votes may be taken. A poll is a formal count of votes on a resolution. It can be useful where a show of hands is inconclusive: it is also sensible where the votes of certain categories of member count for more than those of others and where there is a concern that this would not be recognised on a show of hands where the result is close.

(a) allowing the person appointed under it as a proxy discretion as to how to vote on any ancillary or procedural resolutions put to the meeting; and

(b) appointing that person as a proxy in relation to any adjournment of the general meeting to which it relates as well as the meeting itself.[28]

22A Delivery of proxy notices

(1) A person who is entitled to attend, speak or vote (either on a show of hands or on a poll) at a general meeting remains so entitled in respect of that meeting or any adjournment of it, even though a valid proxy notice has been delivered to the charity by or on behalf of that person.

(2) An appointment under a proxy notice may be revoked by delivering to the charity a notice in writing given by or on behalf of the person by whom or on whose behalf the proxy notice was given.

(3) A notice revoking a proxy appointment only takes effect if it is delivered before the start of the meeting or adjourned meeting to which it relates.

(4) If a proxy notice is not executed by the person appointing the proxy, it must be accompanied by written evidence of the authority of the person who executed it to execute it on the appointor's behalf.

23 Written resolutions

(1) A resolution in writing agreed by a simple majority (or in the case of a special resolution by a majority of not less than 75%) of the members who would have been entitled to vote upon it had it been proposed at a general meeting shall be effective provided that:

(a) a copy of the proposed resolution has been sent to every eligible member;

(b) a simple majority (or in the case of a special resolution a majority of not less than 75%) of members has signified its agreement to the resolution; and

(c) it is contained in an authenticated document which has been received at the registered office within the period of 28 days beginning with the circulation date.

(2) A resolution in writing may comprise several copies to which one or more members have signified their agreement.

(3) In the case of a member that is an organisation, its authorised representative may signify its agreement.[29]

---

[28] Article 22 makes provision for proxy voting. Members of a company have a legal right to appoint proxies under section 324 of the Companies Act 2006. A statement about this right must be contained in a notice calling a meeting of the company (section 325 of the Companies Act 2006). Article 15 deals with such notices.
The provision for proxies is based on the provisions in Schedule 2 of the Companies (Model Articles) Regulations 2008.

[29] Article 23 – This complies with the Companies Act 2006 which provides that if certain requirements are met members may agree written ordinary and special resolutions (sections 288 – 298). What constitutes an authenticated document is explained in section 1146 of the Companies Act 2006. A document sent in hard form is sufficiently authenticated by a signature of the person sending or supplying it. A document sent in electronic form is sufficiently

Votes of members

24 Subject to article 11, every member, whether an individual or an organisation, shall have one vote.

25 Any objection to the qualification of any voter must be raised at the meeting at which the vote is tendered and the decision of the person who is chairing the meeting shall be final.

26
  (1) Any organisation that is a member of the charity may nominate any person to act as its representative at any meeting of the charity.
  (2) The organisation must give written notice to the charity of the name of its representative. The representative shall not be entitled to represent the organisation at any meeting unless the notice has been received by the charity. The representative may continue to represent the organisation until written notice to the contrary is received by the charity.
  (3) Any notice given to the charity will be conclusive evidence that the representative is entitled to represent the organisation or that his or her authority has been revoked. The charity shall not be required to consider whether the representative has been properly appointed by the organisation.

27 **Directors**
  (1) A director must be a natural person aged 16 years or older.[30]
  (2) No one may be appointed a director if he or she would be disqualified from acting under the provisions of article 39.

28 The minimum number of directors shall be [ ] but (unless otherwise determined by ordinary resolution) shall not be subject to any maximum.[31]

29 The first directors shall be those persons notified to Companies House as the first directors of the charity.

30 A director may not appoint an alternate director or anyone to act on his or her behalf at meetings of the directors.

31 **Powers of directors**
  (1) The directors shall manage the business of the charity and may exercise all the powers of the charity unless they are subject to any restrictions imposed by the Companies Acts, the articles or any special resolution.

---

  authenticated (a) if the identity of the sender is confirmed in a manner specified by the company, or (b) where no such manner has been specified, if the communication contains or is accompanied by a statement of the identity of the sender and the company has no reason to doubt the truth of that statement.

[30] Article 27(1) – By 'natural person' we mean a human being rather than a company which can in some circumstances be regarded as a 'person'. The minimum age for a director in this article is 16 years. A statutory provision to this effect came into force on 1 October 2008.

[31] As good operational practice we recommend a minimum of three directors. This will help with the quality of decision making and the sharing of directors' responsibilities and duties. Note that article 42(2) requires a quorum of at least two directors.

(2) No alteration of the articles or any special resolution shall have retrospective effect to invalidate any prior act of the directors.
(3) Any meeting of directors at which a quorum is present at the time the relevant decision is made may exercise all the powers exercisable by the directors.

Retirement of directors

32 At the first annual general meeting all the directors must retire from office unless by the close of the meeting the members have failed to elect sufficient directors to hold a quorate meeting of the directors. At each subsequent annual general meeting one-third of the directors or, if their number is not three or a multiple of three, the number nearest to one-third, must retire from office. If there is only one director he or she must retire.

33
(1) The directors to retire by rotation shall be those who have been longest in office since their last appointment. If any directors became or were appointed directors on the same day those to retire shall (unless they otherwise agree among themselves) be determined by lot.
(2) If a director is required to retire at an annual general meeting by a provision of the articles the retirement shall take effect upon the conclusion of the meeting.

Appointment of directors

34 The charity may by ordinary resolution:
(1) appoint a person who is willing to act to be a director; and
(2) determine the rotation in which any additional directors are to retire.[32]

35 No person other than a director retiring by rotation may be appointed a director at any general meeting unless:
(1) he or she is recommended for re-election by the directors; or
(2) not less than fourteen nor more than thirty-five clear days before the date of the meeting, the charity is given a notice that:
   (a) is signed by a member entitled to vote at the meeting;
   (b) states the member's intention to propose the appointment of a person as a director;
   (c) contains the details that, if the person were to be appointed, the charity would have to file at Companies House;[33] and
   (d) is signed by the person who is to be proposed to show his or her willingness to be appointed.

36 All members who are entitled to receive notice of a general meeting must be given not less than seven nor more than twenty-eight clear days' notice

---

[32] Our guidance *Finding New Trustees: What charities need to know* (CC30) provides guidance on effective methods of recruiting new charity trustees or directors and of familiarising them with the charity.
[33] Certain details of newly appointed directors must be sent to Companies House on Form AP01. This includes details of current and any former name, address, occupation and consent to act.

of any resolution to be put to the meeting to appoint a director other than a director who is to retire by rotation.

37
(1) The directors may appoint a person who is willing to act to be a director.
(2) A director appointed by a resolution of the other directors must retire at the next annual general meeting and must not be taken into account in determining the directors who are to retire by rotation.

38 The appointment of a director, whether by the charity in general meeting or by the other directors, must not cause the number of directors to exceed any number fixed as the maximum number of directors.

39 **Disqualification and removal of directors**
A director shall cease to hold office if he or she:
(1) ceases to be a director by virtue of any provision in the Companies Acts or is prohibited by law from being a director;
(2) is disqualified from acting as a trustee by virtue of sections 178 and 179 of the Charities Act 2011 (or any statutory re-enactment or modification of those provisions);[34]
(3) ceases to be a member of the charity;
(4) in the written opinion, given to the company, of a registered medical practitioner treating that person, has become physically or mentally incapable of acting as a director and may remain so for more than three months;
(5) resigns as a director by notice to the charity (but only if at least two directors will remain in office when the notice of resignation is to take effect); or
(6) is absent without the permission of the directors from all their meetings held within a period of six consecutive months and the directors resolve that his or her office be vacated.

40 **Remuneration of directors**
The directors must not be paid any remuneration unless it is authorised by article 7.

41 **Proceedings of directors**
(1) The directors may regulate their proceedings as they think fit, subject to the provisions of the articles.
(2) Any director may call a meeting of the directors.
(3) The secretary (if any) must call a meeting of the directors if requested to do so by a director.
(4) Questions arising at a meeting shall be decided by a majority of votes.
[Optional
(5) In the case of an equality of votes, the person who is chairing the meeting shall have a second or casting vote.]

---

[34] Our guidance *Finding New Trustees: What charities need to know* (CC30) explains what sections 178 and 179 of this Act cover. In very broad terms, someone who has been convicted of offences involving deception or fraud, or who is an undischarged bankrupt or who has been removed from office as a charity trustee by us, will be disqualified from acting as a director.

[(6) A meeting may be held by suitable electronic means agreed by the directors in which each participant may communicate with all the other participants.]³⁵

42
   (1) No decision may be made by a meeting of the directors unless a quorum is present at the time the decision is purported to be made. ['Present' includes being present by suitable electronic means agreed by the directors in which a participant or participants may communicate with all the other participants.]
   (2) The quorum shall be two or the number nearest to one-third of the total number of directors, whichever is the greater, or such larger number as may be decided from time to time by the directors.
   (3) A director shall not be counted in the quorum present when any decision is made about a matter upon which that director is not entitled to vote.

43 If the number of directors is less than the number fixed as the quorum, the continuing directors or director may act only for the purpose of filling vacancies or of calling a general meeting.

44
   (1) The directors shall appoint a director to chair their meetings and may at any time revoke such appointment.
   (2) If no-one has been appointed to chair meetings of the directors or if the person appointed is unwilling to preside or is not present within ten minutes after the time appointed for the meeting, the directors present may appoint one of their number to chair that meeting.
   (3) The person appointed to chair meetings of the directors shall have no functions or powers except those conferred by the articles or delegated to him or her by the directors.

45
   (1) A resolution in writing or in electronic form agreed by all of the directors entitled to receive notice of a meeting of the directors and to vote upon the resolution shall be as valid and effectual as if it had been passed at a meeting of the directors duly convened and held.
   (2) The resolution in writing may comprise several documents containing the text of the resolution in like form to each of which one or more directors has signified their agreement.

46 Delegation
   (1) The directors may delegate any of their powers or functions to a committee of two or more directors but the terms of any delegation must be recorded in the minute book.

---

[35] We provide guidance on meetings in *Charities and Meetings* (CC48). Article 41(5) is optional: it is common but not obligatory for the chair to have a casting vote at directors' meetings. Article 41(6) is also optional. It permits directors to hold meetings by suitable electronic means where this is agreed by the directors and where each director at the meeting is able to communicate with the other persons attending the meeting. If article 41(6) is adopted, the optional wider definition of 'present' in article 42(1) should also be adopted.

(2) The directors may impose conditions when delegating, including the conditions that:
    (a) the relevant powers are to be exercised exclusively by the committee to whom they delegate;
    (b) no expenditure may be incurred on behalf of the charity except in accordance with a budget previously agreed with the directors.
(3) The directors may revoke or alter a delegation.
(4) All acts and proceedings of any committees must be fully and promptly reported to the directors.

47 Validity of directors' decisions
(1) Subject to article 47(2), all acts done by a meeting of directors, or of a committee of directors, shall be valid notwithstanding the participation in any vote of a director:
    (a) who was disqualified from holding office;
    (b) who had previously retired or who had been obliged by the constitution to vacate office;
    (c) who was not entitled to vote on the matter, whether by reason of a conflict of interests or otherwise;
    if without:
    (d) the vote of that director; and
    (e) that director being counted in the quorum;
    the decision has been made by a majority of the directors at a quorate meeting.
(2) Article 47(1) does not permit a director or a connected person to keep any benefit that may be conferred upon him or her by a resolution of the directors or of a committee of directors if, but for article 47(1), the resolution would have been void, or if the director has not complied with article 8.

48 Seal
If the charity has a seal it must only be used by the authority of the directors or of a committee of directors authorised by the directors. The directors may determine who shall sign any instrument to which the seal is affixed and unless otherwise so determined it shall be signed by a director and by the secretary (if any) or by a second director.

49 Minutes
The directors must keep minutes of all:
(1) appointments of officers made by the directors;
(2) proceedings at meetings of the charity;
(3) meetings of the directors and committees of directors including:
    (a) the names of the directors present at the meeting;
    (b) the decisions made at the meetings; and
    (c) where appropriate the reasons for the decisions.[36]

50 Accounts[37]

---

[36] Using the power to make rules at article 58, the directors can decide in what format the minutes should be kept and how to validate them.

[37] The SORP is available as a free PDF download, but you can also buy a printed copy. Download

(1) The directors must prepare for each financial year accounts as required by the Companies Acts. The accounts must be prepared to show a true and fair view and follow accounting standards issued or adopted by the Accounting Standards Board or its successors and adhere to the recommendations of applicable Statements of Recommended Practice.

(2) The directors must keep accounting records as required by the Companies Act.

51 Annual Report and Return and Register of Charities[38]

(1) The directors must comply with the requirements of the Charities Act 2011 with regard to the:
   (a) transmission of a copy of the statements of account to the Commission;
   (b) preparation of an Annual Report and the transmission of a copy of it to the Commission;
   (c) preparation of an Annual Return and its transmission to the Commission.[39]

(2) The directors must notify the Commission promptly of any changes to the charity's entry on the Central Register of Charities.

52 Means of communication to be used[40]

(1) Subject to the articles, anything sent or supplied by or to the charity under the articles may be sent or supplied in any way in which the Companies Act 2006 provides for documents or information which are authorised or required by any provision of that Act to be sent or supplied by or to the charity.

(2) Subject to the articles, any notice or document to be sent or supplied to a director in connection with the taking of decisions by directors may also be sent or supplied by the means by which that director has asked to be sent or supplied with such notices or documents for the time being.

53 Any notice to be given to or by any person pursuant to the articles:
   (1) must be in writing; or
   (2) must be given in electronic form.

54
   (1) The charity may give any notice to a member either:
      (a) personally; or

---

the SORP as a PDF file (https://www.gov.uk/government/publications/charities-sorp-2005) or find out how to order a printed copy of the SORP (https://www.gov.uk/running-charity).

[38] Guidance available on our website sets out the key accounting requirements for charities. All charities with incomes over £10k must send an Annual Report and Annual Return to us within 10 months of the end of their financial year. Charities with incomes over £25k must in addition send accounts.

[39] The Annual Return provides a summary of key financial data.

[40] There are detailed requirements with regard to electronic communications contained in the Companies Act 2006. Sections 308–309 deal with the manner in which notice is to be given and the content of any notice on a website. Section 333 relates to sending documents relating to meetings etc in electronic form. Sections 1143–1148 and Schedules 4 and 5 deal with sending or supplying documents or information. Section 1168 contains definitions of 'hard copy' and 'electronic form' and other relevant terms.

(b) by sending it by post in a prepaid envelope addressed to the member at his or her address; or
(c) by leaving it at the address of the member; or
(d) by giving it in electronic form to the member's address.
(e) by placing the notice on a website and providing the person with a notification in writing or in electronic form of the presence of the notice on the website. The notification must state that it concerns a notice of a company meeting and must specify the place date and time of the meeting.
(2) A member who does not register an address with the charity or who registers only a postal address that is not within the United Kingdom shall not be entitled to receive any notice from the charity.

55 A member present in person at any meeting of the charity shall be deemed to have received notice of the meeting and of the purposes for which it was called.

56
(1) Proof that an envelope containing a notice was properly addressed, prepaid and posted shall be conclusive evidence that the notice was given.
(2) Proof that an electronic form of notice was given shall be conclusive where the company can demonstrate that it was properly addressed and sent, in accordance with section 1147 of the Companies Act 2006.
(3) In accordance with section 1147 of the Companies Act 2006 notice shall be deemed to be given:
(a) 48 hours after the envelope containing it was posted; or
(b) in the case of an electronic form of communication, 48 hours after it was sent.

Indemnity[41]

[Option 1
[57

---

[41] Article 57 is about the extent to which the directors should be protected ('indemnified') from liability. It reflects changes in the law made by the Companies Act 2006. Three options are given for indemnifying directors. It may be helpful to consult your own legal advisers about which approach is best for your charity.

The options here cater for the needs of most charities. The main differences are to do with whether the company wishes to indemnify its directors in individual cases, or whether this protection should be a right to which they are automatically entitled. Note that none of these options gives the company the power to grant a blanket indemnity to its directors – they are all limited to what is allowed by law and can only be exercised in the interests of the charity.

After considering the options below, choose one and delete the others:

Option 1 gives the company the option to indemnify directors in any circumstances permitted by the Companies Act 2006. It does not confer any right to an indemnity. This option does not explicitly cover officers other than directors, but the general law implies an ability to indemnify them.

Option 2 enables the company to provide a right to an indemnity for directors. A power to indemnify other officers may be implied.

Option 3 enables the company to confer on directors the right to a limited indemnity as set out in the article.

(1) The charity may indemnify a relevant director against any liability incurred in that capacity, to the extent permitted by sections 232 to 234 of the Companies Act 2006.
(2) In this article a 'relevant director' means any director or former director of the charity.]

[Option 2
[57
(1) The charity shall indemnify a relevant director against any liability incurred in that capacity, to the extent permitted by sections 232 to 234 of the Companies Act 2006
(2) In this article a 'relevant director' means any director or former director of the charity.]

[Option 3
[57
(1) The charity shall indemnify a relevant director against any liability incurred in successfully defending legal proceedings in that capacity, or in connection with any application in which relief is granted by the Court from liability for negligence, default, or breach of duty or breach of trust in relation to the charity.
(2) In this article a 'relevant director' means any director or former director of the charity.]

[Optional
57A The charity may indemnify an auditor against any liability incurred by him or her or it
(1) in defending proceedings (whether civil or criminal) in which judgment is given in his or her or its favour or he or she or it is acquitted; or
(2) in connection with an application under section 1157 of the Companies Act 2006 (power of Court to grant relief in case of honest and reasonable conduct) in which relief is granted to him or her or it by the Court.][42]

58 **Rules**
(1) The directors may from time to time make such reasonable and proper rules or bye-laws as they may deem necessary or expedient for the proper conduct and management of the charity.
(2) The bye-laws may regulate the following matters but are not restricted to them:
(a) the admission of members of the charity (including the admission of organisations to membership) and the rights and privileges of such members, and the entrance fees, subscriptions and other fees or payments to be made by members;

---

[42] Article 57A is optional but would permit the charity to indemnify an auditor in the limited circumstances permitted by section 533 of the Companies Act 2006.

(b) the conduct of members of the charity in relation to one another, and to the charity's employees and volunteers;
(c) the setting aside of the whole or any part or parts of the charity's premises at any particular time or times or for any particular purpose or purposes;
(d) the procedure at general meetings and meetings of the directors in so far as such procedure is not regulated by the Companies Acts or by the articles;
(e) generally, all such matters as are commonly the subject matter of company rules.

(3) The charity in general meeting has the power to alter, add to or repeal the rules or bye-laws.
(4) The directors must adopt such means as they think sufficient to bring the rules and bye-laws to the notice of members of the charity.
(5) The rules or bye laws shall be binding on all members of the charity. No rule or bye-law shall be inconsistent with, or shall affect or repeal anything contained in, the articles.

59 Disputes

If a dispute arises between members of the charity about the validity or propriety of anything done by the members of the charity under these articles, and the dispute cannot be resolved by agreement, the parties to the dispute must first try in good faith to settle the dispute by mediation before resorting to litigation.[43]

60 Dissolution

(1) The members of the charity may at any time before, and in expectation of, its dissolution resolve that any net assets of the charity after all its debts and liabilities have been paid, or provision has been made for them, shall on or before the dissolution of the charity be applied or transferred in any of the following ways:
 (a) directly for the Objects; or
 (b) by transfer to any charity or charities for purposes similar to the Objects; or
 (c) to any charity or charities for use for particular purposes that fall within the Objects.
(2) Subject to any such resolution of the members of the charity, the directors of the charity may at any time before and in expectation of its dissolution resolve that any net assets of the charity after all its debts and liabilities have been paid, or provision made for them, shall on or before dissolution of the charity be applied or transferred:
 (a) directly for the Objects; or
 (b) by transfer to any charity or charities for purposes similar to the Objects; or

---

[43] Article 59 It is good practice to include provisions for dealing with any disputes that arise between members of the charity. Litigation can be expensive, and litigation about the internal affairs of a charity would almost certainly constitute 'charity proceedings', which can be taken only with the Commission's authority. We would usually require the parties to a dispute to have tried mediation first.

(c) to any charity or charities for use for particular purposes that fall within the Objects.

(3) In no circumstances shall the net assets of the charity be paid to or distributed among the members of the charity (except to a member that is itself a charity) and if no resolution in accordance with article 60(1) is passed by the members or the directors the net assets of the charity shall be applied for charitable purposes as directed by the Court or the Commission.[44]

61. **Interpretation**

In article 7, sub-clause (2) of article 9 and sub-clause (2) of article 47 'connected person' means:

(1) a child, parent, grandchild, grandparent, brother or sister of the director;

(2) the spouse or civil partner of the director or of any person falling within sub-clause (1) above;

(3) a person carrying on business in partnership with the director or with any person falling within sub-clause (1) or (2) above;

(4) an institution which is controlled –
   (a) by the director or any connected person falling within sub-clause (1), (2), or (3) above; or
   (b) by two or more persons falling within sub-clause 4(a), when taken together

(5) a body corporate in which –
   (a) the director or any connected person falling within sub-clauses (1) to (3) has a substantial interest; or
   (b) two or more persons falling within sub-clause (5)(a) who, when taken together, have a substantial interest.
   (c) Sections 350 – 352 of the Charities Act 2011 apply for the purposes of interpreting the terms used in this article.[45]

---

[44] The charity has power under the Companies Acts to wind up. The directors must comply with company law in using that power and provide Companies House with the required documentation. In these circumstances, directors will need to send to us promptly a copy of the relevant resolution and a copy of the final accounts.

[45] This article explains some of the terms used in some of the other articles.

APPENDIX C

COMPANY NOT HAVING A SHARE CAPITAL[1]

Reproduced with the kind permission of the Charity Commission
https://www.gov.uk/government/publications/setting-up-a-charity-model-governing-documents

MEMORANDUM OF ASSOCIATION

....

....

....

....

....

---

[1] Details about the requirements of the Companies Act 2006 are available from the Companies House website www.companieshouse.gov.uk and our website www.charitycommission.gov.uk. Section 8 of the Companies Act 2006 requires that the Memorandum of Association states that the company's subscribers:
(a) wish to form a company; and
(b) agree to become members of the company.
It also requires the members to authenticate the Memorandum of Association.
In general, the Commission can accept any name but has the power to direct registered charity names to be changed in the circumstances set out in section 42(2) of the Charities Act 2011, which are explained in our guidance *Registering as a Charity* (CC21) and in our Operational Guidance (*Names of charities*) available on our website. In very broad terms, the name should not be offensive, or identical to (or too like) the name of any other charity, or likely to mislead the public about its purposes, activities, status, or connections. Some words and expressions are controlled under the Companies Act 2006 and other legislation. A list of controlled words can be found in Appendices A – C of the Companies House website document 'Incorporation and Names' (GP1).
Authentication by Subscribers: The Memorandum of Association needs to be authenticated by the subscribers stating their names and adding their signatures, or by their use of a form of electronic authentication acceptable to Companies House.
Submission of Documents: The Memorandum of Association should be sent to the Registrar of Companies at Companies House as part of the application to register as a company (section 9 of the Companies Act 2006). The Charity Commission requires a copy of the:
• Memorandum of Association
• Articles of Association
• Certificate of Incorporation (and if applicable the Certificate of Incorporation on Change of Name)

....

Each subscriber to this memorandum of association wishes to form a company under the Companies Act 2006 and agrees to become a member of the company.

Name of each subscriber

Authentication by each subscriber

....

....

....

....

....

....

....

Dated:

....

APPENDIX D

CHARITABLE ASSOCIATIONS: MODEL CONSTITUTION

Reproduced with the kind permission of the Charity Commission https://www.gov.uk/government/publications/setting-up-a-charity-model-governing-documents

It may be appropriate to establish an unincorporated association where the organisation:

- is to be relatively small in terms of assets;
- has a membership;
- is to be run by charity trustees who will be elected by members or appointed to hold office for fixed terms;
- wants to take account of the views of local residents and organisations through membership or as users;
- wishes to carry out its work wholly or partly through the voluntary effort and contributions of its members. Where the organisation is to have a membership but is expected to have considerable resources and/or employ staff and become engaged in charitable purposes which involve commercial risks it is usually more appropriate to take the form of a charitable company for which our *Model Articles of Association* (GD1) can be used.

Guidance to consider before you begin

You may find it helpful to begin by reading the following guidance on our website:

- The comprehensive information under *Start up a charity*
- *Registering as a Charity* (CC21) – its checklist of questions will help you to decide how best to set up the charity
- *Choosing and Preparing a Governing Document* (CC22) – this gives advice on the practicalities of completing the charity's governing document and on the different provisions which may be needed
- *The Essential Trustee – What you need to know* (CC3), which sets out the basics that all charity trustees need to know

Next steps

1. Completing the constitution

Once you have decided to apply to register a charitable association, please read the constitution and its accompanying guidance notes carefully.

Some clauses contain blank spaces that you will need to fill in.

The model is intended to be sufficiently flexible to deal with most eventualities. If you want to include special or complex provisions which are not contained in it you should consider asking a solicitor to help you. Please make clear any changes you make and why they are necessary. This will help us to consider your application as quickly as possible. We cannot guarantee to accept every organisation which uses the model constitution as charitable. We must consider each case separately.

2. Adopting the constitution

Once you have completed the constitution, the organisation's members need to adopt it.

3. Applying to register

To register a new charity, apply online. (The online application material includes *Application for registration – guidance notes*.)

Please attach a copy of your final signed constitution as adopted by the members and your signed *Trustee Declaration* to your application. If you cannot attach these documents to your application please proceed to apply online and we will email you instructions about how to send them to us.

If you cannot apply online, please contact us using the link from our website homepage.

4. How long will it take?

We can normally make a decision in 15 working days if an organisation:

- uses our model wording for its objects (as set out in the *Example charitable objects* on our website);
- shows that its activities that are consistent with the objects;
- shows that any private benefit is incidental and is properly managed; and
- uses our model governing document.

Other applications will need closer consideration and so will take longer (especially where the charity's purposes are novel and/or at the boundaries of what is charitable).

CONSTITUTION

adopted on the .... 20 ....[1]

PART 1

1. **Adoption of the constitution**[2]
    The association and its property will be administered and managed in accordance with the provisions in Parts 1 and 2 of this constitution.

2. **Name**[3]
    The association's name is

    ....

    ....

    ....

    (and in this document it is called the charity).

3. **Objects**[4]
    The charity's objects ('the objects') are

    ....

    ....

---

[1] Insert the date of the meeting at which it was decided to adopt this constitution.

[2] The constitution is in two parts. Part 1 covers the purposes of the charity and how its money and other property can be used. It also contains the powers to change the constitution and to wind the charity up. Part 2 sets out the administrative provisions, including membership, the appointment of charity trustees, members' and trustees' meetings and the powers available to the trustees in running the charity. The provisions in part 1 can only be changed by a two-thirds majority of members present and voting at a meeting whereas those in part 2 can be changed by a simple majority of them.

[3] Insert the name of the charity. In general, the Commission can accept any name unless it infringes the principles set out in section 42 of the Charities Act 2011, which are explained in our guidance *Registering as a Charity* (CC21) and in our Operational Guidance *Names of Charities* on our website. In very broad terms, the name should not be misleading, offensive or likely to be confused with the name of an existing charity.

[4] Insert the purpose for which the charity has been formed. A charity's objects must be expressed in exclusively charitable terms and this calls for precise drafting. Guidance is available in *Choosing and Preparing a Governing Document* (CC22) and example objects covering some of the most common charitable purposes are available on our website. The key elements to include are:
• The purpose itself (eg establishing and running a school);
• The people who can benefit (in our example, school age children); and, if appropriate
• any geographic limits which may be needed to define the area of benefit. This will not always be necessary. If you do include an area of benefit, it is common to define it by reference to a local government area: this has the advantage of clarity and simplicity, but can create problems if the area is subsequently altered or abolished.
If the charity will operate in Scotland and/or Northern Ireland you should include the wording in square brackets to meet the requirements of charity law in that/those countries, deleting as required if the charity works in one of those two countries.

[Nothing in this constitution shall authorise an application of the property of the charity for purposes which are not charitable in accordance with section 7 of the Charities and Trustee Investment (Scotland) Act 2005 and/or section 2 of the Charities Act (Northern Ireland) 2008.]

4. **Application of income and property**
   (1) The income and property of the charity shall be applied solely towards the promotion of the objects.
      (a) A charity trustee is entitled to be reimbursed from the property of the charity or may pay out of such property reasonable expenses properly incurred by him or her when acting on behalf of the charity.
      (b) A charity trustee may benefit from trustee indemnity insurance cover purchased at the charity's expense in accordance with, and subject to the conditions in, section 189 of the Charities Act 2011.[5]
   (2) None of the income or property of the charity may be paid or transferred directly or indirectly by way of dividend bonus or otherwise by way of profit to any member of the charity. This does not prevent a member who is not also a trustee from receiving:
      (a) a benefit from the charity in the capacity of a beneficiary of the charity;
      (b) reasonable and proper remuneration for any goods or services supplied to the charity.[6]

5. **Benefits and payments to charity trustees and connected persons**[7]
   (1) **General provisions**
      No charity trustee or connected person may:
      (a) buy or receive any goods or services from the charity on terms preferential to those applicable to members of the public;

---

[5] Clause 4(1) sets out a trustee's entitlement to reasonable expenses and reflects statutory the provisions in the 2011 Act about a charity trustee's entitlement to benefit from trustee indemnity insurance. It is included in the constitution to inform people involved with the charity.

[6] Clause 4(2) reflects charity law requirements that the income and property of a charity must be applied solely to further its objects and not to benefit the members or charity trustees (except as permitted by the governing document (see clause 5) or other express power). The trustees have a duty to ensure that the funds are correctly applied in accordance with this principle.

[7] Under clause 5, charity trustees may only benefit from their charity if they have express legal authorisation to do so (such as a clause in the constitution). This restriction extends to people closely connected to a trustee ('connected persons' – this term is defined in interpretation clause 34). This clause clarifies the restrictions that apply to the charity trustees. Even where trustees are allowed to benefit from the charity, this must only happen where the benefit is in the interests of the charity. Our guidance *Trustee expenses and payments* (CC11) provides more information about trustee benefits.

This clause permits a minority of the charity trustees or connected persons to receive payments and other benefits in certain instances (such as for goods and services they supply to the charity), subject to the stated controls. The option also allows other types of trustee benefit subject to the Commission's prior consent.

No part of the clause allows trustees to receive payment for acting as a trustee.

(b) sell goods, services or any interest in land to the charity;
(c) be employed by, or receive any remuneration from, the charity;
(d) receive any other financial benefit from the charity;
unless the payment is permitted by sub-clause (2) of this clause, or authorised by the court or the Charity Commission ('the Commission'). In this clause, a 'financial benefit' means a benefit, direct or indirect, which is either money or has a monetary value.

(2) **Scope and powers permitting trustees' or connected persons' benefits**
   (a) A charity trustee or connected person may receive a benefit from the charity in the capacity of a beneficiary of the charity provided that a majority of the trustees do not benefit in this way.
   (b) A charity trustee or connected person may enter into a contract for the supply of services, or of goods that are supplied in connection with the provision of services, to the charity where that is permitted in accordance with, and subject to the conditions in, section 185 of the Charities Act 2011.
   (c) Subject to sub-clause (3) of this clause a charity trustee or connected person may provide the charity with goods that are not supplied in connection with services provided to the charity by the charity trustee or connected person.
   (d) A charity trustee or connected person may receive interest on money lent to the charity at a reasonable and proper rate which must be not more than the Bank of England bank rate (also known as the base rate).[8]
   (e) A charity trustee or connected person may receive rent for premises let by the trustee or connected person to the charity. The amount of the rent and the other terms of the lease must be reasonable and proper. The charity trustee concerned must withdraw from any meeting at which such a proposal or the rent or other terms of the lease are under discussion.
   (f) A charity trustee or connected person may take part in the normal trading and fundraising activities of the charity on the same terms as members of the public.

(3) **Payment for supply of goods only – controls**
   The charity and its charity trustees may only rely upon the authority provided by sub-clause 2(c) of this clause if each of the following conditions is satisfied:
   (a) The amount or maximum amount of the payment for the goods is set out in an agreement in writing between the charity and the charity trustee or connected person supplying the goods ('the supplier') under which the supplier is to supply the goods in question to or on behalf of the charity.

---

[8] If your charity will benefit all local inhabitants in a specific geographical area (eg as a community association) you may wish to substitute the following: 'A trustee or connected person may receive a benefit from the charity as a beneficiary provided that it is available generally to the beneficiaries of the charity.'

(b) The amount or maximum amount of the payment for the goods does not exceed what is reasonable in the circumstances for the supply of the goods in question.
(c) The other charity trustees are satisfied that it is in the best interests of the charity to contract with the supplier rather than with someone who is not a charity trustee or connected person. In reaching that decision the charity trustees must balance the advantage of contracting with a charity trustee or connected person against the disadvantages of doing so.
(d) The supplier is absent from the part of any meeting at which there is discussion of the proposal to enter into a contract or arrangement with him or her or it with regard to the supply of goods to the charity.
(e) The supplier does not vote on any such matter and is not to be counted when calculating whether a quorum of charity trustees is present at the meeting.
(f) The reason for their decision is recorded by the charity trustees in the minute book.
(g) A majority of the charity trustees then in office are not in receipt of remuneration or payments authorised by clause 5.
(4) In sub-clauses (2) and (3) of this clause:
(a) 'the charity' includes any company in which the charity:
(i) holds more than 50% of the shares; or
(ii) controls more than 50% of the voting rights attached to the shares; or
(iii) has the right to appoint one or more trustees to the board of the company.
(b) 'connected person' includes any person within the definition set out in clause 34 (Interpretation).

6. **Dissolution**
(1) If the members resolve to dissolve the charity the trustees will remain in office as charity trustees and be responsible for winding up the affairs of the charity in accordance with this clause.
(2) The trustees must collect in all the assets of the charity and must pay or make provision for all the liabilities of the charity.
(3) The trustees must apply any remaining property or money:
(a) directly for the objects;
(b) by transfer to any charity or charities for purposes the same as or similar to the charity;
(c) in such other manner as the Charity Commission for England and Wales ('the Commission') may approve in writing in advance.
(4) The members may pass a resolution before or at the same time as the resolution to dissolve the charity specifying the manner in which the trustees are to apply the remaining property or assets of the charity and the trustees must comply with the resolution if it is consistent with paragraphs (a) – (c) inclusive in sub-clause (3) above.

(5) In no circumstances shall the net assets of the charity be paid to or distributed among the members of the charity (except to a member that is itself a charity).
(6) The trustees must notify the Commission promptly that the charity has been dissolved. If the trustees are obliged to send the charity's accounts to the Commission for the accounting period which ended before its dissolution, they must send the Commission the charity's final accounts.[9]

7. **Amendment of constitution**
  (1) The charity may amend any provision contained in Part 1 of this constitution provided that:
    (a) no amendment may be made that would have the effect of making the charity cease to be a charity at law;
    (b) no amendment may be made to alter the objects if the change would undermine or work against the previous objects of the charity;
    (c) no amendment may be made to clauses 4 or 5 without the prior written consent of the Commission;
    (d) any resolution to amend a provision of Part 1 of this constitution is passed by not less than two thirds of the members present and voting at a general meeting.
  (2) Any provision contained in Part 2 of this constitution may be amended, provided that any such amendment is made by resolution passed by a simple majority of the members present and voting at a general meeting.
  (3) A copy of any resolution amending this constitution shall be sent to the Commission within twenty one days of it being passed.

PART 2

8. **Membership**[10]
  (1) Membership is open to individuals over eighteen or organisations who are approved by the trustees.[11]
  (2)
    (a) The trustees may only refuse an application for membership if, acting reasonably and properly, they consider it to be in the best interests of the charity to refuse the application.
    (b) The trustees must inform the applicant in writing of the reasons for the refusal within twenty-one days of the decision.

---

[9] The Charities Act 2011 sets out the accounting obligations on charities: see our website for further guidance.
[10] For advice and guidance on best practice for running membership organisations, see *Membership Charities* (RS7) on the Charity Commission's website.
[11] The law says people under 18 cannot be trustees or take on the administrative rights and duties of full members. Associations can have separate junior membership arrangements if it is clear that they do not have the rights and responsibilities of administration of full members, like voting. See Charity Commission's website for detailed guidance on involving younger people under Running a charity – good practice for charities.

(c) The trustees must consider any written representations the applicant may make about the decision. The trustees' decision following any written representations must be notified to the applicant in writing but shall be final.

(3) Membership is not transferable to anyone else.

(4) The trustees must keep a register of names and addresses of the members which must be made available to any member upon request.[12]

9. **Termination of membership**

Membership is terminated if:

(1) the member dies or, if it is an organisation, ceases to exist;

(2) the member resigns by written notice to the charity unless, after the resignation, there would be less than two members;

(3) any sum due from the member to the charity is not paid in full within six months of it falling due;[13]

(4) the member is removed from membership by a resolution of the trustees that it is in the best interests of the charity that his or her membership is terminated. A resolution to remove a member from membership may only be passed if:

(a) the member has been given at least twenty one days' notice in writing of the meeting of the trustees at which the resolution will be proposed and the reasons why it is to be proposed;

(b) the member or, at the option of the member, the member's representative (who need not be a member of the charity has been allowed to make representations to the meeting.

10. **General meetings**[14]

(1) The charity must hold a general meeting within twelve months of the date of the adoption of this constitution.

(2) An annual general meeting must be held in each subsequent year and not more than fifteen months may elapse between successive annual general meetings.

(3) All general meetings other than annual general meetings shall be called special general meetings.

(4) The trustees may call a special general meeting at any time.

(5) The trustees must call a special general meeting if requested to do so in writing by at least ten members or one tenth of the membership, which ever is the greater. The request must state the nature of the business that is to be discussed. If the trustees fail to hold the meeting

---

[12] It is very important for the good administration of the charity to keep the register of members up to date: failure to do so can result in a number of problems, including serious difficulties with the calling of annual or extraordinary general meetings. The trustees must ensure that they handle personal data in accordance with the requirements of the Data Protection Act 1998.

[13] The notice for any general meeting should remind members of this requirement. The Charity Commission recommends that there should be a reasonable gap between the deadline for payment of subscriptions (or any other regular payments by members to the charity) and the holding of a general meeting to reduce the risk of this becoming an administrative problem for the charity.

[14] See the Charity Commission's guidance on meetings in *Charities and Meetings* (CC48), produced in association with ICSA (The Institute of Chartered Secretaries and Administrators).

within twenty-eight days of the request, the members may proceed to call a special general meeting but in doing so they must comply with the provisions of this constitution.

11. Notice
(1) The minimum period of notice required to hold any general meeting of the charity is fourteen clear days from the date on which the notice is deemed to have been given.[15]
(2) A general meeting may be called by shorter notice, if it is so agreed by all the members entitled to attend and vote.
(3) The notice must specify the date, time and place of the meeting and the general nature of the business to be transacted. If the meeting is to be an annual general meeting, the notice must say so.
(4) The notice must be given to all the members and to the trustees.

12. Quorum
(1) No business shall be transacted at any general meeting unless a quorum is present.[16]
(2) A quorum is:
  (a) [ ] members entitled to vote upon the business to be conducted at the meeting;[17] or
  (b) one tenth of the total membership at the time,
  whichever is the greater.
(3) The authorised representative of a member organisation shall be counted in the quorum.
(4) If:
  (a) a quorum is not present within half an hour from the time appointed for the meeting; or
  (b) during a meeting a quorum ceases to be present,
  the meeting shall be adjourned to such time and place as the trustees shall determine.
(5) The trustees must re-convene the meeting and must give at least seven clear days' notice of the re-convened meeting stating the date time and place of the meeting.
(6) If no quorum is present at the re-convened meeting within fifteen minutes of the time specified for the start of the meeting the members present at that time shall constitute the quorum for that meeting.[18]

13. Chair

---

[15] 'Clear days' does not include the day on which the notice would be received by the member or the day on which the meeting is held – see sub-clause 31(5)(c). Section 332 of the Charities Act 2011 sets out how notice may be given by post. In broad terms, the charity may send notice to each trustee at the UK address held in the charity's records: no notice is required for trustees living outside the UK.

[16] This means that a quorum must be present when a matter is being discussed and voted on, in order for a decision on it to be validly made. If the meeting subsequently becomes inquorate, this will not invalidate earlier, quorate decisions.

[17] Insert the figure for the quorum. This should be set with care. If it is too high, any absences may make it difficult to have a valid meeting. If it is too low, a small minority may be able to impose its views unreasonably. Note that sub-clauses 12(4)–(6) set out the procedure for dealing with situations where the meeting is inquorate.

[18] Note that this provision permits the re-scheduled meeting to proceed without a quorum being

(1) General meetings shall be chaired by the person who has been elected as Chair.
(2) If there is no such person or he or she is not present within fifteen minutes of the time appointed for the meeting a trustee nominated by the trustees shall chair the meeting.
(3) If there is only one trustee present and willing to act, he or she shall chair the meeting.
(4) If no trustee is present and willing to chair the meeting within fifteen minutes after the time appointed for holding it, the members present and entitled to vote must choose one of their number to chair the meeting.

14. Adjournments[19]
(1) The members present at a meeting may resolve that the meeting shall be adjourned.
(2) The person who is chairing the meeting must decide the date time and place at which meeting is to be re-convened unless those details are specified in the resolution.
(3) No business shall be conducted at an adjourned meeting unless it could properly have been conducted at the meeting had the adjournment not taken place.
(4) If a meeting is adjourned by a resolution of the members for more than seven days, at least seven clear days' notice shall be given of the re-convened meeting stating the date time and place of the meeting.

15. Votes
(1) Each member shall have one vote but if there is an equality of votes the person who is chairing the meeting shall have a casting vote in addition to any other vote he or she may have.
(2) A resolution in writing signed by each member (or in the case of a member that is an organisation, by its authorised representative) who would have been entitled to vote upon it had it been proposed at a general meeting shall be effective. It may comprise several copies each signed by or on behalf of one or more members.

16. Representatives of other bodies[20]
(1) Any organisation that is a member of the charity may nominate any person to act as its representative at any meeting of the charity.
(2) The organisation must give written notice to the charity of the name of its representative. The nominee shall not be entitled to represent the organisation at any meeting unless the notice has been received by

---

present within 15 minutes of the specified start time. It also means that the number of members present 15 minutes after the scheduled start of the meeting will form the quorum if the quorum required at sub-clause 12(2) is not achieved.

[19] This is a discretionary power for the members to adjourn a quorate meeting – when the meeting is reconvened it must be quorate. This provision differs from the adjournment provisions in Clause 12 which are not discretionary and must be used where a general meeting is not quorate.

[20] Organisations which are members ('corporate members') enjoy the same rights and duties as individual members. Our research report *Membership Charities* (RS7) provides advice and guidance on managing corporate members.

the charity. The nominee may continue to represent the organisation until written notice to the contrary is received by the charity.

(3) Any notice given to the charity will be conclusive evidence that the nominee is entitled to represent the organisation or that his or her authority has been revoked. The charity shall not be required to consider whether the nominee has been properly appointed by the organisation.

17. **Officers and trustees**
    (1) The charity and its property shall be managed and administered by a committee comprising the officers and other members elected in accordance with this constitution. The officers and other members of the committee shall be the trustees of the Charity and in this constitution are together called 'the trustees'.
    (2) The charity shall have the following officers:
       (a) A chair,
       (b) A secretary,
       (c) A treasurer.
    (3) A trustee must be a member of the charity or the nominated representative of an organisation that is a member of the charity.
    (4) No one may be appointed a trustee if he or she would be disqualified from acting under the provisions of clause 20.
    (5) The number of trustees shall be not less than three but (unless otherwise determined by a resolution of the charity in general meeting) shall not be subject to any maximum.
    (6) The first trustees (including officers) shall be those persons elected as trustees and officers at the meeting at which this constitution is adopted.
    (7) A trustee may not appoint anyone to act on his or her behalf at meetings of the trustees.

18. **Appointment of trustees**[21]
    (1) The charity in general meeting shall elect the officers and the other trustees.
    (2) The trustees may appoint any person who is willing to act as a trustee. Subject to sub-clause 5(b) of this clause, they may also appoint trustees to act as officers.
    (3) Each of the trustees shall retire with effect from the conclusion of the annual general meeting next after his or her appointment but shall be eligible for re-election at that annual general meeting.
    (4) No-one may be elected a trustee or an officer at any annual general meeting unless prior to the meeting the charity is given a notice that:
       (a) is signed by a member entitled to vote at the meeting;
       (b) states the member's intention to propose the appointment of a person as a trustee or as an officer;
       (c) is signed by the person who is to be proposed to show his or her willingness to be appointed.

---

[21] *Finding New Trustees: What charities need to know* (CC30) provides guidance on effective methods of recruiting new charity trustees and of familiarising them with the charity.

(5)
  (a) The appointment of a trustee, whether by the charity in general meeting or by the other trustees, must not cause the number of trustees to exceed any number fixed in accordance with this constitution as the maximum number of trustees.
  (b) The trustees may not appoint a person to be an officer if a person has already been elected or appointed to that office and has not vacated the office.

19. **Powers of trustees**[22]
  (1) The trustees must manage the business of the charity and have the following powers in order to further the objects (but not for any other purpose):
  (a) to raise funds. In doing so, the trustees must not undertake any taxable permanent trading activity and must comply with any relevant statutory regulations;[23]
  (b) to buy, take on lease or in exchange, hire or otherwise acquire any property and to maintain and equip it for use;[24]
  (c) to sell, lease or otherwise dispose of all or any part of the property belonging to the charity. In exercising this power, the trustees must comply as appropriate with sections 117 – 122 of the Charities Act 2011;[25]
  (d) to borrow money and to charge the whole or any part of the property belonging to the charity as security for repayment of the money borrowed. The trustees must comply as appropriate with sections 124 – 126 of the Charities Act 2011, if they intend to mortgage land;[26]

---

[22] It is sensible to set out all the powers that the charity will commonly need, for the avoidance of doubt and to remind trustees of the conditions that have to be met when they exercise those powers. Some of these powers are implicit in a charity's objects (for example, if the object is to provide a school, the trustees have an implicit power to acquire premises). Other powers are given by statute, often only if specific conditions are met. For example, the Trustee Act 2000 gives trustees power to acquire and dispose of land, to borrow money in many circumstances, to delegate much of the running of the charity and to invest. However, there are some things that can be done only if the charity's governing document provides express power to do them.

[23] This sub-clause provides a general power to raise funds through a wide variety of methods. The only restriction here is that it does not allow the charity to engage in substantial permanent trading for the purpose of raising funds. (Trading on a small scale is allowed. HM Revenue and Customs provide guidance on the tax treatment of different sorts of trading). The terms of this power do not prevent trading in order to carry out the charity's object – for example, an educational charity can charge fees for the educational services it provides.

[24] This power is helpful if the charity is to acquire property either for use as office premises or functionally (such as a playground or school site). *Acquiring Land* (CC33) contains further guidance on the issue. See also notes to sub-clause 19(1)(d) and clause 29.

[25] This power enables the trustees to dispose of property belonging to the charity (for example, by selling or leasing it). Sections 117–122 of the Charities Act 2011 apply to most charities and require compliance with certain conditions to ensure that charity property is disposed of for the best terms reasonably obtainable. Our guidance *Disposing of Charity Land* (CC28) provides more information about this.

[26] This provides the trustees with a power to borrow. It also makes clear that if this power involves securing the loan on land of the charity, it must comply with the requirements of sections 124–126 of the Charities Act 2011. Briefly, the Act requires that the trustees take

(e) to co-operate with other charities, voluntary bodies and statutory authorities and to exchange information and advice with them;

(f) to establish or support any charitable trusts, associations or institutions formed for any of the charitable purposes included in the objects;

(g) to acquire, merge with or enter into any partnership or joint venture arrangement with any other charity formed for any of the objects;

(h) to set aside income as a reserve against future expenditure but only in accordance with a written policy about reserves;

(i) to obtain and pay for such goods and services as are necessary for carrying out the work of the charity;[27]

(j) to open and operate such bank and other accounts as the trustees consider necessary and to invest funds and to delegate the management of funds in the same manner and subject to the same conditions as the trustees of a trust are permitted to do by the Trustee Act 2000;[28]

(k) to do all such other lawful things as are necessary for the achievement of the objects.

(2) No alteration of this constitution or any special resolution shall have retrospective effect to invalidate any prior act of the trustees.

(3) Any meeting of trustees at which a quorum is present at the time the relevant decision is made may exercise all the powers exercisable by the trustees.

20. Disqualification and removal of trustees[29]

A trustee shall cease to hold office if he or she:

---

advice and provide certain certificates / statements when they are borrowing money by way of mortgage.

The Charity Commission provide detailed information on this in their Operational Guidance *Borrowing and Mortgages* on their website.

[27] This power cannot be used if the goods or services are being provided by a trustee: see Clause 5.

[28] Bank accounts – the trustees can make rules (under clause 32) to allow others associated with the operation of the charity such as employees or volunteers to sign cheques and other orders in relation to the charity's bank accounts so long as these activities are properly managed so as to reduce the risk of fraud. For example, the trustees might allow two senior volunteers to sign cheques up to a defined face value, with a limit on the total value of cheques which they are authorised to sign in any one month. For charities which operate electronic bank accounts, there is guidance on trustee duties and operational best practice in *Internal Controls for Charities* (CC8) on our website. With regard to the delegation and management of funds, the Trustee Act 2000 provides wide powers of investment and requires the charity to take advice and to consider the need to invest in a range of different investments. Our guidance *Investment of Charitable Funds: Basic Principles* (CC14) provides more information about charity investments. The powers to employ agents, nominees and custodians are of particular use where the charity wishes to use an investment manager.

[29] See Charity Commission guidance *Finding New Trustees: What charities need to know* (CC30) which explains what sections 178 and 179 of this Act covers. In very broad terms, someone who has been convicted of offences involving deception or fraud, or who is an undischarged bankrupt or who has been removed from office as a charity trustee by us will be disqualified for acting as a trustee.

(1) is disqualified from acting as a trustee by virtue of sections 178 and 179 of the Charities Act 2011 (or any statutory re-enactment or modification of that provision);
(2) ceases to be a member of the charity;
(3) in the written opinion, given to the charity, of a registered medical practitioner treating that person, has become physically or mentally incapable of acting as a trustee and may remain so for more than three months;
(4) resigns as a trustee by notice to the charity (but only if at least two trustees will remain in office when the notice of resignation is to take effect); or
(5) is absent without the permission of the trustees from all their meetings held within a period of six consecutive months and the trustees resolve that his or her office be vacated.

21. **Proceedings of trustees**[30]
    (1) The trustees may regulate their proceedings as they think fit, subject to the provisions of this constitution.
    (2) Any trustee may call a meeting of the trustees.
    (3) The secretary must call a meeting of the trustees if requested to do so by a trustee.
    (4) Questions arising at a meeting must be decided by a majority of votes.
    (5) In the case of an equality of votes, the person who chairs the meeting shall have a second or casting vote.
    (6) No decision may be made by a meeting of the trustees unless a quorum is present at the time the decision is purported to be made.
    (7) The quorum shall be two or the number nearest to one-third of the total number of trustees, whichever is the greater or such larger number as may be decided from time to time by the trustees.[31]
    (8) A trustee shall not be counted in the quorum present when any decision is made about a matter upon which that trustee is not entitled to vote.
    (9) If the number of trustees is less than the number fixed as the quorum, the continuing trustees or trustee may act only for the purpose of filling vacancies or of calling a general meeting.
    (10) The person elected as the Chair shall chair meetings of the trustees.
    (11) If the Chair is unwilling to preside or is not present within ten minutes after the time appointed for the meeting, the trustees present may appoint one of their number to chair that meeting.
    (12) The person appointed to chair meetings of the trustees shall have no functions or powers except those conferred by this constitution or delegated to him or her in writing by the trustees.
    (13) A resolution in writing signed by all the trustees entitled to receive notice of a meeting of trustees or of a committee of trustees and to vote upon the resolution shall be as valid and effectual as if it had

---

[30] See further guidance on meetings in *Charities and Meetings* (CC48).
[31] Where the total number of trustees is the mid-point between two numbers which can be divided by three, we recommend rounding up to the next multiple of three.

been passed at a meeting of the trustees or (as the case may be) a committee of trustees duly convened and held.

(14) The resolution in writing may comprise several documents containing the text of the resolution in like form each signed by one or more trustees.

22. **Conflicts of interests and conflicts of loyalties**[32]

A charity trustee must:
(1) declare the nature and extent of any interest, direct or indirect, which he or she has in a proposed transaction or arrangement with the charity or in any transaction or arrangement entered into by the charity which has not been previously declared; and
(2) absent himself or herself from any discussions of the charity trustees in which it is possible that a conflict will arise between his or her duty to act solely in the interests of the charity and any personal interest (including but not limited to any personal financial interest).

Any charity trustee absenting himself or herself from any discussions in accordance with this clause must not vote or be counted as part of the quorum in any decision of the charity trustees on the matter.

23. **Saving provisions**[33]
    (1) Subject to sub-clause (2) of this clause, all decisions of the charity trustees, or of a committee of the charity trustees, shall be valid notwithstanding the participation in any vote of a charity trustee:
        (a) who is disqualified from holding office;
        (b) who had previously retired or who had been obliged by this constitution to vacate office;
        (c) who was not entitled to vote on the matter, whether by reason of a conflict of interests or otherwise;
        if, without the vote of that charity trustee and that charity trustee being counted in the quorum, the decision has been made by a majority of the charity trustees at a quorate meeting.
    (2) Sub-clause (1) of this clause does not permit a charity trustee to keep any benefit that may be conferred upon him or her by a resolution of the charity trustees or of a committee of charity trustees if, but for sub-clause (1), the resolution would have been void, or if the charity trustee has not complied with clause 22 (Conflicts of interests and conflicts of loyalties).

24. **Delegation**
    (1) The trustees may delegate any of their powers or functions to a committee of two or more trustees but the terms of any such delegation must be recorded in the minute book.
    (2) The trustees may impose conditions when delegating, including the conditions that:
        (a) the relevant powers are to be exercised exclusively by the committee to whom they delegate;

---

[32] This reflects good practice on managing conflicts of interests and conflicts of loyalties.
[33] This reduces the risk of trustees' decisions being declared invalid for purely technical reasons.

(b) no expenditure may be incurred on behalf of the charity except in accordance with a budget previously agreed with the trustees.
(3) The trustees may revoke or alter a delegation.
(4) All acts and proceedings of any committees must be fully and promptly reported to the trustees.

25. **Irregularities in proceedings**
    (1) Subject to sub-clause (2) of this clause, all acts done by a meeting of Trustees, or of a committee of trustees, shall be valid notwithstanding the participation in any vote of a trustee:
        (a) who was disqualified from holding office;
        (b) who had previously retired or who had been obliged by the constitution to vacate office;
        (c) who was not entitled to vote on the matter, whether by reason of a conflict of interests or otherwise;
        if, without:
        (d) the vote of that trustee; and
        (e) that trustee being counted in the quorum,
        the decision has been made by a majority of the trustees at a quorate meeting.
    (2) Sub-clause (1) of this clause does not permit a trustee to keep any benefit that may be conferred upon him or her by a resolution of the trustees or of a committee of trustees if the resolution would otherwise have been void.[34]
    (3) No resolution or act of
        (a) the trustees
        (b) any committee of the trustees
        (c) the charity in general meeting
        shall be invalidated by reason of the failure to give notice to any trustee or member or by reason of any procedural defect in the meeting unless it is shown that the failure or defect has materially prejudiced a member or the beneficiaries of the charity.

26. **Minutes**[35]
    The trustees must keep minutes of all:
    (1) appointments of officers and trustees made by the trustees;
    (2) proceedings at meetings of the charity;
    (3) meetings of the trustees and committees of trustees including:
        (a) the names of the trustees present at the meeting;
        (b) the decisions made at the meetings; and
        (c) where appropriate the reasons for the decisions.

27. **Accounts, Annual Report, Annual Return**[36]

---

[34] See clause 5 (and in particular sub-clauses 5(2) and 5(3)) which sets out the restrictions on trustee benefits and the procedures to be followed if a benefit is to be allowed to a trustee.

[35] Using the power to make rules at clause 32, the trustees can decide in what format the minutes should be kept and how to validate them.

[36] The key accounting requirements for charities are set out on our website. All registered charities with incomes over £10k must send accounts, Annual Report and Annual Return to us within 10 months of the end of their financial year.

(1) The trustees must comply with their obligations under the Charities Act 2011 with regard to:
  (a) the keeping of accounting records for the charity;
  (b) the preparation of annual statements of account for the charity;
  (c) the transmission of the statements of account to the Commission;
  (d) the preparation of an Annual Report and its transmission to the Commission;
  (e) the preparation of an Annual Return and its transmission to the Commission.[37]
(2) Accounts must be prepared in accordance with the provisions of any Statement of Recommended Practice issued by the Commission, unless the trustees are required to prepare accounts in accordance with the provisions of such a Statement prepared by another body.[38]

28. **Registered particulars**[39]
The trustees must notify the Commission promptly of any changes to the charity's entry on the Central Register of Charities.

29. **Property**[40]
(1) The trustees must ensure the title to:
  (a) all land held by or in trust for the charity that is not vested in the Official Custodian of Charities; and
  (b) all investments held by or on behalf of the charity, is vested either in a corporation entitled to act as custodian trustee or in not less than three individuals appointed by them as holding trustees.
(2) The terms of the appointment of any holding trustees must provide that they may act only in accordance with lawful directions of the trustees and that if they do so they will not be liable for the acts and defaults of the trustees or of the members of the charity.
(3) The trustees may remove the holding trustees at any time.

30. **Repair and insurance**[41]

---

[37] The Annual Return provides a summary of key financial data and is used by us for monitoring purposes to detect issues which might require our attention or guidance.

[38] The Statement of Recommended Practice for charities (SORP 2005) is available as a free PDF download, but you can also buy a printed copy. Download the SORP as a PDF file (https://www.gov.uk/government/publications/charities-sorp-2005) or find out how to order a printed copy of the SORP (https://www.gov.uk/running-charity).

[39] A charity's entry includes its name, correspondence address, objects, governing document (and any amendment) and names of its trustees. The Commission issues to every charity an Annual Update form and Annual Return on which these details can conveniently be supplied, although changes to the correspondent details should be provided as soon as possible.

[40] When the trustees acquire land for the charity, the ownership of the land cannot rest with the charity directly as it has no separate legal identity. The trustees will therefore need to ensure that title to the charity's land is held in the name of individuals ('holding trustees') or a company, in trust on behalf of the charity. Typically this can be some or all of the trustees, the Official Custodian for Charities (see our guidance *The Official Custodian for Charities' Land Holding Service* (CC13)) or a nominee.

[41] These are the minimum requirements and trustees should consider if any other forms of insurance are needed.

The trustees must keep in repair and insure to their full value against fire and other usual risks all the buildings of the charity (except those buildings that are required to be kept in repair and insured by a tenant). They must also insure suitably in respect of public liability and employer's liability.

31. Notices
(1) Any notice required by this constitution to be given to or by any person must be:
   (a) in writing; or
   (b) given using electronic communications.
(2) The charity may give any notice to a member either:
   (a) personally; or
   (b) by sending it by post in a prepaid envelope addressed to the member at his or her address; or
   (c) by leaving it at the address of the member; or
   (d) by giving it using electronic communications to the member's address.
(3) A member who does not register an address with the charity or who registers only a postal address that is not within the United Kingdom shall not be entitled to receive any notice from the charity.
(4) A member present in person at any meeting of the charity shall be deemed to have received notice of the meeting and of the purposes for which it was called.
(5)
   (a) Proof that an envelope containing a notice was properly addressed, prepaid and posted shall be conclusive evidence that the notice was given.
   (b) Proof that a notice contained in an electronic communication was sent in accordance with guidance issued by the Institute of Chartered Secretaries and Administrators shall be conclusive evidence that the notice was given.
   (c) A notice shall be deemed to be given 48 hours after the envelope containing it was posted or, in the case of an electronic communication, 48 hours after it was sent.

32. Rules[42]
(1) The trustees may from time to time make rules or bye-laws for the conduct of their business.
(2) The bye-laws may regulate the following matters but are not restricted to them:
   (a) the admission of members of the charity (including the admission of organisations to membership) and the rights and privileges of such members, and the entrance fees, subscriptions and other fees or payments to be made by members;

---

[42] Rules are effectively the internal procedures adopted by the trustees for the proper administration of the charity. They cannot be used to change any of the provisions in this constitution. Clause 7 of this constitution sets out the procedure for amending the provisions of this constitution.

(b) the conduct of members of the charity in relation to one another, and to the charity's employees and volunteers;
(c) the setting aside of the whole or any part or parts of the charity's premises at any particular time or times or for any particular purpose or purposes;
(d) the procedure at general meeting and meetings of the trustees in so far as such procedure is not regulated by this constitution;
(e) the keeping and authenticating of records. (If regulations made under this clause permit records of the charity to be kept in electronic form and requires a trustee to sign the record, the regulations must specify a method of recording the signature that enables it to be properly authenticated.)[43]
(f) generally, all such matters as are commonly the subject matter of the rules of an unincorporated association.
(3) The charity in general meeting has the power to alter, add to or repeal the rules or bye-laws.
(4) The trustees must adopt such means as they think sufficient to bring the rules and bye-laws to the notice of members of the charity.
(5) The rules or bye-laws shall be binding on all members of the charity. No rule or bye-law shall be inconsistent with, or shall affect or repeal anything contained in, this constitution.

33. Disputes[44]

If a dispute arises between members of the charity about the validity or propriety of anything done by the members under this constitution, and the dispute cannot be resolved by agreement, the parties to the dispute must first try in good faith to settle the dispute by mediation before resorting to litigation.

34. Interpretation

In this constitution 'connected person' means:
(1) a child, parent, grandchild, grandparent, brother or sister of the trustee;
(2) the spouse or civil partner of the trustee or of any person falling within sub-clause (1) above;
(3) a person carrying on business in partnership with the trustee or with any person falling within sub-clause (1) or (2) above;
(4) an institution which is controlled –
  (a) by the trustee or any connected person falling within sub-clause (1), (2), or (3) above; or
  (b) by two or more persons falling within sub-clause (4)(a), when taken together

---

[43] The Electronic Communications Act 2000 and the Electronic Signatures Regulations 2002 permit electronic signatures to be accepted as evidence, subject to certain conditions. This sub-clause summarises those conditions.

[44] It is good practice to include provisions for dealing with any disputes that arise between members of the charity. Litigation can be expensive, and litigation about the internal affairs of a charity would almost certainly constitute 'charity proceedings', which can be taken only with the Commission's authority. We would usually require the parties to a dispute to have tried mediation first.

(5) a body corporate in which –
  (a) the charity trustee or any connected person falling within sub-clauses (1) to (3) has a substantial interest; or
  (b) two or more persons falling within sub-clause (5)(a) who, when taken together, have a substantial interest.
(6) Sections 350 – 352 of the Charities Act 2011 apply for the purposes of interpreting the terms used in this clause.

Signatures

....
....
....
....
....
....
....

APPENDIX E

CHARITABLE INCORPORATED ORGANISATION: MODEL CONSTITUTION FOR A CIO WITH A VOTING MEMBERSHIP (IN ADDITION TO THE CHARITY TRUSTEES)

Reproduced with the kind permission of the Charity Commission https://www.gov.uk/government/publications/setting-up-a-charity-model-governing-documents

('Association' model constitution)

This document is a Charity Commission model constitution for a Charitable Incorporated Organisation (CIO). If you want to set up a CIO, you will find it easiest to use one of our model constitutions.

This guidance briefly explains:
- What a CIO is
- How to decide whether the CIO is the right form for your charity
- How to choose the right model constitution
- How to complete the model constitution and register as a charity
- Where to get more information and advice

There are notes explaining key points about each clause in the model constitution, to help you decide how to complete it.

We also have more detailed guidance on CIOs available on our website.

What is a Charitable Incorporated Organisation?

The Charitable Incorporated Organisation (CIO) is a new legal form for a charity. It has been created in response to requests from the charitable sector. It is a new incorporated form of charity which is not a limited company or subject to company regulation.

The Charities Act 2011 creates the basic legal framework for the CIO. This framework is completed by regulations:

- the Charitable Incorporated Organisations (General) Regulations 2012 ('General Regulations'); and
- the Charitable Incorporated Organisations (Insolvency and Dissolution) Regulations 2012 ('Dissolution Regulations').

Is the CIO the right structure for our charity?

Choosing the right legal structure and governing document is one of the first and most important decisions that the founders of a charity need to make. It will affect:

- how easy it will be to set up and run the charity
- how easy it will be to make changes in the future
- whether the charity can have a voting membership
- whether the charity can itself own premises, employ staff or enter contracts, or whether the trustees will have to do this personally.

With the introduction of the CIO, there are four main legal forms that charities may take. We produce model governing documents for each of these forms:

- Trust (governing document: trust deed; could also be created by a will)
- Unincorporated association (governing document: constitution or rules)
- Company limited by guarantee (governing document: memorandum and articles of association for company formed before September 2009; articles of association for company formed since then)
- CIO (governing document: constitution)

An incorporated form, CIO or company limited by guarantee, may be more suitable for a charity that will:

- own land in its own name
- control substantial funds or assets
- enter into contracts, for example by employing staff, or
- engage in charitable activities involving financial risks

Some points to note about CIOs:

- A CIO is a corporate body (like a company) that can own property, employ staff and enter into other contracts in its own name (rather than in the names of the trustees).
- Members of a company limited by guarantee have limited liability for its debts if it winds up (they only have to pay a fixed amount). Members of a CIO may either have no liability at all or (like a company) limited liability for its debts.
- Because they have additional legal protection, members of a corporate body (company or CIO) must comply with extra regulations.
- Unlike companies, CIOs do not have to register with Companies House.

- Unlike companies, CIOs will not be fined for administrative errors like late filing of accounts, but some breaches of the CIO Regulations are legal offences.
- All CIOs must register with the Commission, regardless of their income. This means that an exempt charity cannot be a CIO, and CIO may be unsuitable for other types of charity that don't have to register. (See our *guidance on types of charity that don't have to register*.)
- CIOs must produce accounts under charity law, not company law. This allows smaller CIOs (income below £250,000) to produce simpler receipts and payments accounts.
- To simplify the CIO framework, there is currently no provision for CIOs to issue debentures, or for a register of charges (mortgages etc) over CIO property.

For more information on other legal forms, see our guidance on choosing your charity's governing document. Another useful source of advice is the Get Legal website and online decision tool (www.getlegal.org.uk).

Why are there two different model constitutions for a CIO?

Like companies (which must have both members and company directors) all CIOs must have members and charity trustees. Some CIOs may want the only members to be the charity trustees; others may want a wider membership open to other people. We have produced two model constitutions for CIOs:

- the **'foundation'** model is for charities whose **only** voting members will be the charity trustees
- the **'association'** model (this model) is for charities that will have a wider membership, including voting members other than the charity trustees

In practice a CIO using the 'foundation' model will be like an incorporated charitable trust, run by a small group of people (the charity trustees) who make all key decisions. Charity trustees may be appointed for an unlimited time and they will probably appoint new charity trustees.

A CIO using the 'association' model will have a wider voting membership who must make certain decisions (such as amending the constitution), will usually appoint some or all of the charity trustees (who will serve for fixed terms), and may be involved in the work of the CIO.

There are not two different forms of CIO. A CIO with the 'foundation' model could change to the 'association' model if it wanted a wider voting membership. (This could also happen the other way around, but members who were not trustees would be giving up their membership.) Some of the changes would need our approval.

Why use one of the Commission's model CIO constitutions?

A CIO's constitution **must** be in the form to be specified by Commission regulations (or as near to that form as the circumstances allow). These regulations will specify that the constitution should be in the form of one of our model constitutions. This still allows some flexibility, as explained in the guidance notes on the model. The constitution **must** be in English if the CIO's principal office is in England, but may be in English or Welsh if the principal office is in Wales.

A CIO's constitution **must** include certain provisions to comply with the Charities Act 2011 (the 2011 Act) and the General Regulations. However the 2011 Act and General Regulations do not prescribe an exact wording.

There are other provisions that **must** be included **if** they apply to a particular CIO. If they do not fully apply, the constitution **must** explain to what extent or how they apply.

We have included other provisions in this model constitution because:
- they reflect good practice that we recommend
- they remind the trustees about a legal requirement
- the constitution would not work properly without them, or
- charities have said that it would be a useful option and it would be helpful to have standard wording

Using one of the Commission's models will help to ensure that you include all of the constitutional provisions that your CIO will need:
- to meet the requirements of the law
- to comply with good practice, and
- to be practical and workable

The guidance notes will prompt you to think about whether you may need to include particular powers.

The 2011 Act and the General Regulations don't require you to use a particular wording, but the wording in our models has been carefully considered and also informed by specialists in the charity sector. Using one of our models will also mean that there will be fewer questions for us to ask and consider when you apply for charity registration.

How do we become a CIO?

(i) *New charities*
   To set up and register a new CIO, follow the procedure set out below under Next steps.

(ii) *Existing charitable trusts and unincorporated associations*
   An existing unincorporated charity can only change to a CIO by:
   - setting up and registering a new CIO (in the same way as for a new charity), then

- transferring its property and operations to the CIO.

You should check whether your charity can transfer its property in this way, or whether you need authorisation from the Commission. Once the transfer is complete, the original charity can normally be wound up and removed from the register, but different arrangements may apply to charities with permanent endowment (see below).

(iii) Existing charities with permanent endowment

Some charitable trusts have property (land or investments) that cannot be expended as income. Property restricted in this way is called permanent endowment. This may include land that must be used in a particular way for the purposes of the charity.

- Often, these charities have no power to wind up or transfer their permanent endowment.
- CIOs cannot hold permanent endowment as part of their own (corporate) property.

The General Regulations make special provision to enable charities with permanent endowment to transfer to a CIO. The trustees of the permanently endowed charity need to:

- set up and register a new CIO with the Commission, then
- make a vesting declaration under section 310 of the 2011 Act (as amended by the General Regulations), transferring all property of the original charity to the new CIO.

The vesting declaration will:

- transfer expendable property to the CIO as part of its corporate property
- vest legal title to the permanent endowment in the CIO, to be held on its original trusts
- appoint the CIO as trustee for the permanent endowment trust and give it the powers of a trust corporation for that trust
- mean that the CIO and the permanent endowment trust are treated as a single charity for registration and accounting purposes (they won't need to register separately or produce separate accounts).

If charities use a vesting declaration to carry out a merger, they must record it in the *Register of Mergers*. Vesting declarations are legal documents, so you may need advice from a solicitor or other professional. There are circumstances in which permanent endowment can be spent; it is not absolutely protected.

For further information see our general guidance on CIOs.

(iv) Existing charitable companies and industrial and provident societies

Once all of the provisions are in force, it will also be possible for an existing charitable company or charitable industrial and provident society to convert directly into a CIO; there are specific procedures for this.

To manage demand, the Commission is phasing in the introduction of the CIO and not all of these options will be available immediately. Please see our general guidance on CIOs for details.

What guidance should we consider before we begin?

- There is comprehensive guidance on *setting up and registering a charity* on our website.
- We also have more detailed **guidance on CIOs**.
- *The Essential Trustee* sets out the basics that all charity trustees need to know.

Next steps

1. Completing the constitution
   Please note – we are publishing the model constitutions in this format (PDF) to help charities and their professional advisers to prepare for the implementation of the CIO. We are currently looking into more flexible and user-friendly formats that will make it easier for promoters to complete the constitution.
   Once you have decided to apply to register a CIO and have chosen the correct model constitution, please read the constitution and accompanying guidance notes carefully. In the guidance notes we say that something '**must**' be included in the constitution if it is a legal requirement in the 2011 Act or the Regulations. We say that something '**should**' be included if we consider it to be minimum good practice. We 'recommend' that you include other provisions to help ensure the smooth running of the CIO in future.
   There are guidance notes on each clause explaining what it is for, and whether you **must** or **should** include (all or part of) it, and whether it **may** or **should** be amended to fit the circumstances. Even where clauses are completely optional, however, we advise you to follow the model provisions or suggested alternatives unless there is a particular need, in the interests of your charity, to do otherwise.
   Some clauses contain options for you to choose from and blank spaces that you will need to fill in.
   If you want to add any special or complex provisions that you have drafted yourself, you may need advice from a solicitor or other adviser. We may need more time to look at any specialist changes. Please make clear what changes you make, and why they are necessary. This will help us to consider your application as quickly as possible. We cannot guarantee to accept every organisation which uses one of our models as charitable. We must consider each case separately.
   When you have finished, please check that you have:
   - filled in all the blanks;
   - deleted any clauses which you don't need; and
   - numbered the remaining clauses (and sub-clauses) in sequence (including cross-references).

2. Applying to register
   To register a new charity, apply online. If you cannot apply online, please contact Charity Commission Direct. The best way to contact us is by email.

3. How long will it take?
   We can normally make a decision in 40 working days if an organisation:

- can use our model wording for its objects (*Example charitable objects* on our website);
- shows that its activities are or will be consistent with the objects;
- shows that any private benefit is only incidental and is properly managed; and
- uses our model governing document.

Other applications will need closer consideration and so will take longer.

Constitution of a Charitable Incorporated Organisation with voting members other than its charity trustees

('Association' Model Constitution)

Date of constitution (last amended):[1]

....

1. Name[2]
   The name of the Charitable Incorporated Organisation ("the CIO") is

....

....

2. National location of principal office[3]
   The CIO must have a principal office in England or Wales. The principal office of the CIO is in [England][Wales].
3. Object[s][4]
   The object[s] of the CIO [is][are] ....
   ....
   ....

   Nothing in this constitution shall authorise an application of the property of the CIO for the purposes which are not charitable in accordance with

---

[1] Inserting the date of the constitution is good practice, and helps to ensure everyone is working from the same document. The date to enter here is the date the constitution, or any amendment to it, has been registered by the Commission, as this is when it comes into effect. Leave this undated until the constitution has been registered. You should send a dated version when the date of registration has been confirmed.

[2] You **must** include the name of the CIO in the constitution. In general, the Commission can accept any charity name unless it would be misleading, offensive or too similar to the name of an existing charity (unless the CIO is replacing that charity). The Commission has powers to require a charity to change its name if this happens. Further information on this is provided in our publication *Registering as a charity* (CC21) and in our Operational Guidance (OG330 – *Names of charities*), which are available on our website. There are also legal restrictions on using the same name as an existing company (unless it is a charitable company that is converting to a CIO) or as a former company or CIO that underwent insolvent liquidation – if in doubt seek professional advice.

[3] The constitution **must** state whether the CIO's principal office is in England or Wales.

[4] The CIO **must** have exclusively charitable objects which you must set out in the constitution. Guidance on appropriate wording for objects is available on our website. The key elements to include are:
  • the purpose or purposes for which the CIO is being established;
  • the people who can benefit; and if appropriate
  • any geographic limits defining the area of benefit. If you include an area of benefit, it is common to define it by reference to a local government area: this has the advantage of clarity and simplicity, but can create problems if the area is subsequently altered or abolished. If this happens in future, contact the Commission for advice on amending the objects.
  NB. If you cannot fit your objects in the space provided, please include them on a separate piece of paper and submit this with the constitution.
  If the CIO needs to be recognised as a charity in Scotland and/or Northern Ireland you will need to include the relevant parts of the wording in square brackets to meet the requirements of charity law in those countries.

[section 7 of the Charities and Trustee Investment (Scotland) Act 2005] and [section 2 of the Charities Act (Northern Ireland) 2008].

4. Powers[5]

The CIO has power to do anything which is calculated to further its object[s] or is conducive or incidental to doing so. In particular, the CIO's powers include power to:

(1) borrow money and to charge the whole or any part of its property as security for the repayment of the money borrowed. The CIO must comply as appropriate with sections 124 and 125 of the Charities Act 2011 if it wishes to mortgage land;

(2) buy, take on lease or in exchange, hire or otherwise acquire any property and to maintain and equip it for use;

(3) sell, lease or otherwise dispose of all or any part of the property belonging to the CIO. In exercising this power, the CIO must comply as appropriate with sections 117 and 119-123 of the Charities Act 2011;

(4) employ and remunerate such staff as are necessary for carrying out the work of the CIO. The CIO may employ or remunerate a charity trustee only to the extent that it is permitted to do so by clause 6 (Benefits and payments to charity trustees and connected persons) and provided it complies with the conditions of that clause;

(5) deposit or invest funds, employ a professional fund-manager, and arrange for the investments or other property of the CIO to be held in the name of a nominee, in the same manner and subject to the same conditions as the trustees of a trust are permitted to do by the Trustee Act 2000;

5. **Application of income and property**[6]

(1) The income and property of the CIO must be applied solely towards the promotion of the objects.

    (a) A charity trustee is entitled to be reimbursed from the property of the CIO or may pay out of such property reasonable expenses properly incurred by him or her when acting on behalf of the CIO.

---

[5] The Charities Act 2011 gives a CIO power to do 'anything which is calculated to further its purposes or is conducive or incidental to doing so'. Strictly speaking, this is the only power a CIO needs. It can, however, be helpful to state certain powers explicitly in the constitution. In particular, a stated power to borrow [(1)] may reassure potential lenders. For this reason we recommend that you include the example powers set out in the model (these include powers to buy, sell and lease property, employ staff and delegate investment management to a professional fund-manager). You **may** add other express powers here if you wish to.

You **may** include a constitutional provision restricting the general power in the 2011 Act. You **must only** include such a restriction if it is in the CIO's interests. You **must not** restrict the CIO's powers in a way that prevents it from disposing of its property. Restrictions on the powers are not provided for in this model and we recommend that you seek appropriate advice if you are considering this.

[6] We recommend that you include this clause.

(b) A charity trustee may benefit from trustee indemnity insurance cover purchased at the CIO's expense in accordance with, and subject to the conditions in, section 189 of the Charities Act 2011.[7]

(2) None of the income or property of the CIO may be paid or transferred directly or indirectly by way of dividend, bonus or otherwise by way of profit to any member of the CIO. This does not prevent a member who is not also a charity trustee receiving:
   (a) a benefit from the CIO as a beneficiary of the CIO;
   (b) reasonable and proper remuneration for any goods or services supplied to the CIO.[8]

(3) Nothing in this clause shall prevent a charity trustee or connected person receiving any benefit or payment which is authorised by Clause 6.

6. Benefits and payments to charity trustees and connected persons[9]
   (1) General provisions
   No charity trustee or connected person may:
   (a) buy or receive any goods or services from the CIO on terms preferential to those applicable to members of the public;
   (b) sell goods, services, or any interest in land to the CIO;
   (c) be employed by, or receive any remuneration from, the CIO;
   (d) receive any other financial benefit from the CIO;
   unless the payment or benefit is permitted by sub-clause (2) of this clause, or authorised by the court or the prior written consent of the Charity Commission ("the Commission") has been obtained. In this

---

[7] This sub-clause reflects the statutory provisions in the Charities Act 2011 about a CIO charity trustee's entitlement to reasonable expenses and that they may benefit from trustee indemnity insurance. We recommend that you include it in the constitution, to inform people involved with the charity.

[8] This sub-clause reflects charity law requirements that the income and property of a CIO must be applied solely to further its objects and not to benefit the members or charity trustees (except as permitted by the governing document (see clause 6) or other express power). The trustees have a duty to ensure that the funds are correctly applied in accordance with this principle.

[9] Charity trustees may only benefit from their charity if they have express legal authorisation to do so (such as a clause in the constitution). This restriction extends to people closely connected to a trustee ('connected persons' – this term is defined in the interpretation clause). You **should** include this clause so that charity trustees are clear about the restrictions that apply to them; and unless you include it, the default legal position will apply. Even where trustees are allowed to benefit from the CIO, this must only happen where the benefit is in the interests of the CIO. Our guidance *Trustee expenses and payments* (CC11) provides more information about trustee benefits.

The model clause permits a minority of the charity trustees or connected persons to receive payments and other benefits in certain instances (such as for goods and services they supply to the CIO), subject to the stated controls. The option also allows other types of trustee benefit, subject to the Commission's prior consent.

You may restrict the benefits that the charity trustees will be allowed receive by altering these clauses, but if you later need to undo any of the restrictions it will require the Commission's consent to do so. Trustees do not have to use these powers just because they have them – we suggest you may find it simpler to keep to the model wording.

None of these options allows the trustees to receive payment for acting as a trustee.

clause, a "financial benefit" means a benefit, direct or indirect, which is either money or has a monetary value.

(2) **Scope and powers permitting trustees' or connected persons' benefits**
  (a) A charity trustee or connected person may receive a benefit from the CIO as a beneficiary of the CIO provided that a majority of the trustees do not benefit in this way.[10]
  (b) A charity trustee or connected person may enter into a contract for the supply of services, or of goods that are supplied in connection with the provision of services, to the CIO where that is permitted in accordance with, and subject to the conditions in, section 185 to 188 of the Charities Act 2011.
  (c) Subject to sub-clause (3) of this clause a charity trustee or connected person may provide the CIO with goods that are not supplied in connection with services provided to the CIO by the charity trustee or connected person.
  (d) A charity trustee or connected person may receive interest on money lent to the CIO at a reasonable and proper rate which must be not more than the Bank of England bank rate (also known as the base rate).[11]
  (e) A charity trustee or connected person may receive rent for premises let by the trustee or connected person to the CIO. The amount of the rent and the other terms of the lease must be reasonable and proper. The charity trustee concerned must withdraw from any meeting at which such a proposal or the rent or other terms of the lease are under discussion.
  (f) A charity trustee or connected person may take part in the normal trading and fundraising activities of the CIO on the same terms as members of the public.

(3) **Payment for supply of goods only – controls**
  The CIO and its charity trustees may only rely upon the authority provided by sub-clause (2)(c) of this clause if each of the following conditions is satisfied:
  (a) The amount or maximum amount of the payment for the goods is set out in a written agreement between the CIO and the charity trustee or connected person supplying the goods ("the supplier").
  (b) The amount or maximum amount of the payment for the goods does not exceed what is reasonable in the circumstances for the supply of the goods in question.
  (c) The other charity trustees are satisfied that it is in the best interests of the CIO to contract with the supplier rather than with someone who is not a charity trustee or connected person.

---

[10] If all of the trustees will benefit from the activities of the CIO (for example, by using facilities available to all inhabitants of the area, such as a community centre), you may wish to substitute the following wording: "A charity trustee or connected person may receive a benefit from the CIO as a beneficiary provided that it is available generally to the beneficiaries of the CIO'.

[11] The CIO should document the amount of, and the terms of, the trustee's or connected person's loan.

In reaching that decision the charity trustees must balance the advantage of contracting with a charity trustee or connected person against the disadvantages of doing so.
- (d) The supplier is absent from the part of any meeting at which there is discussion of the proposal to enter into a contract or arrangement with him or her or it with regard to the supply of goods to the CIO.
- (e) The supplier does not vote on any such matter and is not to be counted when calculating whether a quorum of charity trustees is present at the meeting.
- (f) The reason for their decision is recorded by the charity trustees in the minute book.
- (g) A majority of the charity trustees then in office are not in receipt of remuneration or payments authorised by clause 6.

(4) In sub-clauses (2) and (3) of this clause:
- (a) "the CIO" includes any company in which the CIO:
  - (i) holds more than 50% of the shares; or
  - (ii) controls more than 50% of the voting rights attached to the shares; or
  - (iii) has the right to appoint one or more directors to the board of the company;
- (b) "connected person" includes any person within the definition set out in clause [30] (Interpretation);

7. **Conflicts of interest and conflicts of loyalty**[12]
   A charity trustee must:
   (1) declare the nature and extent of any interest, direct or indirect, which he or she has in a proposed transaction or arrangement with the CIO or in any transaction or arrangement entered into by the CIO which has not previously been declared; and
   (2) absent himself or herself from any discussions of the charity trustees in which it is possible that a conflict of interest will arise between his or her duty to act solely in the interests of the CIO and any personal interest (including but not limited to any financial interest).

   Any charity trustee absenting himself or herself from any discussions in accordance with this clause must not vote or be counted as part of the quorum in any decision of the charity trustees on the matter.

8. **Liability of members to contribute to the assets of the CIO if it is wound up**[13]

---

[12] The General Regulations provide that a charity trustee of a CIO must not take part in any decision from which they would directly or indirectly benefit personally, unless they cannot reasonably be regarded as having a conflict of interest. This clause reminds the trustees of this requirement and also reflects wider good practice on managing conflicts of interest and conflicts of loyalty. We recommend that you include it.

[13] The constitution must state whether members of the CIO *either*: (a) have no liability to contribute to the assets of the CIO if it is wound up [option 1]; *or* (b) will be liable to contribute up to a maximum amount each if the CIO cannot meet its financial obligations when it is wound up [option 2]. Choose one option and delete the other. There is no preference or requirement in the legal framework for members to be liable to contribute anything. If you

Option 1

If the CIO is wound up, the members of the CIO have no liability to contribute to its assets and no personal responsibility for settling its debts and liabilities.

Option 2

(1) If the CIO is wound up, each member of the CIO is liable to contribute to the assets of the CIO such amount (but not more than £[. . .]) as may be required for payment of the debts and liabilities of the CIO contracted before that person or organisation ceases to be a member, for payment of the costs, charges and expenses of winding up, and for adjustment of the rights of the contributing members among themselves.

(2) In sub-clause (1) of this clause "member" includes any person or organisation that was a member of the CIO within 12 months before the commencement of the winding up.

(3) But subject to that, the members of the CIO have no liability to contribute to its assets if it is wound up, and accordingly have no personal responsibility for the settlement of its debts and liabilities beyond the amount that they are liable to contribute.

9. **Membership of the CIO**[14]
   (1) **Admission of new members**
       (a) **Eligibility**
           Membership of the CIO is open to anyone who is interested in furthering its purposes, and who, by applying for membership, has indicated his, her or its agreement to become a member and acceptance of the duty of members set out in sub-clause (3) of this clause.
           A member may be an individual, a corporate body, or [an individual or corporate body representing] an organisation which is not incorporated.[15]
       (b) **Admission procedure**

---

choose option 2, you must insert the maximum amount (normally a nominal sum such as £1 or £10) for which members will be individually liable.

[14] A CIO must have one or more members.
If all of the CIO's voting members will also be trustees and there will be no other voting members, you should use the Foundation Model Constitution.
According to sub-clause (1)(a) and (b), you must state in the constitution who is eligible to be a member and how someone becomes a member.
It is possible to include more restrictive membership provisions (for example requiring members to be 'approved' by the charity trustees); in that case the membership refusal provisions (clause 9(1)(b)(iii)) would also need to be changed. Membership must not be unreasonably restricted if the members are also the beneficiaries of the CIO as that would affect public benefit.

[15] Normally, the members of a charity are individuals, but corporate bodies (eg companies) can also be members. In a few cases, charities say they also have unincorporated bodies (eg local associations that are part of a national federation) as members. Legal experts disagree about this, but charities asked us not to prevent it by default. If a CIO will have unincorporated members, they should either be represented by a person they nominate (keep the words in square brackets) or act as members in their own right (delete the words in square brackets). The CIO will need to make rules to govern how any unincorporated members exercise their rights

The charity trustees:
(i) may require applications for membership to be made in any reasonable way that they decide;
(ii) [shall, if they approve an application for membership, notify the applicant of their decision within [21 days];]
(iii) may refuse an application for membership if they believe that it is in the best interests of the CIO for them to do so;
(iv) shall, if they decide to refuse an application for membership, give the applicant their reasons for doing so, within [21 days] of the decision being taken, and give the applicant the opportunity to appeal against the refusal; and
(v) shall give fair consideration to any such appeal, and shall inform the applicant of their decision, but any decision to confirm refusal of the application for membership shall be final.

(2) **Transfer of membership**
Membership of the CIO cannot be transferred to anyone else [except in the case of an individual or corporate body representing an organisation which is not incorporated, whose membership may be transferred by the unincorporated organisation to a new representative. Such transfer of membership does not take effect until the CIO has received written notification of the transfer].[16]

(3) **Duty of members**
It is the duty of each member of the CIO to exercise his or her powers as a member of the CIO in the way he or she decides in good faith would be most likely to further the purposes of the CIO.[17]

(4) **Termination of membership**
(a) Membership of the CIO comes to an end if:
(i) the member dies, or, in the case of an organisation (or the representative of an organisation) that organisation ceases to exist; or
(ii) the member sends a notice of resignation to the charity trustees; or
(iii) any sum of money owed by the member to the CIO is not paid in full within six months of its falling due; or
(iv) the charity trustees decide that it is in the best interests of the CIO that the member in question should be removed from membership, and pass a resolution to that effect.
(b) Before the charity trustees take any decision to remove someone from membership of the CIO they must:

---

and duties as members, for example, attending meetings and voting, or meeting any liability to contribute funds in the event of the CIO winding up.

[16] We recommend you include this provision, otherwise the charity's membership records could become unworkable and the charity would lose control over membership. Include the words in square brackets if the membership includes representatives of unincorporated organisations (see clause 9(1)(a)); otherwise remove them.

[17] This is the legal duty of each member of the CIO as set out in the Charities Act 2011. You may find it helpful to set this out in the constitution. The constitution cannot change the members' legal duty.

(i) inform the member of the reasons why it is proposed to remove him, her or it from membership;

(ii) give the member at least 21 clear days notice in which to make representations to the charity trustees as to why he, she or it should not be removed from membership;

(iii) at a duly constituted meeting of the charity trustees, consider whether or not the member should be removed from membership;

(iv) consider at that meeting any representations which the member makes as to why the member should not be removed; and

(v) allow the member, or the member's representative, to make those representations in person at that meeting, if the member so chooses.[18]

(5) **Membership fees**

The CIO may require members to pay reasonable membership fees to the CIO.[19]

[(6) **Informal or associate (non-voting) membership**

(a) The charity trustees may create associate or other classes of non-voting membership, and may determine the rights and obligations of any such members (including payment of membership fees), and the conditions for admission to, and termination of membership of any such class of members.

(b) Other references in this constitution to "members" and "membership" do not apply to non-voting members, and non-voting members do not qualify as members for any purpose under the Charities Acts, General Regulations or Dissolution Regulations.][20]

10. **Members' decisions**[21]

(1) **General provisions**

Except for those decisions that must be taken in a particular way as indicated in sub-clause (4) of this clause, decisions of the members of

---

[18] The General Regulations state that the constitution must contain provision for retirement and termination of membership. The suggestions here are based on experience and good practice.

[19] Charities have discretion to set and charge membership fees, but it may be advisable to state this in the constitution to avoid any misunderstanding.

Classes of membership – Some charities have different categories or classes of members with different voting rights. The General Regulations require that if this applies to the CIO, the different categories of members and their voting rights must be set out in the constitution. We are unable to provide a model clause for this as it will need to be drafted to reflect the CIO's particular circumstances. You may need professional advice on a suitable wording.

We do not advise CIOs to have different classes of membership, but it is permissible where the trustees consider it to be in the interests of the CIO.

[20] We advise CIOs to include this power if they will have or may consider having an informal (associate) membership. Membership of this kind does not count as membership for legal purposes, for example in terms of voting rights, legal obligations to act in the interests of the charity or any liability to contribute to the assets of the CIO on dissolution.

Details of any informal members should not be included in the Register of Members.

[21] These provisions reflect provisions in the General Regulations that govern decision-making by members. We recommend they are included in the constitution for clarity.

the CIO may be taken either by vote at a general meeting as provided in sub-clause (2) of this clause or by written resolution as provided in sub-clause (3) of this clause.

(2) **Taking ordinary decisions by vote**
Subject to sub-clause (4) of this clause, any decision of the members of the CIO may be taken by means of a resolution at a general meeting. Such a resolution may be passed by a simple majority of votes cast at the meeting [(including votes cast by postal or email ballot, and proxy votes)].[22]

(3) **Taking ordinary decisions by written resolution without a general meeting**
   (a) Subject to sub-clause (4) of this clause, a resolution in writing agreed by a simple majority of all the members who would have been entitled to vote upon it had it been proposed at a general meeting shall be effective, provided that:
      (i) a copy of the proposed resolution has been sent to all the members eligible to vote; and
      (ii) a simple majority of members has signified its agreement to the resolution in a document or documents which are received at the principal office within the period of 28 days beginning with the circulation date. The document signifying a member's agreement must be authenticated by their signature (or in the case of an organisation which is a member, by execution according to its usual procedure), by a statement of their identity accompanying the document, or in such other manner as the CIO has specified.
   (b) The resolution in writing may comprise several copies to which one or more members has signified their agreement.
   (c) Eligibility to vote on the resolution is limited to members who are members of the CIO on the date when the proposal is first circulated in accordance with paragraph (a) above.
   (d) Not less than 10% of the members of the CIO may request the charity trustees to make a proposal for decision by the members.
   (e) The charity trustees must within 21 days of receiving such a request comply with it if:
      (i) The proposal is not frivolous or vexatious, and does not involve the publication of defamatory material;
      (ii) The proposal is stated with sufficient clarity to enable effect to be given to it if it is agreed by the members; and
      (iii) Effect can lawfully be given to the proposal if it is so agreed.
   (f) Sub-clauses (a) to (c) of this clause apply to a proposal made at the request of members.[23]

---

[22] This clause describes the usual mechanism for making decisions at general meetings. We recommend that it is included in the constitution to reduce the possibility of disagreements about decision-making by members.

[23] This power (to take decisions other than by resolution at a general meeting) is optional, but if the CIO intends to use it, it must be included in the constitution.

Model Constitution for a CIO with a Voting Membership   165

(4) **Decisions that must be taken in a particular way**
[(a) Any decision to remove a trustee must be taken in accordance with clause [15(2)].]
(b) Any decision to amend this constitution must be taken in accordance with clause [28] of this constitution (Amendment of Constitution).
(c) Any decision to wind up or dissolve the CIO must be taken in accordance with clause [29] of this constitution (Voluntary winding up or dissolution). Any decision to amalgamate or transfer the undertaking of the CIO to one or more other CIOs must be taken in accordance with the provisions of the Charities Act 2011.[24]

11. **General meetings of members**[25]
    (1) Types of general meeting
    There must be an annual general meeting (AGM) of the members of the CIO. The first AGM must be held within 18 months of the registration of the CIO, and subsequent AGMs must be held at intervals of not more than 15 months. The AGM must receive the annual statement of accounts (duly audited or examined where applicable) and the trustees' annual report, and must elect trustees as required under clause [13].
    Other general meetings of the members of the CIO may be held at any time.
    All general meetings must be held in accordance with the following provisions.
    (2) Calling general meetings
       (a) The charity trustees:
           (i) must call the annual general meeting of the members of the CIO in accordance with sub-clause (1) of this clause, and identify it as such in the notice of the meeting; and

---

[24] This clause highlights when special provisions apply to a decision, and we recommend you include it. Only include (a) if you are including the corresponding optional power to remove charity trustees.
A CIO may include further restrictions in its constitution controlling how particular decisions must be taken (this is called 'a provision for entrenchment'). CIOs considering this should seek professional advice.

[25] The General Regulations state that the constitution must include provisions about the holding and calling of general meetings, including: procedure at general meetings; the appointment of a Chair; the minimum number of members who can form a quorum; whether members can demand a poll; and the procedure for conducting a poll. Whilst it is not a legal requirement, we strongly recommend that CIOs with a wider voting membership include provisions along these lines and do not include provisions allowing them to opt out of holding general meetings including an annual general meeting. Certain decisions (such as amendments to the constitution) must be made by the members rather than the trustees, and general meetings are the usual way that membership-based charities make such decisions. Members' meetings are also an important method both of communicating with members and being accountable to them.
Except where indicated as legal or regulatory requirements, the provisions in this clause are examples based on recommended good practice.

(ii) may call any other general meeting of the members at any time.
(b) The charity trustees must, within 21 days, call a general meeting of the members of the CIO if:
  (i) they receive a request to do so from at least 10% of the members of the CIO; and
  (ii) the request states the general nature of the business to be dealt with at the meeting, and is authenticated by the member(s) making the request.
(c) If, at the time of any such request, there has not been any general meeting of the members of the CIO for more than 12 months, then sub-clause (b)(i) of this clause shall have effect as if 5% were substituted for 10%.
(d) Any such request may include particulars of a resolution that may properly be proposed, and is intended to be proposed, at the meeting.
(e) A resolution may only properly be proposed if it is lawful, and is not defamatory, frivolous or vexatious.
(f) Any general meeting called by the charity trustees at the request of the members of the CIO must be held within 28 days from the date on which it is called.
(g) If the charity trustees fail to comply with this obligation to call a general meeting at the request of its members, then the members who requested the meeting may themselves call a general meeting.
(h) A general meeting called in this way must be held not more than 3 months after the date when the members first requested the meeting.
(i) The CIO must reimburse any reasonable expenses incurred by the members calling a general meeting by reason of the failure of the charity trustees to duly call the meeting, but the CIO shall be entitled to be indemnified by the charity trustees who were responsible for such failure.

(3) Notice of general meetings
(a) The charity trustees, or, as the case may be, the relevant members of the CIO, must give at least 14 clear days notice of any general meeting to all of the members, and to any charity trustee of the CIO who is not a member.
(b) If it is agreed by not less than 90% of all members of the CIO, any resolution may be proposed and passed at the meeting even though the requirements of sub-clause (3)(a) of this clause have not been met. This sub-clause does not apply where a specified period of notice is strictly required by another clause in this constitution, by the Charities Act 2011 or by the General Regulations.
(c) The notice of any general meeting must:
  (i) state the time and date of the meeting;
  (ii) give the address at which the meeting is to take place;

(iii) give particulars of any resolution which is to be moved at the meeting, and of the general nature of any other business to be dealt with at the meeting; and

(iv) if a proposal to alter the constitution of the CIO is to be considered at the meeting, include the text of the proposed alteration;

(v) include, with the notice for the AGM, the annual statement of accounts and trustees' annual report, details of persons standing for election or re-election as trustee, or where allowed under clause [22] (Use of electronic communication), details of where the information may be found on the CIO's website.

(d) Proof that an envelope containing a notice was properly addressed, prepaid and posted; or that an electronic form of notice was properly addressed and sent, shall be conclusive evidence that the notice was given. Notice shall be deemed to be given 48 hours after it was posted or sent.

(e) The proceedings of a meeting shall not be invalidated because a member who was entitled to receive notice of the meeting did not receive it because of accidental omission by the CIO.

(4) **Chairing of general meetings**

The person nominated as chair by the charity trustees under clause [19](2) (Chairing of meetings), shall, if present at the general meeting and willing to act, preside as chair of the meeting. Subject to that, the members of the CIO who are present at a general meeting shall elect a chair to preside at the meeting.

(5) **Quorum at general meetings**

(a) No business may be transacted at any general meeting of the members of the CIO unless a quorum is present when the meeting starts.

(b) Subject to the following provisions, the quorum for general meetings shall be the greater of [5]% or [three] members. An organisation represented by a person present at the meeting in accordance with sub-clause (7) of this clause, is counted as being present in person.[26]

(c) If the meeting has been called by or at the request of the members and a quorum is not present within 15 minutes of the starting time specified in the notice of the meeting, the meeting is closed.

(d) If the meeting has been called in any other way and a quorum is not present within 15 minutes of the starting time specified in the notice of the meeting, the chair must adjourn the meeting. The date, time and place at which the meeting will resume must

---

[26] The General Regulations require that the Constitution must specify a quorum. We suggest that the quorum should be 5% (or three) of the members. You may choose a different figure. If it is set too high, any absences may make it difficult to hold a valid meeting; if it is too low, a small minority may be able to impose their views unreasonably.

[either be announced by the chair or] be notified to the CIO's members at least seven clear days before the date on which it will resume.[27]

(e) If a quorum is not present within 15 minutes of the start time of the adjourned meeting, the member or members present at the meeting constitute a quorum.

(f) If at any time during the meeting a quorum ceases to be present, the meeting may discuss issues and make recommendations to the trustees but may not make any decisions. If decisions are required which must be made by a meeting of the members, the meeting must be adjourned.

(6) **Voting at general meetings**

(a) Any decision other than one falling within clause [10(4)] (Decisions that must be taken in a particular way) shall be taken by a simple majority of votes cast at the meeting [(including proxy and postal votes)]. Every member has one vote [unless otherwise provided in the rights of a particular class of membership under this constitution].

(b) A resolution put to the vote of a meeting shall be decided on a show of hands, unless (before or on the declaration of the result of the show of hands) a poll is duly demanded. A poll may be demanded by the chair or by at least 10% of the members present in person or by proxy at the meeting.

(c) A poll demanded on the election of a person to chair the meeting or on a question of adjournment must be taken immediately. A poll on any other matter shall be taken, and the result of the poll shall be announced, in such manner as the chair of the meeting shall decide, provided that the poll must be taken, and the result of the poll announced, within 30 days of the demand for the poll.

(d) A poll may be taken:
 (i) at the meeting at which it was demanded; or
 (ii) at some other time and place specified by the chair; or
 (iii) through the use of postal or electronic communications.[28]

---

[27] This model constitution does not require formal notice to be repeated for an adjourned meeting, but provision for this may be made in the constitution by deleting the wording in square brackets. (This may help to ensure that there is a better attendance at the adjourned meeting.)

[28] The General Regulations require that, if members are to have the right to demand a poll, this must be set out in the constitution, including provisions governing the manner in which it will be conducted. The provisions suggested here reflect good practice.

Proxy voting – The General Regulations stipulate that members can only vote by proxy if there is a specific provision in the constitution, which must set out: (a) how a member appoints a proxy; (b) the rights of the proxy; and (c) how the appointment is terminated. For recommended wording (which does not form part of the model), please see the Appendix to this constitution.

Postal voting – The General Regulations stipulate that members can only use postal votes if there is a specific provision in the constitution, which must make provision about the circumstances in which, and the way in which, such votes may be given. For recommended wording (which does not form part of the model), please see the Appendix to this constitution.

[(e) In the event of an equality of votes, whether on a show of hands or on a poll, the chair of the meeting shall have a second, or casting vote.]

(f) Any objection to the qualification of any voter must be raised at the meeting at which the vote is cast and the decision of the chair of the meeting shall be final.

(7) **Representation of [organisations and] corporate members**

A[n organisation or a]corporate body that is a member of the CIO may, in accordance with its usual decision-making process, authorise a person to act as its representative at any general meeting of the CIO.

The representative is entitled to exercise the same powers on behalf of the [organisation or] corporate body as the [organisation or] corporate body could exercise as an individual member of the CIO.[29]

(8) **Adjournment of meetings**

The chair may with the consent of a meeting at which a quorum is present (and shall if so directed by the meeting) adjourn the meeting to another time and/or place. No business may be transacted at an adjourned meeting except business which could properly have been transacted at the original meeting.

12. Charity trustees

(1) **Functions and duties of charity trustees**

The charity trustees shall manage the affairs of the CIO and may for that purpose exercise all the powers of the CIO. It is the duty of each charity trustee:

(a) to exercise his or her powers and to perform his or her functions as a trustee of the CIO in the way he or she decides in good faith would be most likely to further the purposes of the CIO; and

(b) to exercise, in the performance of those functions, such care and skill as is reasonable in the circumstances having regard in particular to:

(i) any special knowledge or experience that he or she has or holds himself or herself out as having; and

(ii) if he or she acts as a charity trustee of the CIO in the course of a business or profession, to any special knowledge or experience that it is reasonable to expect of a person acting in the course of that kind of business or profession.[30]

(2) **Eligibility for trusteeship**[31]

---

[29] If the CIO will have corporate members, the General Regulations require that the constitution must include provision explaining how they will be represented at general meetings.
  If the CIO will have unincorporated members (see clause 9 – Membership of the CIO) you should include references to organisations in this clause. Otherwise you should delete the words in square brackets.

[30] This clause explains the charity trustees' legal function, legal duty to act in good faith, and statutory duty of care. We recommend that these should be set out in the constitution. The trustees cannot adopt a lower duty of care.

[31] You should include provisions setting out who is eligible to be a charity trustee of the CIO. Sub-clause (a) requires all trustees to be individuals. It is legally permissible for a corporate

(a) Every charity trustee must be a natural person.
(b) No one may be appointed as a charity trustee:
- if he or she is under the age of 16 years; or
- if he or she would automatically cease to hold office under the provisions of clause [15(1)(f)].
(c) No one is entitled to act as a charity trustee whether on appointment or on any re-appointment until he or she has expressly acknowledged, in whatever way the charity trustees decide, his or her acceptance of the office of charity trustee.
[(d) At least one of the trustees of the CIO must be 18 years of age or over. If there is no trustee aged at least 18 years, the remaining trustee or trustees may act only to call a meeting of the charity trustees, or appoint a new charity trustee.][32]
(3) **Number of charity trustees**[33]
Option 1

---

body to be a charity trustee, but we would advise against a trustee body including both individuals and one or more corporate bodies. Where the CIO will have corporate members we recommend that they should not be elected as trustees; only individuals or nominees of these bodies should be eligible for election.

This clause and those that follow are drafted on the basis that the CIO will be governed by a trustee body made up of a number of individuals. If there is a good reason why the CIO will be administered by a single trustee (eg a corporation) or have any other trusteeship arrangement, you will need to amend clauses 12-16, and should seek your own professional advice.

The suggested provisions in (b) reflect the law and (c) is based on good practice. There are offences under the General Regulations concerning legally disqualified individuals acting as trustees.

If there are to be additional conditions for trustee eligibility (beyond the legal restrictions), these **must** be stated in the constitution. For example, some charities add requirements to ensure that trustees have particular knowledge or experience (eg of the locality in which the CIO operates or of issues relevant to the people that the CIO serves).

[32] This sub-clause contains an optional restriction on the proportion of charity trustees who are under 18. The Commission encourages charities to involve young people in their governance in whatever ways are appropriate in the circumstances, but advises against having a board made up entirely of people under 18. CIO trustees cannot be under 16.

[33] The General Regulations require that the constitution **must** state the minimum number of charity trustees, **if** more than one.

We recommend setting and including minimum and maximum numbers of charity trustees.

A CIO can have a fixed number of trustees or a range between a maximum and minimum (which will give the CIO more flexibility). Option 1a provides for a specified maximum number. Option 1b provides for no maximum limit. Option 2 provides for other trustee appointment arrangements in accordance with clause 13 (see below).

Choose Clause 12(3) Option 1 (and Option 1a *or* b) and Clause 13 Option 1 *or* choose Clause 12(3) Option 2 and Clause 13 Option 2 (selecting the relevant parts of each section). Delete the options that you have not chosen.

For good practice, a CIO should have at least three charity trustees. If the number of trustees falls below the minimum specified in the constitution, the provisions in clause 12(3) will enable the remaining charity trustees to appoint new trustees and prevent the CIO from becoming inoperable.

A CIO should have enough charity trustees to effectively carry out their duties, but not too many so that it becomes impractical to hold effective trustee meetings where everyone can participate in decision making. We suggest a maximum of 12 trustees, but you **may** choose a higher or lower number depending on the CIO's needs.

(a) There must be at least [three] charity trustees. If the number falls below this minimum, the remaining trustee or trustees may act only to call a meeting of the charity trustees, or appoint a new charity trustee.

Option 1a

(b) The maximum number of charity trustees is [12]. The charity trustees may not appoint any charity trustee if as a result the number of charity trustees would exceed the maximum.

Option 1b

(b) There is no maximum number of charity trustees that may be appointed to the CIO.

Option 2

(a) There should be: [Not less than ... nor more than] ... elected trustees; [... ex officio trustee[s]; and [Not less than ... nor more than] ... nominated trustees].

(b) There must be at least [three] charity trustees. If the number falls below this minimum, the remaining trustee or trustees may act only to call a meeting of the charity trustees, or appoint a new charity trustee.

(c) The maximum number of charity trustees that can be appointed is as provided in sub-clause (a) of this clause. No trustee appointment may be made in excess of these provisions.

(4) **First charity trustees**[34]

The first charity trustees of the CIO are –

....
....
....
....
....

13. Appointment of charity trustees[35]

Option 1[36]

[(1) At the first annual general meeting of the members of the CIO all the charity trustees shall retire from office;]

(2) At every [subsequent] annual general meeting of the members of the CIO, one-third of the charity trustees shall retire from office. If the number of charity trustees is not three or a multiple of three, then the number nearest to one-third shall retire from office, but if there is only one charity trustee, he or she shall retire;

---

[34] The General Regulations require that the constitution **must** include the names of the first charity trustees.

[35] The constitution must make provision about the appointment of one or more persons to be charity trustees. This clause contains two options. Choose the corresponding options in Clause 12 (3) and Clause 13.

[36] Option 1 provides for new trustees to be appointed by the membership ('elected) and retire by rotation. This is the simplest, and likely to be the usual, arrangement for most association CIOs.
The mechanism for election and retirement in this clause reflects good practice. You may wish to include provision for all trustees to retire at the first AGM [(1)] but this is not essential.

(3) The charity trustees to retire by rotation shall be those who have been longest in office since their last appointment or reappointment. If any trustees were last appointed or reappointed on the same day those to retire shall (unless they otherwise agree among themselves) be determined by lot;

(4) The vacancies so arising may be filled by the decision of the members at the annual general meeting; any vacancies not filled at the annual general meeting may be filled as provided in sub-clause (5) of this clause;

(5) The members or the charity trustees may at any time decide to appoint a new charity trustee, whether in place of a charity trustee who has retired or been removed in accordance with clause [15] (Retirement and removal of charity trustees), or as an additional charity trustee, provided that the limit specified in clause [12(3)] on the number of charity trustees would not as a result be exceeded;[37]

(6) A person so appointed by the members of the CIO shall retire in accordance with the provisions of sub-clauses (2) and (3) of this clause. A person so appointed by the charity trustees shall retire at the conclusion of the next annual general meeting after the date of his or her appointment, and shall not be counted for the purpose of determining which of the charity trustees is to retire by rotation at that meeting.

Option 2[38]

(1) **Elected charity trustees**

[(a) At the first annual general meeting of the members of the CIO all the elected charity trustees shall retire from office;]

(b) At every [subsequent] annual general meeting of the members of the CIO, one-third of the elected charity trustees shall retire from office. If the number of elected charity trustees is not three or a multiple of three, then the number nearest to one-third shall retire from office, but if there is only one charity trustee, he or she shall retire;

(c) The charity trustees to retire by rotation shall be those who have been longest in office since their last appointment or reappointment. If any trustees were last appointed or reappointed on the same day those to retire shall (unless they otherwise agree among themselves) be determined by lot;

---

[37] This sub-clause allows the existing charity trustees or the members to appoint additional trustees to temporarily fill vacancies or to bring additional skills and experience onto the trustee board. We recommend that you include this power.

[38] Option 2 provides for new trustees to be appointed in different ways including election by members, ex-officio (ie by virtue of holding a certain office, eg the local vicar) and nomination by another organisation. If you use option 2 you will need to amend it to meet the CIO's particular circumstances depending on the combination of different methods of appointment that will apply. These additional appointment methods are usually only appropriate for charities operating in particular local areas or with links to particular bodies, and where it is desired to involve members of local councils, local churches or other external organisations on the trustee body.

You may wish to include provision for all elected trustees to retire at the first AGM [(1)(a)] but this is not essential.

(d) The vacancies so arising may be filled by the decision of the members at the annual general meeting; any vacancies not filled at the annual general meeting may be filled as provided in sub-clause (e) of this clause;

(e) The members or the charity trustees may at any time decide to appoint a new charity trustee, whether in place of a charity trustee who has retired or been removed in accordance with clause [15] (Retirement and removal of charity trustees), or as an additional charity trustee, provided that the limit specified in clause [12(3)] on the number of charity trustees would not as a result be exceeded;[39]

(f) A person so appointed by the members of the CIO shall retire in accordance with the provisions of sub-clauses (b) and (c) of this clause. A person so appointed by the charity trustees shall retire at the conclusion of the annual general meeting next following the date of his appointment, and shall not be counted for the purpose of determining which of the charity trustees is to retire by rotation at that meeting.

[(2) **Ex officio charity trustee[s]**

The [insert role] for the time being ("the office holder") shall automatically, by virtue of holding that office ("ex officio"), be a charity trustee.

If unwilling to act as a charity trustee, the office holder may:

(a) before accepting appointment as a charity trustee, give notice in writing to the trustees of his or her unwillingness to act in that capacity; or

(b) after accepting appointment as a charity trustee, resign under the provisions contained in clause 15 (Retirement and removal of charity trustees).

The office of ex officio charity trustee will then remain vacant until the office holder ceases to hold office.]

[(3) **Nominated Charity Trustee[s]**

(a) [insert name of appointing body] ("the appointing body") may appoint [insert number] charity trustees.

(b) Any appointment must be made at a meeting held according to the ordinary practice of the appointing body.

(c) Each appointment must be for a term of [3] years.

(d) The appointment will be effective from the later of:
   (i) the date of the vacancy; or
   (ii) the date on which the CIO is informed of the appointment.

(e) The person appointed need not be a member of the appointing body.

---

[39] This sub-clause allows the existing charity trustees or the members to appoint additional trustees to temporarily fill vacancies or to bring additional skills and experience onto the trustee board. We recommend that you include this power.

(f) A trustee appointed by the appointing body has the same duty under Clause 12(1) as the other charity trustees to act in the way he or she decides in good faith would be most likely to further the purposes of the CIO.]

14. Information for new charity trustees[40]
The charity trustees will make available to each new charity trustee, on or before his or her first appointment:
    (a) a copy of this constitution and any amendments made to it; and
    (b) a copy of the CIO's latest trustees' annual report and statement of accounts.

15. Retirement and removal of charity trustees
(1) A charity trustee ceases to hold office if he or she:
    (a) retires by notifying the CIO in writing (but only if enough charity trustees will remain in office when the notice of resignation takes effect to form a quorum for meetings);
    (b) is absent without the permission of the charity trustees from all their meetings held within a period of six months and the trustees resolve that his or her office be vacated;
    (c) dies;
    (d) in the written opinion, given to the company, of a registered medical practitioner treating that person, has become physically or mentally incapable of acting as a director and may remain so for more than three months;
    (e) [is removed by the members of the CIO in accordance with sub-clause (2) of this clause;] or
    (f) is disqualified from acting as a charity trustee by virtue of section 178-180 of the Charities Act 2011 (or any statutory re-enactment or modification of that provision).[41]

[(2) A charity trustee shall be removed from office if a resolution to remove that trustee is proposed at a general meeting of the members called for that purpose and properly convened in accordance with clause [11], and the resolution is passed by a [two-thirds] majority of votes cast at the meeting.

(3) A resolution to remove a charity trustee in accordance with this clause shall not take effect unless the individual concerned has been given at least 14 clear days' notice in writing that the resolution is to be proposed, specifying the circumstances alleged to justify removal from office, and has been given a reasonable opportunity of making oral and/or written representations to the members of the CIO.][42]

---

[40] This clause represents good practice; we recommend that you include it. It is vital for new trustees to have easy access to the information and training that they need to become effective members of the trustee body.

[41] The General Regulations require that the constitution must contain provisions setting out how charity trustees may retire or otherwise cease to hold office. The provisions in the model follow recommended good practice.

[42] This is an optional power allowing the members to remove a charity trustee. The members may

16. **Reappointment of charity trustees**[43]
    Any person who retires as a charity trustee by rotation or by giving notice to the CIO is eligible for reappointment. [A charity trustee who has served for [three] consecutive terms may not be reappointed for a [fourth] consecutive term but may be reappointed after an interval of at least [three years].]

17. **Taking of decisions by charity trustees**[44]
    Any decision may be taken either:
    - at a meeting of the charity trustees; or
    - by resolution in writing or electronic form agreed by all of the charity trustees, which may comprise either a single document or several documents containing the text of the resolution in like form to each of which one or more charity trustees has signified their agreement.

18. **Delegation by charity trustees**[45]
    (1) The charity trustees may delegate any of their powers or functions to a committee or committees, and, if they do, they must determine the terms and conditions on which the delegation is made. The charity trustees may at any time alter those terms and conditions, or revoke the delegation.
    (2) This power is in addition to the power of delegation in the General Regulations and any other power of delegation available to the charity trustees, but is subject to the following requirements -

    (a) a committee may consist of two or more persons, but at least one member of each committee must be a charity trustee;

    (b) the acts and proceedings of any committee must be brought to the attention of the charity trustees as a whole as soon as is reasonably practicable; and

    (c) the charity trustees shall from time to time review the arrangements which they have made for the delegation of their powers.

19. **Meetings and proceedings of charity trustees**[46]

---

only remove trustees if a power to do so is included in the constitution. This power should be exercised only in the interests of the charity, and it is important that the process is fair and transparent (as provided in (3)).

[43] This clause will help to ensure clarity about reappointing trustees who have retired. We recommend that you include it. There is an optional provision to limit the number of consecutive terms that a trustee can serve for, which may help to encourage regular turnover and change on the trustee board. (It is good practice to aim for a balance between continuity and change.)

[44] The power to take decisions by resolution in writing or electronic form outside meetings is optional, but if the trustees intend to use it, it **must** be included in the constitution. Such a decision must be unanimous (ie all of the trustees must agree).

[45] This power is optional. We recommend you include it as a matter of good practice. The General Regulations give charity trustees of a CIO automatic power to delegate tasks to sub-committees, staff or agents; but without this additional constitutional power, the trustees will be unable to delegate any power to make decisions.
Sub-clauses (2)(a)-(c) reflect minimum good practice and are safeguards that **should** not be removed or diminished.

[46] The General Regulations require that the Constitution **must** include provisions for the calling and running of meetings including the minimum number of trustees who shall form a quorum,

(1) **Calling meetings**
   (a) Any charity trustee may call a meeting of the charity trustees.
   (b) Subject to that, the charity trustees shall decide how their meetings are to be called, and what notice is required.
(2) **Chairing of meetings**
   The charity trustees may appoint one of their number to chair their meetings and may at any time revoke such appointment. If no-one has been so appointed, or if the person appointed is unwilling to preside or is not present within 10 minutes after the time of the meeting, the charity trustees present may appoint one of their number to chair that meeting.
(3) **Procedure at meetings**
   (a) No decision shall be taken at a meeting unless a quorum is present at the time when the decision is taken. The quorum is [two] charity trustees, or the number nearest to [one third] of the total number of charity trustees, whichever is greater, or such larger number as the charity trustees may decide from time to time. A charity trustee shall not be counted in the quorum present when any decision is made about a matter upon which he or she is not entitled to vote.[47]
   (b) Questions arising at a meeting shall be decided by a majority of those eligible to vote.
   [(c) In the case of an equality of votes, the chair shall have a second or casting vote.][48]
(4) **Participation in meetings by electronic means**[49]
   (a) A meeting may be held by suitable electronic means agreed by the charity trustees in which each participant may communicate with all the other participants.
   (b) Any charity trustee participating at a meeting by suitable electronic means agreed by the charity trustees in which a participant or participants may communicate with all the other participants shall qualify as being present at the meeting.
   (c) Meetings held by electronic means must comply with rules for meetings, including chairing and the taking of minutes.

20. **Saving provisions**[50]

---

appointment of a chair and, if trustees will be able to demand a poll (a counted vote, normally with voting papers), the procedure for conducting such a poll. The provisions in this model are good practice recommendations.
(We have not included provision for trustees to have a poll as feedback from our consultations suggested that most charities did not feel it was appropriate. If this power is required, please see clause 11(6)(b-e) for a suitable wording.)

[47] We recommend that the quorum for trustee meetings should not be less than one third of the number of trustees.
[48] It is common, but not obligatory, for the Chair to have a casting vote. You may include or delete this power.
[49] This clause is optional, but will be required if one or more of the CIO's trustees may from time to time participate in meetings by telephone or similar means.
[50] We recommend that you include this clause to reduce the risk of trustees' decisions being declared invalid for purely technical reasons. This is, however, also covered in the General Regulations.

(1) Subject to sub-clause (2) of this clause, all decisions of the charity trustees, or of a committee of charity trustees, shall be valid notwithstanding the participation in any vote of a charity trustee:
- who was disqualified from holding office;
- who had previously retired or who had been obliged by the constitution to vacate office;
- who was not entitled to vote on the matter, whether by reason of a conflict of interest or otherwise;

if, without the vote of that charity trustee and that charity trustee being counted in the quorum, the decision has been made by a majority of the charity trustees at a quorate meeting.

(2) Sub-clause (1) of this clause does not permit a charity trustee to keep any benefit that may be conferred upon him or her by a resolution of the charity trustees or of a committee of charity trustees if, but for clause (1), the resolution would have been void, or if the charity trustee has not complied with clause 7 (Conflicts of interest).

21. Execution of documents[51]
(1) The CIO shall execute documents either by signature or by affixing its seal (if it has one).
(2) A document is validly executed by signature if it is signed by at least two of the charity trustees.
(3) If the CIO has a seal:
 (a) it must comply with the provisions of the General Regulations; and
 (b) it must only be used by the authority of the charity trustees or of a committee of charity trustees duly authorised by the charity trustees. The charity trustees may determine who shall sign any document to which the seal is affixed and unless otherwise determined it shall be signed by two charity trustees.

22. Use of electronic communications[52]
[(1) **General**]
The CIO will comply with the requirements of the Communications Provisions in the General Regulations and in particular:
 (a) the requirement to provide within 21 days to any member on request a hard copy of any document or information sent to the member otherwise than in hard copy form;

---

[51] We recommend that you include this clause, for clarity about how documents may be validly executed on behalf of the CIO. It includes provision for use of a seal, which the General Regulations stipulate **must** be included if the CIO is to have a seal (but there is no requirement to have one). The General Regulations require the full name of the CIO to be clearly written on the seal, and failure to comply with this is an offence.

[52] The General Regulations include provisions governing the use of electronic communication, and we recommend that CIO trustees familiarise themselves with the requirements. Failure to comply with the requirement to provide a hard copy would constitute an offence.
The General Regulations state that if the CIO intends to automatically use electronic communication or a website to send formal communications to members, this **must** be stated in the constitution, which must also set out the circumstances in which this will happen. For suggested wording, please see the appendix to this constitution.

(b) any requirements to provide information to the Commission in a particular form or manner.

23. **Keeping of Registers**[53]

    The CIO must comply with its obligations under the General Regulations in relation to the keeping of, and provision of access to, registers of its members and charity trustees.

24. **Minutes**[54]

    The charity trustees must keep minutes of all:
    (1) appointments of officers made by the charity trustees;
    (2) proceedings at general meetings of the CIO;
    (3) meetings of the charity trustees and committees of charity trustees including:
    - the names of the trustees present at the meeting;
    - the decisions made at the meetings; and
    - where appropriate the reasons for the decisions;
    (4) decisions made by the charity trustees otherwise than in meetings.

25. **Accounting records, accounts, annual reports and returns, register maintenance**[55]

    (1) The charity trustees must comply with the requirements of the Charities Act 2011 with regard to the keeping of accounting records, to the preparation and scrutiny of statements of accounts, and to the preparation of annual reports and returns. The statements of accounts, reports and returns must be sent to the Charity Commission, regardless of the income of the CIO, within 10 months of the financial year end.

    (2) The charity trustees must comply with their obligation to inform the Commission within 28 days of any change in the particulars of the CIO entered on the Central Register of Charities.

26. **Rules**[56]

    The charity trustees may from time to time make such reasonable and proper rules or bye-laws as they may deem necessary or expedient for the proper conduct and management of the CIO, but such rules or bye-laws must not be inconsistent with any provision of this constitution. Copies of any such rules or bye-laws currently in force must be made available to any member of the CIO on request.

27. **Disputes**[57]

---

[53] This clause reflects the requirements in the General Regulations that the CIO keeps registers of members and charity trustees and makes this information available for inspection by interested persons. This does not have to be stated in the constitution but is included to serve as a reminder.

[54] This clause reflects the requirements of the General Regulations regarding record keeping. We recommend that this clause is included, to remind the trustees of their responsibilities.

[55] This clause reflects the trustees' duties under the Charities Act 2011. We recommend that this clause is included, to remind the trustees of their responsibilities.

[56] We recommend that this power **should** be included for clarity, but charities automatically have this power and an express power is not needed. It is important that members are made aware of, and can easily obtain, copies of any rules.

[57] It is good practice to include provisions for dealing with any disputes that arise between

If a dispute arises between members of the CIO about the validity or propriety of anything done by the members under this constitution, and the dispute cannot be resolved by agreement, the parties to the dispute must first try in good faith to settle the dispute by mediation before resorting to litigation.

28. **Amendment of constitution**[58]
    As provided by clauses 224–227 of the Charities Act 2011:
    (1) This constitution can only be amended:
        (a) by resolution agreed in writing by all members of the CIO; or
        (b) by a resolution passed by a 75% majority of votes cast at a general meeting of the members of the CIO.
    (2) Any alteration of clause 3 (Objects), clause [29] (Voluntary winding up or dissolution), this clause, or of any provision where the alteration would provide authorisation for any benefit to be obtained by charity trustees or members of the CIO or persons connected with them, requires the prior written consent of the Charity Commission.
    (3) No amendment that is inconsistent with the provisions of the Charities Act 2011 or the General Regulations shall be valid.
    (4) A copy of any resolution altering the constitution, together with a copy of the CIO's constitution as amended, must be sent to the Commission within 15 days from the date on which the resolution is passed. The amendment does not take effect until it has been recorded in the Register of Charities.

29. **Voluntary winding up or dissolution**[59]
    (1) As provided by the Dissolution Regulations, the CIO may be dissolved by resolution of its members. Any decision by the members to wind up or dissolve the CIO can only be made:
        (a) at a general meeting of the members of the CIO called in accordance with clause [11] (Meetings of Members), of which not less than 14 days' notice has been given to those eligible to attend and vote:

---

members of the CIO. Litigation can be expensive, and litigation about the internal affairs of a charity would almost certainly constitute "charity proceedings", which can be taken only with the Commission's authority. We would usually require the parties to a dispute to have tried mediation first.

[58] This reflects the CIOs' statutory power of amendment in sections 224–227 of the Charities Act 2011. A CIO's constitution **should** include these provisions for ease of reference. The constitution of a CIO cannot override the statutory power of constitutional amendment, but the General Regulations provide that you **may** include additional restrictions in some or all cases, for example requiring a longer period of notice before the meeting, or a higher majority, for certain changes. Additional restrictions are not provided for in this model and if you are considering this, we recommend that you take appropriate advice. To request the Commission's consent to an amendment or to inform the Commission of an amendment, please complete our online form which is available at http://forms.charitycommission.gov.uk/contact-us/get-our-permission/change-your-governing-document/amend-governing-document/.

[59] This clause reflects the provisions of the Charities Act 2011, the General Regulations and Dissolution Regulations. We recommend that it is included in the constitution for ease of reference. It also highlights that there are other requirements in the Dissolution Regulations that the trustees must comply with, as there are offences for non-compliance. To inform the Commission of your CIO's dissolution, please complete our online form.

                (i) by a resolution passed by a 75% majority of those voting, or
                (ii) by a resolution passed by decision taken without a vote and without any expression of dissent in response to the question put to the general meeting; or
            (b) by a resolution agreed in writing by all members of the CIO.
    (2) Subject to the payment of all the CIO's debts:
        (a) Any resolution for the winding up of the CIO, or for the dissolution of the CIO without winding up, may contain a provision directing how any remaining assets of the CIO shall be applied.
        (b) If the resolution does not contain such a provision, the charity trustees must decide how any remaining assets of the CIO shall be applied.
        (c) In either case the remaining assets must be applied for charitable purposes the same as or similar to those of the CIO.[60]
    (3) The CIO must observe the requirements of the Dissolution Regulations in applying to the Commission for the CIO to be removed from the Register of Charities, and in particular:
        (a) the charity trustees must send with their application to the Commission:
            (i) a copy of the resolution passed by the members of the CIO;
            (ii) a declaration by the charity trustees that any debts and other liabilities of the CIO have been settled or otherwise provided for in full; and
            (iii) a statement by the charity trustees setting out the way in which any property of the CIO has been or is to be applied prior to its dissolution in accordance with this constitution;
        (b) the charity trustees must ensure that a copy of the application is sent within seven days to every member and employee of the CIO, and to any charity trustee of the CIO who was not privy to the application.
    (4) If the CIO is to be wound up or dissolved in any other circumstances, the provisions of the Dissolution Regulations must be followed.[61]
30. Interpretation[62]
    In this constitution:

"connected person" means:
(a) child, parent, grandchild, grandparent, brother or sister of the charity trustee;

---

[60] The constitution **must** contain directions about how its property will be applied if it is wound up. Any assets remaining after the payment of debts **must** be applied for charitable purposes that are similar to those of the CIO.

[61] It is essential for trustees to be aware that if the CIO is unable to meet its financial obligations in full when it is wound up, the provisions in sub-clauses (1)–(3) do not apply, and the relevant provisions of the Dissolution Regulations must be followed. Failure to do so is not only an offence, but it could lead to personal liability for the trustees.

[62] This clause explains some terms used in the rest of the constitution.

(b) the spouse or civil partner of the charity trustee or of any person falling within sub-clause (a) above;
(c) a person carrying on business in partnership with the charity trustee or with any person falling within sub-clause (a) or (b) above;
(d) an institution which is controlled –
  (i) by the charity trustee or any connected person falling within sub-clause (a), (b), or (c) above; or
  (ii) by two or more persons falling within sub-clause (d)(i), when taken together.
(e) a body corporate in which –
  (i) the charity trustee or any connected person falling within sub-clauses (a) to (c) has a substantial interest; or
  (ii) two or more persons falling within sub-clause (e)(i) who, when taken together, have a substantial interest.

Section 118 of the Charities Act 2011 apply for the purposes of interpreting the terms used in this constitution.

"General Regulations" means the Charitable Incorporated Organisations (General) Regulations 2012.

"Dissolution Regulations" means the Charitable Incorporated Organisations (Insolvency and Dissolution) Regulations 2012.

The "Communications Provisions" means the Communications Provisions in [Part 10, Chapter 4] of the General Regulations.

"charity trustee" means a charity trustee of the CIO.

A "poll" means a counted vote or ballot, usually (but not necessarily) in writing.

APPENDIX

The following provisions do not form part of the 'Association' model constitution but are available as options under clauses 11 (General meetings of members) and 22 (Use of electronic communications). For CIOs intending to include these powers in their constitutions, we recommend that you use the following wording. Notes on these clauses are included with the explanatory notes accompanying the clauses in the model.

11. **General meetings of members**
    (7) **Proxy voting**
        (a) Any member of the CIO may appoint another person as a proxy to exercise all or any of that member's rights to attend, speak and vote at a general meeting of the CIO. Proxies must be appointed by a notice in writing (a "proxy notice") which:
            (i) states the name and address of the member appointing the proxy;
            (ii) identifies the person appointed to be that member's proxy and the general meeting in relation to which that person is appointed;

        (iii) is signed by or on behalf of the member appointing the proxy, or is authenticated in such manner as the CIO may determine; and
        (iv) is delivered to the CIO in accordance with the constitution and any instructions contained in the notice of the general meeting to which they relate.
  (b) The CIO may require proxy notices to be delivered in a particular form, and may specify different forms for different purposes.
  (c) Proxy notices may (but do not have to) specify how the proxy appointed under them is to vote (or that the proxy is to abstain from voting) on one or more resolutions.
  (d) Unless a proxy notice indicates otherwise, it must be treated as:
        (i) allowing the person appointed under it as a proxy discretion as to how to vote on any ancillary or procedural resolutions put to the meeting; and
        (ii) appointing that person as a proxy in relation to any adjournment of the general meeting to which it relates as well as the meeting itself.
  (e) A member who is entitled to attend, speak or vote (either on a show of hands or on a poll) at a general meeting remains so entitled in respect of that meeting or any adjournment of it, even though a valid proxy notice has been delivered to the CIO by or on behalf of that member.
  (f) An appointment under a proxy notice may be revoked by delivering to the CIO a notice in writing given by or on behalf of the member by whom or on whose behalf the proxy notice was given.
  (g) A notice revoking a proxy appointment only takes effect if it is delivered before the start of the meeting or adjourned meeting to which it relates.
  (h) If a proxy notice is not signed or authenticated by the member appointing the proxy, it must be accompanied by written evidence that the person who signed or authenticated it on that member's behalf had authority to do so.

(8) **Postal Voting**
  (a) The CIO may, if the charity trustees so decide, allow the members to vote by post or electronic mail ("email") to elect charity trustees or to make a decision on any matter that is being decided at a general meeting of the members.
  (b) The charity trustees must appoint at least two persons independent of the CIO to serve as scrutineers to supervise the conduct of the postal/email ballot and the counting of votes.
  (c) If postal and/or email voting is to be allowed on a matter, the CIO must send to members of the CIO not less than [21] days before the deadline for receipt of votes cast in this way:
        (i) a notice by email, if the member has agreed to receive notices in this way under clause [22] (Use of electronic

communications), including an explanation of the purpose of the vote and the voting procedure to be followed by the member, and a voting form capable of being returned by email or post to the CIO, containing details of the resolution being put to a vote, or of the candidates for election, as applicable;

(ii) a notice by post to all other members, including a written explanation of the purpose of the postal vote and the voting procedure to be followed by the member; and a postal voting form containing details of the resolution being put to a vote, or of the candidates for election, as applicable.

(d) The voting procedure must require all forms returned by post to be in an envelope with the member's name and signature, and nothing else, on the outside, inside another envelope addressed to 'The Scrutineers for [name of CIO]', at the CIO's principal office or such other postal address as is specified in the voting procedure.

(e) The voting procedure for votes cast by email must require the member's name to be at the top of the email, and the email must be authenticated in the manner specified in the voting procedure.

(f) Email votes must be returned to an email address used only for this purpose and must be accessed only by a scrutineer.

(g) The voting procedure must specify the closing date and time for receipt of votes, and must state that any votes received after the closing date or not complying with the voting procedure will be invalid and not be counted.

(h) The scrutineers must make a list of names of members casting valid votes, and a separate list of members casting votes which were invalid. These lists must be provided to a charity trustee or other person overseeing admission to, and voting at, the general meeting. A member who has cast a valid postal or email vote must not vote at the meeting, and must not be counted in the quorum for any part of the meeting on which he, she or it has already cast a valid vote. A member who has cast an invalid vote by post or email is allowed to vote at the meeting and counts towards the quorum.

(i) For postal votes, the scrutineers must retain the internal envelopes (with the member's name and signature). For email votes, the scrutineers must cut off and retain any part of the email that includes the member's name. In each case, a scrutineer must record on this evidence of the member's name that the vote has been counted, or if the vote has been declared invalid, the reason for such declaration.

(j) Votes cast by post or email must be counted by all the scrutineers before the meeting at which the vote is to be taken. The scrutineers must provide to the person chairing the meeting written confirmation of the number of valid votes received by post and email and the number of votes received which were invalid.

(k) The scrutineers must not disclose the result of the postal/email ballot until after votes taken by hand or by poll at the meeting, or by poll after the meeting, have been counted. Only at this point shall the scrutineers declare the result of the valid votes received, and these votes shall be included in the declaration of the result of the vote.

(l) Following the final declaration of the result of the vote, the scrutineers must provide to a charity trustee or other authorised person bundles containing the evidence of members submitting valid postal votes; evidence of members submitting valid email votes; evidence of invalid votes; the valid votes; and the invalid votes.

(m) Any dispute about the conduct of a postal or email ballot must be referred initially to a panel set up by the charity trustees, to consist of two trustees and two persons independent of the CIO. If the dispute cannot be satisfactorily resolved by the panel, it must be referred to the Electoral Reform Services.

20. **Use of electronic communications**

(2) **To the CIO**

Any member or charity trustee of the CIO may communicate electronically with the CIO to an address specified by the CIO for the purpose, so long as the communication is authenticated in a manner which is satisfactory to the CIO.

(3) **By the CIO**

(a) Any member or charity trustee of the CIO, by providing the CIO with his or her email address or similar, is taken to have agreed to receive communications from the CIO in electronic form at that address, unless the member has indicated to the CIO his or her unwillingness to receive such communications in that form.

(b) The charity trustees may, subject to compliance with any legal requirements, by means of publication on its website –
 (i) provide the members with the notice referred to in clause 11(3) (Notice of general meetings);
 (ii) give charity trustees notice of their meetings in accordance with clause 19(1) (Calling meetings); [and
 (iii) submit any proposal to the members or charity trustees for decision by written resolution or postal vote in accordance with the CIO's powers under clause 10 (Members' decisions), 10(3) (Decisions taken by resolution in writing), or [[the provisions for postal voting] (if you have included this optional provision, please insert the correct clause number here)].

(c) The charity trustees must:

(i) take reasonable steps to ensure that members and charity trustees are promptly notified of the publication of any such notice or proposal;

(ii) send any such notice or proposal in hard copy form to any member or charity trustee who has not consented to receive communications in electronic form.

APPENDIX F

CHARITABLE INCORPORATED ORGANISATION: MODEL CONSTITUTION FOR A CIO WHOSE ONLY VOTING MEMBERS ARE ITS CHARITY TRUSTEES

Reproduced with the kind permission of the Charity Commission https://www.gov.uk/government/publications/setting-up-a-charity-model-governing-documents

('Foundation' model constitution)

This document is a Charity Commission model constitution for a Charitable Incorporated Organisation (CIO). If you want to set up a CIO, you will find it easiest to use one of our model constitutions.

This guidance briefly explains:
- What a CIO is
- How to decide whether the CIO is the right form for your charity
- How to choose the right model constitution
- How to complete the model constitution and register as a charity
- Where to get more information and advice

There are notes explaining key points about each clause in the model constitution, to help you decide how to complete it.

We also have more detailed guidance on CIOs available on our website.

What is a Charitable Incorporated Organisation?

The Charitable Incorporated Organisation (CIO) is a new legal form for a charity. It has been created in response to requests from the charitable sector. It is a new incorporated form of charity which is not a limited company or subject to company regulation.

The Charities Act 2011 creates the basic legal framework for the CIO. This framework is completed by regulations:

- the Charitable Incorporated Organisations (General) Regulations 2012 ('General Regulations'); and
- the Charitable Incorporated Organisations (Insolvency and Dissolution) Regulations 2012 ('Dissolution Regulations').

Is the CIO the right structure for our charity?

Choosing the right legal structure and governing document is one of the first and most important decisions that the founders of a charity need to make. It will affect:

- how easy it will be to set up and run the charity
- how easy it will be to make changes in the future
- whether the charity can have a voting membership
- whether the charity can itself own premises, employ staff or enter contracts, or whether the trustees will have to do this personally.

With the introduction of the CIO, there are four main legal forms that charities may take. We produce model governing documents for each of these forms:

- Trust (governing document: trust deed; could also be created by a will)
- Unincorporated association (governing document: constitution or rules)
- Company limited by guarantee (governing document: memorandum and articles of association for company formed before September 2009; articles of association for company formed since then)
- CIO (governing document: constitution)

An incorporated form, CIO or company limited by guarantee, may be more suitable for a charity that will:

- own land in its own name
- control substantial funds or assets
- enter into contracts, for example by employing staff, or
- engage in charitable activities involving financial risks

Some points to note about CIOs:

- A CIO is a corporate body (like a company) that can own property, employ staff and enter into other contracts in its own name (rather than in the names of the trustees).
- Members of a company limited by guarantee have limited liability for its debts if it winds up (they only have to pay a fixed amount). Members of a CIO may either have no liability at all or (like a company) limited liability for its debts.
- Because they have additional legal protection, members of a corporate body (company or CIO) must comply with extra regulations.
- Unlike companies, CIOs do not have to register with Companies House.

- Unlike companies, CIOs will not be fined for administrative errors like late filing of accounts, but some breaches of the CIO Regulations are legal offences.
- All CIOs must register with the Commission, regardless of their income. This means that an exempt charity cannot be a CIO, and CIO may be unsuitable for other types of charity that don't have to register. (See our guidance on types of charity that don't have to register.)
- CIOs must produce accounts under charity law, not company law. This allows smaller CIOs (income below £250,000) to produce simpler receipts and payments accounts.
- To simplify the CIO framework, there is currently no provision for CIOs to issue debentures, or for a register of charges (mortgages etc) over CIO property.

For more information on other legal forms, see our guidance on choosing your charity's governing document. Another useful source of advice is the Get Legal website and online decision tool (www.getlegal.org.uk).

Why are there two different model constitutions for a CIO?

Like companies (which must have both members and company directors) all CIOs must have members and charity trustees. Some CIOs may want the only members to be the charity trustees; others may want a wider membership open to other people. We have produced two model constitutions for CIOs:
- the **'foundation'** model is for charities whose **only** voting members will be the charity trustees
- the **'association'** model (this model) is for charities that will have a wider membership, including voting members other than the charity trustees

In practice a CIO using the 'foundation' model will be like an incorporated charitable trust, run by a small group of people (the charity trustees) who make all key decisions. Charity trustees may be appointed for an unlimited time and they will probably appoint new charity trustees.

A CIO using the 'association' model will have a wider voting membership who must make certain decisions (such as amending the constitution), will usually appoint some or all of the charity trustees (who will serve for fixed terms), and may be involved in the work of the CIO.

There are not two different forms of CIO. A CIO with the 'foundation' model could change to the 'association' model if it wanted a wider voting membership. (This could also happen the other way around, but members who were not trustees would be giving up their membership.) Some of the changes would need our approval.

Why use one of the Commission's model CIO constitutions?

A CIO's constitution **must** be in the form to be specified by Commission regulations (or as near to that form as the circumstances allow). These regulations will specify that the constitution should be in the form of one of our model constitutions. This still allows some flexibility, as explained in the guidance notes on the model. The constitution **must** be in English if the CIO's principal office is in England, but may be in English or Welsh if the principal office is in Wales.

A CIO's constitution **must** include certain provisions to comply with the Charities Act 2011 (the 2011 Act) and the General Regulations. However the 2011 Act and General Regulations do not prescribe an exact wording.

There are other provisions that **must** be included **if** they apply to a particular CIO. If they do not fully apply, the constitution **must** explain to what extent or how they apply.

We have included other provisions in this model constitution because:
- they reflect good practice that we recommend
- they remind the trustees about a legal requirement
- the constitution would not work properly without them, or
- charities have said that it would be a useful option and it would be helpful to have standard wording

Using one of the Commission's models will help to ensure that you include all of the constitutional provisions that your CIO will need:
- to meet the requirements of the law
- to comply with good practice, and
- to be practical and workable

The guidance notes will prompt you to think about whether you may need to include particular powers.

The 2011 Act and the General Regulations don't require you to use a particular wording, but the wording in our models has been carefully considered and also informed by specialists in the charity sector. Using one of our models will also mean that there will be fewer questions for us to ask and consider when you apply for charity registration.

How do we become a CIO?

(i) *New charities*
   To set up and register a new CIO, follow the procedure set out below under Next steps.

(ii) *Existing charitable trusts and unincorporated associations*
   An existing unincorporated charity can only change to a CIO by:
   - setting up and registering a new CIO (in the same way as for a new charity), then

Model Constitution for CIO – Only Voting Members are its Charity Trustees 191

- transferring its property and operations to the CIO.

You should check whether your charity can transfer its property in this way, or whether you need authorisation from the Commission. Once the transfer is complete, the original charity can normally be wound up and removed from the register, but different arrangements may apply to charities with permanent endowment (see below).

(iii) *Existing charities with permanent endowment*

Some charitable trusts have property (land or investments) that cannot be expended as income. Property restricted in this way is called permanent endowment. This may include land that must be used in a particular way for the purposes of the charity.

- Often, these charities have no power to wind up or transfer their permanent endowment.
- CIOs cannot hold permanent endowment as part of their own (corporate) property.

The General Regulations make special provision to enable charities with permanent endowment to transfer to a CIO. The trustees of the permanently endowed charity need to:

- set up and register a new CIO with the Commission, then
- make a vesting declaration under section 310 of the 2011 Act (as amended by the General Regulations), transferring all property of the original charity to the new CIO.

The vesting declaration will:

- transfer expendable property to the CIO as part of its corporate property
- vest legal title to the permanent endowment in the CIO, to be held on its original trusts
- appoint the CIO as trustee for the permanent endowment trust and give it the powers of a trust corporation for that trust
- mean that the CIO and the permanent endowment trust are treated as a single charity for registration and accounting purposes (they won't need to register separately or produce separate accounts).

If charities use a vesting declaration to carry out a merger, they must record it in the Register of Mergers. Vesting declarations are legal documents, so you may need advice from a solicitor or other professional. There are circumstances in which permanent endowment can be spent; it is not absolutely protected.

For further information see our general guidance on CIOs.

(iv) *Existing charitable companies and industrial and provident societies*

Once all of the provisions are in force, it will also be possible for an existing charitable company or charitable industrial and provident society to convert directly into a CIO; there are specific procedures for this.

To manage demand, the Commission is phasing in the introduction of the CIO and not all of these options will be available immediately. Please see our general guidance on CIOs for details.

What guidance should we consider before we begin?

- There is comprehensive guidance on setting up and registering a charity on our website.
- We also have more detailed **guidance on CIOs**.
- *The Essential Trustee* sets out the basics that all charity trustees need to know.

Next steps

1. Completing the constitution
   Please note – we are publishing the model constitutions in this format (PDF) to help charities and their professional advisers to prepare for the implementation of the CIO. We are currently looking into more flexible and user-friendly formats that will make it easier for promoters to complete the constitution.

   Once you have decided to apply to register a CIO and have chosen the correct model constitution, please read the constitution and accompanying guidance notes carefully. In the guidance notes we say that something '**must**' be included in the constitution if it is a legal requirement in the 2011 Act or the General or Dissolution Regulations. We say that something '**should**' be included if we consider it to be minimum good practice. We 'recommend' that you include other provisions to help ensure the smooth running of the CIO in future.

   There are guidance notes on each clause explaining what it is for, and whether you **must** or **should** include (all or part of) it, and whether it **may** or **should** be amended to fit the circumstances. Even where clauses are completely optional, however, we advise you to follow the model provisions or suggested alternatives unless there is a particular need, in the interests of your charity, to do otherwise.

   Some clauses contain options for you to choose from and blank spaces that you will need to fill in.

   If you want to add any special or complex provisions that you have drafted yourself, you may need advice from a solicitor or other adviser. We may need more time to look at any specialist changes. Please make clear what changes you make, and why they are necessary. This will help us to consider your application as quickly as possible. We cannot guarantee to accept every organisation which uses one of our models as charitable. We must consider each case separately.

   When you have finished, please check that you have:
   - filled in all the blanks,
   - deleted any clauses which you don't need; and
   - numbered the remaining clauses (and sub-clauses) in sequence (including cross-references).

2. Applying to register
   To register a new charity, apply online. If you cannot apply online, please contact Charity Commission Direct. The best way to contact us is by email. If you need to speak to someone over the phone you can call our contact centre on 0845 300 0218.

3. How long will it take?

We can normally make a decision in 40 working days if an organisation:
- can use our model wording for its objects (Example charitable objects on our website);
- shows that its activities are or will be consistent with the objects;
- shows that any private benefit is only incidental and is properly managed; and
- uses our model governing document.

Other applications will need closer consideration and so will take longer.

Constitution of a Charitable Incorporated Organisation whose only voting members are its charity trustees

('Foundation' model constitution)

Date of constitution (last amended):[1]

....

1. Name[2]
   The name of the Charitable Incorporated Organisation ("the CIO") is.
   ....

2. National location of principal office[3]
   The CIO must have a principal office in England or Wales. The principal office of the CIO is in [England][Wales].

3. Object[s][4]
   The object[s] of the CIO [is][are]
   ....

   Nothing in this constitution shall authorise an application of the property of the CIO for the purposes which are not charitable in accordance with [section 7 of the Charities and Trustee Investment (Scotland) Act 2005] and [section 2 of the Charities Act (Northern Ireland) 2008].

---

[1] Inserting the date of the constitution is good practice, and helps to ensure everyone is working from the same document. The date to enter here is the date the constitution, or any amendment to it, has been registered by the Commission, as this is when it comes into effect. Leave this undated until the constitution has been registered. You should send a dated version when the date of registration has been confirmed.

[2] You **must** include the name of the CIO in the constitution. In general, the Commission can accept any charity name unless it would be misleading, offensive or too similar to the name of an existing charity (unless the CIO is replacing that charity). The Commission has powers to require a charity to change its name if this happens. Further information on this is provided in our publication *Registering as a charity* (CC21) and in our Operational Guidance (OG330 – *Names of charities*), which are available on our website. There are also legal restrictions on using the same name as an existing company (unless it is a charitable company that is converting to a CIO) or as a former company or CIO that underwent insolvent liquidation – if in doubt seek professional advice.

[3] The constitution **must** state whether the CIO's principal office is in England or Wales.

[4] The CIO **must** have exclusively charitable objects which you **must** set out in the constitution. Guidance on appropriate wording for objects is available on our website. The key elements to include are:
- the purpose or purposes for which the CIO is being established;
- the people who can benefit; and if appropriate
- any geographic limits defining the area of benefit. If you include an area of benefit, it is common to define it by reference to a local government area: this has the advantage of clarity and simplicity, but can create problems if the area is subsequently altered or abolished. If this happens in future, contact the Commission for advice on amending the objects.

NB. If you cannot fit your objects in the space provided, please include them on a separate piece of paper and submit this with the constitution.

If the CIO needs to be recognised as a charity in Scotland and/or Northern Ireland you will need to include the relevant parts of the wording in square brackets to meet the requirements of charity law in those countries.

4. Powers[5]

The CIO has power to do anything which is calculated to further its object[s] or is conducive or incidental to doing so. In particular, the CIO's powers include power to:

(1) borrow money and to charge the whole or any part of its property as security for the repayment of the money borrowed. The CIO must comply as appropriate with sections 124 and 125 of the Charities Act 2011 if it wishes to mortgage land;

(2) buy, take on lease or in exchange, hire or otherwise acquire any property and to maintain and equip it for use;

(3) sell, lease or otherwise dispose of all or any part of the property belonging to the CIO. In exercising this power, the CIO must comply as appropriate with sections 117 and 119-123 of the Charities Act 2011;

(4) employ and remunerate such staff as are necessary for carrying out the work of the CIO. The CIO may employ or remunerate a charity trustee only to the extent that it is permitted to do so by clause 6 (Benefits and payments to charity trustees and connected persons) and provided it complies with the conditions of that clause;

(5) deposit or invest funds, employ a professional fund-manager, and arrange for the investments or other property of the CIO to be held in the name of a nominee, in the same manner and subject to the same conditions as the trustees of a trust are permitted to do by the Trustee Act 2000;

5. **Application of income and property**[6]

(1) The income and property of the CIO must be applied solely towards the promotion of the objects.

   (a) A charity trustee is entitled to be reimbursed from the property of the CIO or may pay out of such property reasonable expenses properly incurred by him or her when acting on behalf of the CIO.

   (b) A charity trustee may benefit from trustee indemnity insurance cover purchased at the CIO's expense in accordance with, and subject to the conditions in, section 189 of the Charities Act 2011.[7]

---

[5] The Charities Act 2011 gives a CIO power to do 'anything which is calculated to further its purposes or is conducive or incidental to doing so'. Strictly speaking, this is the only power a CIO needs. It can, however, be helpful to state certain powers explicitly in the constitution. In particular, a stated power to borrow [(1)] may reassure potential lenders. For this reason we recommend that you include the example powers set out in the model (these include powers to buy, sell and lease property, employ staff and delegate investment management to a professional fund-manager). You **may** add other express powers here if you wish to.

You **may** include a constitutional provision restricting the general power in the 2011 Act. You **must only** include such a restriction if it is in the CIO's interests. You **must not** restrict the CIO's powers in a way that prevents it from disposing of its property. Restrictions on the powers are not provided for in this model and we recommend that you seek appropriate advice if you are considering this.

[6] We recommend that you include this clause.

[7] This sub-clause reflects the statutory provisions in the Charities Act 2011 about a CIO charity

(2) None of the income or property of the CIO may be paid or transferred directly or indirectly by way of dividend, bonus or otherwise by way of profit to any member of the CIO.[8]

(3) Nothing in this clause shall prevent a charity trustee or connected person receiving any benefit or payment which is authorised by Clause 6.

6. Benefits and payments to charity trustees and connected persons[9]
   (1) General provisions
       No charity trustee or connected person may:
       (a) buy or receive any goods or services from the CIO on terms preferential to those applicable to members of the public;
       (b) sell goods, services, or any interest in land to the CIO;
       (c) be employed by, or receive any remuneration from, the CIO;
       (d) receive any other financial benefit from the CIO;
       unless the payment or benefit is permitted by sub-clause (2) of this clause, or authorised by the court or the prior written consent of the Charity Commission ("the Commission") has been obtained. In this clause, a "financial benefit" means a benefit, direct or indirect, which is either money or has a monetary value.

   (2) Scope and powers permitting trustees' or connected persons' benefits
       (a) A charity trustee or connected person may receive a benefit from the CIO as a beneficiary of the CIO provided that a majority of the trustees do not benefit in this way.[10]

---

trustee's entitlement to reasonable expenses and that they may benefit from trustee indemnity insurance. We recommend that you include it in the constitution, to inform people involved with the charity.

[8] This sub-clause reflects charity law requirements that the income and property of a CIO must be applied solely to further its objects and not to benefit the members or charity trustees (except as permitted by the governing document (see clause 6) or other express power). The trustees have a duty to ensure that the funds are correctly applied in accordance with this principle.

[9] Charity trustees may only benefit from their charity if they have express legal authorisation to do so (such as a clause in the constitution). This restriction extends to people closely connected to a trustee ('connected persons' – this term is defined in the interpretation clause). You **should** include this clause so that charity trustees are clear about the restrictions that apply to them; and unless you include it, the default legal position will apply. Even where trustees are allowed to benefit from the CIO, this must only happen where the benefit is in the interests of the CIO. Our guidance *Trustee expenses and payments* (CC11) provides more information about trustee benefits.

The model clause permits a minority of the charity trustees or connected persons to receive payments and other benefits in certain instances (such as for goods and services they supply to the CIO), subject to the stated controls. The option also allows other types of trustee benefit, subject to the Commission's prior consent.

You may restrict the benefits that the charity trustees will be allowed receive by altering these clauses, but if you later need to undo any of the restrictions it will require the Commission's consent to do so. Trustees do not have to use these powers just because they have them – we suggest you may find it simpler to keep to the model wording.

None of these options allows the trustees to receive payment for acting as a trustee.

[10] If all of the trustees will benefit from the activities of the CIO (for example, by using facilities available to all inhabitants of the area, such as a community centre), you may wish to substitute the following wording: "A charity trustee or connected person may receive a benefit from the CIO as a beneficiary provided that it is available generally to the beneficiaries of the CIO."

(b) A charity trustee or connected person may enter into a contract for the supply of services, or of goods that are supplied in connection with the provision of services, to the CIO where that is permitted in accordance with, and subject to the conditions in, section 185 to 188 of the Charities Act 2011.

(c) Subject to sub-clause (3) of this clause a charity trustee or connected person may provide the CIO with goods that are not supplied in connection with services provided to the CIO by the charity trustee or connected person.

(d) A charity trustee or connected person may receive interest on money lent to the CIO at a reasonable and proper rate which must be not more than the Bank of England bank rate (also known as the base rate).[11]

(e) A charity trustee or connected person may receive rent for premises let by the trustee or connected person to the CIO. The amount of the rent and the other terms of the lease must be reasonable and proper. The charity trustee concerned must withdraw from any meeting at which such a proposal or the rent or other terms of the lease are under discussion.

(f) A charity trustee or connected person may take part in the normal trading and fundraising activities of the CIO on the same terms as members of the public.

(3) **Payment for supply of goods only – controls**

The CIO and its charity trustees may only rely upon the authority provided by sub-clause (2)(c) of this clause if each of the following conditions is satisfied:

(a) The amount or maximum amount of the payment for the goods is set out in a written agreement between the CIO and the charity trustee or connected person supplying the goods ("the supplier").

(b) The amount or maximum amount of the payment for the goods does not exceed what is reasonable in the circumstances for the supply of the goods in question.

(c) The other charity trustees are satisfied that it is in the best interests of the CIO to contract with the supplier rather than with someone who is not a charity trustee or connected person. In reaching that decision the charity trustees must balance the advantage of contracting with a charity trustee or connected person against the disadvantages of doing so.

(d) The supplier is absent from the part of any meeting at which there is discussion of the proposal to enter into a contract or arrangement with him or her or it with regard to the supply of goods to the CIO.

(e) The supplier does not vote on any such matter and is not to be counted when calculating whether a quorum of charity trustees is present at the meeting.

---

[11] The CIO should document the amount of, and the terms of, the trustee's or connected person's loan.

(f) The reason for their decision is recorded by the charity trustees in the minute book.
(g) A majority of the charity trustees then in office are not in receipt of remuneration or payments authorised by clause 6.
(4) In sub-clauses (2) and (3) of this clause:
  (a) "the CIO" includes any company in which the CIO:
    (i) holds more than 50% of the shares; or
    (ii) controls more than 50% of the voting rights attached to the shares; or
    (iii) has the right to appoint one or more directors to the board of the company;
  (b) "connected person" includes any person within the definition set out in clause [30] (Interpretation);

7. **Conflicts of interest and conflicts of loyalty**[12]
A charity trustee must:
(1) declare the nature and extent of any interest, direct or indirect, which he or she has in a proposed transaction or arrangement with the CIO or in any transaction or arrangement entered into by the CIO which has not previously been declared; and
(2) absent himself or herself from any discussions of the charity trustees in which it is possible that a conflict of interest will arise between his or her duty to act solely in the interests of the CIO and any personal interest (including but not limited to any financial interest).

Any charity trustee absenting himself or herself from any discussions in accordance with this clause must not vote or be counted as part of the quorum in any decision of the charity trustees on the matter.

8. **Liability of members to contribute to the assets of the CIO if it is wound up**[13]

Option 1

If the CIO is wound up, the members of the CIO have no liability to contribute to its assets and no personal responsibility for settling its debts and liabilities.

Option 2

(1) If the CIO is wound up, each member of the CIO is liable to contribute to the assets of the CIO such amount (but not more than £[...]) as may be

---

[12] The General Regulations provide that a charity trustee of a CIO must not take part in any decision from which they would directly or indirectly benefit personally, unless they cannot reasonably be regarded as having a conflict of interest. This clause reminds the trustees of this requirement and also reflects wider good practice on managing conflicts of interest and conflicts of loyalty. We recommend that you include it.

[13] The constitution **must** state whether members of the CIO *either*: (a) have no liability to contribute to the assets of the CIO if it is wound up [**option 1**]; *or* (b) will be liable to contribute up to a maximum amount each if the CIO cannot meet its financial obligations when it is wound up [**option 2**]. **Choose one option and delete the other.** There is no preference or requirement in the legal framework for members to be liable to contribute anything. If you choose option 2, you **must** insert the maximum amount (normally a nominal sum such as £1 or £10) for which members will be individually liable.

required for payment of the debts and liabilities of the CIO contracted before that person or organisation ceases to be a member, for payment of the costs, charges and expenses of winding up, and for adjustment of the rights of the contributing members among themselves.

(2) In sub-clause (1) of this clause "member" includes any person or organisation that was a member of the CIO within 12 months before the commencement of the winding up.

(3) But subject to that, the members of the CIO have no liability to contribute to its assets if it is wound up, and accordingly have no personal responsibility for the settlement of its debts and liabilities beyond the amount that they are liable to contribute.

9. **Charity trustees**
   (1) **Functions and duties of charity trustees**
   The charity trustees shall manage the affairs of the CIO and may for that purpose exercise all the powers of the CIO. It is the duty of each charity trustee:
   (a) to exercise his or her powers and to perform his or her functions as a trustee of the CIO in the way he or she decides in good faith would be most likely to further the purposes of the CIO; and
   (b) to exercise, in the performance of those functions, such care and skill as is reasonable in the circumstances having regard in particular to:
       (i) any special knowledge or experience that he or she has or holds himself or herself out as having; and
       (ii) if he or she acts as a charity trustee of the CIO in the course of a business or profession, to any special knowledge or experience that it is reasonable to expect of a person acting in the course of that kind of business or profession.[14]
   (2) **Eligibility for trusteeship**[15]

---

[14] This clause explains the charity trustees' legal function, legal duty to act in good faith, and statutory duty of care. We recommend that these should be set out in the constitution. The trustees cannot adopt a lower duty of care.

[15] You should include provisions setting out who is eligible to be a charity trustee of the CIO. Sub-clause (a) requires all trustees to be individuals. It is legally permissible for a corporate body to be a charity trustee, but we would advise against a trustee body including both individuals and one or more corporate bodies. Where the CIO will have corporate members we recommend that they should not be elected as trustees; only individuals or nominees of these bodies should be eligible for election.
This clause and those that follow are drafted on the basis that the CIO will be governed by a trustee body made up of a number of individuals. If there is a good reason why the CIO will be administered by a single trustee (eg a corporation) or have any other trusteeship arrangement, you will need to amend clauses 12-16, and should seek your own professional advice.
The suggested provisions in (b) reflect the law and (c) is based on good practice. There are offences under the General Regulations concerning legally disqualified individuals acting as trustees.
If there are to be additional conditions for trustee eligibility (beyond the legal restrictions), these **must** be stated in the constitution. For example, some charities add requirements to ensure that trustees have particular knowledge or experience (eg of the locality in which the CIO operates or of issues relevant to the people that the CIO serves).

(a) Every charity trustee must be a natural person.
(b) No one may be appointed as a charity trustee:
- if he or she is under the age of 16 years; or
- if he or she would automatically cease to hold office under the provisions of clause [12(1)(e)].
(c) No one is entitled to act as a charity trustee whether on appointment or on any re-appointment until he or she has expressly acknowledged, in whatever way the charity trustees decide, his or her acceptance of the office of charity trustee.
[(d) At least one of the trustees of the CIO must be 18 years of age or over. If there is no trustee aged at least 18 years, the remaining trustee or trustees may act only to call a meeting of the charity trustees, or appoint a new charity trustee.][16]

(3) **Number of charity trustees**[17]

Option 1

(a) There must be at least [three] charity trustees. If the number falls below this minimum, the remaining trustee or trustees may act only to call a meeting of the charity trustees, or appoint a new charity trustee.

Option 1a

(b) The maximum number of charity trustees is [12]. The charity trustees may not appoint any charity trustee if as a result the number of charity trustees would exceed the maximum.

Option 1b

(b) There is no maximum number of charity trustees that may be appointed to the CIO.

Option 2

(a) There should be:

---

[16] This sub-clause contains an optional restriction on the proportion of charity trustees who are under 18. The Commission encourages charities to involve young people in their governance in whatever ways are appropriate in the circumstances, but advises against having a board made up entirely of people under 18. CIO trustees cannot be under 16.

[17] The General Regulations require that the constitution **must** state the minimum number of charity trustees, **if** more than one.
We recommend setting and including minimum and maximum numbers of charity trustees.
A CIO can have a fixed number of trustees or a range between a maximum and minimum (which will give the CIO more flexibility). Option 1a provides for a specified maximum number. Option 1b provides for no maximum limit. Option 2 provides for other trustee appointment arrangements in accordance with clause 13 (see below).
Choose Clause 12(3) Option 1 (and Option 1a *or* b) and Clause 13 Option 1 *or* choose Clause 12(3) Option 2 and Clause 13 Option 2 (selecting the relevant parts of each section). Delete the options that you have not chosen.
For good practice, a CIO should have at least three charity trustees. If the number of trustees falls below the minimum specified in the constitution, the provisions in clause 12(3) will enable the remaining charity trustees to appoint new trustees and prevent the CIO from becoming inoperable.
A CIO should have enough charity trustees to effectively carry out their duties, but not too many so that it becomes impractical to hold effective trustee meetings where everyone can participate in decision making. We suggest a maximum of 12 trustees, but you **may** choose a higher or lower number depending on the CIO's needs.

[Not less than . . . nor more than] . . . elected trustees; [. . . ex officio trustee[s]; and

[Not less than . . . nor more than] . . . nominated trustees].

(b) There must be at least [three] charity trustees. If the number falls below this minimum, the remaining trustee or trustees may act only to call a meeting of the charity trustees, or appoint a new charity trustee.

(c) The maximum number of charity trustees that can be appointed is as provided in sub-clause (a) of this clause. No trustee appointment may be made in excess of these provisions.

(4) **First charity trustees**[18]

The first charity trustees are as follows[, and are appointed for the following terms] –

.... [for [4] years]
.... [for [3] years]
.... [for [2] years]

10. **Appointment of charity trustees**[19]

Option 1[20]

(1) Apart from the first charity trustees, every trustee must be appointed [for a term of [three] years] by a resolution passed at a properly convened meeting of the charity trustees.

(2) In selecting individuals for appointment as charity trustees, the charity trustees must have regard to the skills, knowledge and experience needed for the effective administration of the CIO.

Option 2[21]

(1) **Appointed charity trustees**

(a) Apart from the first charity trustees, every appointed trustee must be appointed [for a term of [three] years] by a resolution passed at a properly convened meeting of the charity trustees.

---

[18] The General Regulations require that the constitution **must** include the names of the first charity trustees.
[19] The constitution must make provision about the appointment of one or more persons to be charity trustees. This clause contains two options. Choose the corresponding options in Clause 9(3) and Clause 10.
[20] Option 1 provides for new trustees to be appointed by the current trustees. This is the simplest, and likely to be the usual, arrangement for most foundation CIOs.
[21] Option 2 provides for new trustees to be appointed in different ways including appointment by the current trustees, ex-officio (ie by virtue of holding a certain office, eg the local vicar) and nomination by another organisation. If you use option 2 you will need to amend it to meet the CIO's particular circumstances depending on the combination of different methods of appointment that will apply. These additional appointment methods are usually only appropriate for charities operating in particular local areas or with links to particular bodies, and where it is desired to involve members of local councils, local churches or other external organisations on the trustee body.
It is good practice for trustees to be appointed for a fixed term, but you may instead provide for appointed trustees to be appointed indefinitely (ie for life or until they retire), in which case, delete the words in square brackets in clauses 9(4) and 10(1).

(b) In selecting individuals for appointment as appointed charity trustees, the charity trustees must have regard to the skills, knowledge and experience needed for the effective administration of the CIO.

[(2) Ex officio Trustee[s]
  (a) The [insert role] for the time being ("the office holder") shall automatically ("ex-officio") be a charity trustee, for as long as he or she holds that office.
  (b) If unwilling to act as a charity trustee, the office holder may:
      (i) before accepting appointment as a charity trustee, give notice in writing to the trustees of his or her unwillingness to act in that capacity; or
      (ii) after accepting appointment as a charity trustee, resign under the provisions contained in clause [12] (Retirement and removal of charity trustees).
  The office of ex officio charity trustee will then remain vacant until the office holder ceases to hold office.]

[(3) Nominated Trustee[s]
  (a) [insert name of appointing body] ("the appointing body") may appoint [insert number] charity trustees.
  (b) Any appointment must be made at a meeting held according to the ordinary practice of the appointing body.
  (c) Each appointment must be for a term of [three] years.
  (d) The appointment will be effective from the later of:
      (i) the date of the vacancy; and
      (ii) the date on which the charity trustees or their secretary or clerk are informed of the appointment.
  (e) The person appointed need not be a member of the appointing body.
  (f) A trustee appointed by the appointing body has the same duty under clause 9(1) as the other charity trustees to act in the way he or she decides in good faith would be most likely to further the purposes of the CIO].

11 Information for new charity trustees[22]

The charity trustees will make available to each new charity trustee, on or before his or her first appointment:
(a) a copy of the current version of this constitution; and
(b) a copy of the CIO's latest Trustees' Annual Report and statement of accounts.

12. Retirement and removal of charity trustees

(1) A charity trustee ceases to hold office if he or she:
  (a) retires by notifying the CIO in writing (but only if enough charity trustees will remain in office when the notice of resignation takes effect to form a quorum for meetings);

---

[22] This clause represents good practice; we recommend that you include it. It is vital for new trustees to have easy access to the information and training that they need in order to become effective members of the trustee body.

(b) is absent without the permission of the charity trustees from all their meetings held within a period of six months and the trustees resolve that his or her office be vacated;
(c) dies;
(d) in the written opinion, given to the company, of a registered medical practitioner treating that person, has become physically or mentally incapable of acting as a director and may remain so for more than three months;
(e) is disqualified from acting as a charity trustee by virtue of section 178-180 of the Charities Act 2011 (or any statutory re-enactment or modification of that provision).
(2) Any person retiring as a charity trustee is eligible for reappointment.
[(3) A charity trustee who has served for [three] consecutive terms may not be reappointed for a [fourth] consecutive term but may be reappointed after an interval of at least [one year].][23]

13. **Taking of decisions by charity trustees**[24]
Any decision may be taken either:
- at a meeting of the charity trustees; or
- by resolution in writing or electronic form agreed by all of the charity trustees, which may comprise either a single document or several documents containing the text of the resolution in like form to each of which one or more charity trustees has signified their agreement.

14. **Delegation by charity trustees**[25]
(1) The charity trustees may delegate any of their powers or functions to a committee or committees, and, if they do, they must determine the terms and conditions on which the delegation is made. The charity trustees may at any time alter those terms and conditions, or revoke the delegation.
(2) This power is in addition to the power of delegation in the General Regulations and any other power of delegation available to the charity trustees, but is subject to the following requirements –
(a) a committee may consist of two or more persons, but at least one member of each committee must be a charity trustee;

---

[23] The General Regulations require that the constitution must contain provisions setting out how charity trustees (and members) may retire or otherwise cease to hold office. The provisions in the model follow recommended good practice. There is an optional provision (sub clause (3)) to ensure that trustees do not serve for more than three consecutive terms, which may help to encourage regular turnover and change on the trustee board. (It is good practice to aim for a balance between continuity and change.)

[24] The power to take decisions by resolution in writing or electronic form outside meetings is optional, but if the trustees intend to use it, it **must** be included in the constitution. Such a decision must be unanimous (ie all of the trustees must agree).

[25] This power is optional. We recommend you include it as a matter of good practice. The General Regulations give charity trustees of a CIO automatic power to delegate tasks to sub-committees, staff or agents; but without this additional constitutional power, the trustees will be unable to delegate any power to make decisions.
Sub-clauses (2)(a)–(c) reflect minimum good practice and are safeguards that **should** not be removed or diminished.

(b) the acts and proceedings of any committee must be brought to the attention of the charity trustees as a whole as soon as is reasonably practicable; and
　　　(c) the charity trustees shall from time to time review the arrangements which they have made for the delegation of their powers.

15. **Meetings of charity trustees**[26]
    (1) **Calling meetings**
　　　(a) Any charity trustee may call a meeting of the charity trustees.
　　　(b) Subject to that, the charity trustees shall decide how their meetings are to be called, and what notice is required.
    (2) **Chairing of meetings**
    The charity trustees may appoint one of their number to chair their meetings and may at any time revoke such appointment. If no-one has been so appointed, or if the person appointed is unwilling to preside or is not present within 10 minutes after the time of the meeting, the charity trustees present may appoint one of their number to chair that meeting.
    (3) **Procedure at meetings**
　　　(a) No decision shall be taken at a meeting unless a quorum is present at the time when the decision is taken. The quorum is two charity trustees, or the number nearest to one third of the total number of charity trustees, whichever is greater, or such larger number as the charity trustees may decide from time to time. A charity trustee shall not be counted in the quorum present when any decision is made about a matter upon which he or she is not entitled to vote.[27]
　　　(b) Questions arising at a meeting shall be decided by a majority of those eligible to vote.
　　　[(c) In the case of an equality of votes, the person who chairs the meeting shall have a second or casting vote.][28]
    (4) **Participation in meetings by electronic means**[29]
　　　(a) A meeting may be held by suitable electronic means agreed by the charity trustees in which each participant may communicate with all the other participants.

---

[26] The General Regulations require that the Constitution **must** include provisions for the calling and running of meetings including the minimum number of trustees who shall form a quorum, appointment of a chair and, if trustees will be able to demand a poll (a counted vote, normally with voting papers), the procedure for conducting such a poll. The provisions in this model are good practice recommendations.
(We have not included provision for trustees to have a poll as feedback from our consultations suggested that most charities did not feel it was appropriate. If this power is required, please see clause 11(6)(b–e) for a suitable wording.)

[27] We recommend that the quorum for trustee meetings should not be less than one third of the number of trustees.

[28] It is common, but not obligatory, for the Chair to have a casting vote. You may include or delete this power.

[29] This clause is optional, but will be required if one or more of the CIO's trustees may from time to time participate in meetings by telephone or other electronic means where participants may not be able to see and hear each other.

(b) Any charity trustee participating at a meeting by suitable electronic means agreed by the charity trustees in which a participant or participants may communicate with all the other participants shall qualify as being present at the meeting.
(c) Meetings held by electronic means must comply with rules for meetings, including chairing and the taking of minutes.

16. **Membership of the CIO**[30]
    (1) The members of the CIO shall be its charity trustees for the time being. The only persons eligible to be members of the CIO are its charity trustees. Membership of the CIO cannot be transferred to anyone else.
    (2) Any member and charity trustee who ceases to be a charity trustee automatically ceases to be a member of the CIO.

[17. **Informal or associate (non-voting) membership**[31]
    (1) The charity trustees may create associate or other classes of non-voting membership, and may determine the rights and obligations of any such members (including payment of membership fees), and the conditions for admission to, and termination of membership of any such class of members.
    (2) Other references in this constitution to "members" and "membership" do not apply to non-voting members, and non-voting members do not qualify as members for any purpose under the Charities Acts, General Regulations or Dissolution Regulations.]

18. **Decisions which must be made by the members of the CIO**[32]
    (1) Any decision to:
        (a) amend the constitution of the CIO;
        (b) amalgamate the CIO with, or transfer its undertaking to, one or more other CIOs, in accordance with the Charities Act 2011; or
        (c) wind up or dissolve the CIO (including transferring its business to any other charity)
        must be made by a resolution of the members of the CIO (rather than a resolution of the charity trustees).[33]
    (2) Decisions of the members may be made either:

---

[30] A CIO must have one or more members. In this model constitution the charity trustees are the only members and become members automatically. If the CIO is going to have a wider voting membership you will need use the Association Model Constitution.
The constitution must set out who is eligible for membership and how someone becomes a member. The constitution must contain provision for retirement and termination of membership. This model clause fulfils these requirements.
The General Regulations have been drafted on the basis that all members of a 'foundation' CIO will be charity trustees, and they will case to be members of the CIO when they cease to be trustees.

[31] Informal or associate (non-voting) membership – We advise CIOs to include this power if they contemplate having an informal (associate) membership. Membership of this kind does not count as membership for legal purposes, for example in terms of voting rights, legal obligations to act in the interests of the charity or any liability to contribute to the assets of the CIO on dissolution.

[32] We recommend that you include these powers and provisions in full.

[33] This sub-clause acts as a reminder that certain decisions must be made by the members, rather than by the trustees (although in practice they are the same persons).

(a) by resolution at a general meeting; or
(b) by resolution in writing, in accordance with sub-clause (4) of this clause.[34]

(3) Any decision specified in sub-clause (1) of this clause must be made in accordance with the provisions of clause [28] (amendment of constitution), clause [29] (Voluntary winding up or dissolution), or the provisions of the Charities Act 2011, the General Regulations or the Dissolution Regulations as applicable. Those provisions require the resolution to be agreed by a 75% majority of those members voting at a general meeting, or agreed by all members in writing.[35]

(4) Except where a resolution in writing must be agreed by all the members, such a resolution may be agreed by a simple majority of all the members who are entitled to vote on it. Such a resolution shall be effective provided that:
(a) a copy of the proposed resolution has been sent to all the members eligible to vote; and
(b) the required majority of members has signified its agreement to the resolution in a document or documents which are received at the principal office within the period of 28 days beginning with the circulation date. The document signifying a member's agreement must be authenticated by their signature, by a statement of their identity accompanying the document, or in such other manner as the CIO has specified.

The resolution in writing may comprise several copies to which one or more members has signified their agreement. Eligibility to vote on the resolution is limited to members who are members of the CIO on the date when the proposal is first circulated.[36]

19. **General meetings of members**[37]
(1) **Calling of general meetings of members**
The charity trustees may designate any of their meetings as a general meeting of the members of the CIO. The purpose of such a meeting is to discharge any business which must by law be discharged by a resolution of the members of the CIO as specified in clause [18] (Decisions which must be made by the members of the CIO).[38]
(2) **Notice of general meetings of members**

---

[34] This sub-clause allows decisions of the members to be made at a general meeting or by written resolution.

[35] The decisions specified in sub-clause (1) are subject to special requirements; this sub-clause acts as a reminder of those requirements.

[36] This sub-clause sets out the procedure for written resolutions.

[37] The General Regulations state that the constitution must make provision about the holding and calling of general meetings, and procedure at such meetings including the minimum number of members who shall form a quorum, whether members can demand a poll, and the procedure for conducting such a poll. The provisions in this clause are good practice recommendations.

[38] In a CIO with the 'foundation' model constitution, all of the members are trustees, so the trustees may decide which of their meetings should be treated as a general meeting of the members (subject to the notice requirements in (2)).

(a) The minimum period of notice required to hold a general meeting of the members of the CIO is [14] days.[39]

20. **Saving provisions**[40]
    (1) Subject to sub-clause (2) of this clause, all decisions of the charity trustees, or of a committee of charity trustees, shall be valid notwithstanding the participation in any vote of a charity trustee:
    • who was disqualified from holding office;
    • who had previously retired or who had been obliged by the constitution to vacate office;
    • who was not entitled to vote on the matter, whether by reason of a conflict of interest or otherwise;
    if, without the vote of that charity trustee and that charity trustee being counted in the quorum, the decision has been made by a majority of the charity trustees at a quorate meeting.
    (2) Sub-clause (1) of this clause does not permit a charity trustee to keep any benefit that may be conferred upon him or her by a resolution of the charity trustees or of a committee of charity trustees if, but for clause (1), the resolution would have been void, or if the charity trustee has not complied with clause 7 (Conflicts of interest).

21. **Execution of documents**[41]
    (1) The CIO shall execute documents either by signature or by affixing its seal (if it has one).
    (2) A document is validly executed by signature if it is signed by at least two of the charity trustees.
    (3) If the CIO has a seal:
    (a) it must comply with the provisions of the General Regulations; and
    (b) it must only be used by the authority of the charity trustees or of a committee of charity trustees duly authorised by the charity trustees. The charity trustees may determine who shall sign any document to which the seal is affixed and unless otherwise determined it shall be signed by two charity trustees.

22. **Use of electronic communications**[42]

---

[39] The minimum period of notice for general meetings should be reasonable in the CIO's particular circumstances, to enable as many members (trustees) as possible to participate in such decisions. For the decisions mentioned in clause 18(1) the period of notice is specified as 14 days in the General Regulations.
[40] We recommend that you include this clause to reduce the risk of trustees' decisions being declared invalid for purely technical reasons. This is, however, also covered in the General Regulations.
[41] We recommend that you include this clause, for clarity about how documents may be validly executed on behalf of the CIO. It includes provision for use of a seal, which the General Regulations stipulate **must** be included if the CIO is to have a seal (but there is no requirement to have one). The General Regulations require the full name of the CIO to be clearly written on the seal, and failure to comply with this is an offence.
[42] The General Regulations include provisions governing the use of electronic communication, and we recommend that CIO trustees familiarise themselves with the requirements. Failure to comply with the requirement to provide a hard copy would constitute an offence.
The General Regulations state that if the CIO intends to automatically use electronic

[(1) **General**]
The CIO will comply with the requirements of the Communications Provisions in the General Regulations and in particular:
  (a) the requirement to provide within 21 days to any member on request a hard copy of any document or information sent to the member otherwise than in hard copy form;
  (b) any requirements to provide information to the Commission in a particular form or manner.

23. **Keeping of Registers**[43]
The CIO must comply with its obligations under the General Regulations in relation to the keeping of, and provision of access to, a (combined) register of its members and charity trustees.

24. **Minutes**[44]
The charity trustees must keep minutes of all:
(1) appointments of officers made by the charity trustees;
(2) proceedings at general meetings of the CIO;
(3) meetings of the charity trustees and committees of charity trustees including:
  - the names of the trustees present at the meeting;
  - the decisions made at the meetings; and
  - where appropriate the reasons for the decisions;
(4) decisions made by the charity trustees otherwise than in meetings.

25. **Accounting records, accounts, annual reports and returns, register maintenance**[45]
(1) The charity trustees must comply with the requirements of the Charities Act 2011 with regard to the keeping of accounting records, to the preparation and scrutiny of statements of accounts, and to the preparation of annual reports and returns. The statements of accounts, reports and returns must be sent to the Charity Commission, regardless of the income of the CIO, within 10 months of the financial year end.
(2) The charity trustees must comply with their obligation to inform the Commission within 28 days of any change in the particulars of the CIO entered on the Central Register of Charities.

26. **Rules**[46]

---

communication or a website to send formal communications to members, this **must** be stated in the constitution, which must also set out the circumstances in which this will happen. For suggested wording, please see the appendix to this constitution.

[43] This clause reflects the requirements in the General Regulations that the CIO keeps registers of members and charity trustees and makes this information available for inspection by interested persons. This does not have to be stated in the constitution but is included to serve as a reminder.

[44] This clause reflects the requirements of the General Regulations regarding record keeping. We recommend that this clause is included, to remind the trustees of their responsibilities.

[45] This clause reflects the trustees' duties under the Charities Act 2011. We recommend that this clause is included, to remind the trustees of their responsibilities.

[46] We recommend that this power **should** be included for clarity, but charities automatically have this power and it does not have to be stated in the constitution. It is important that members are made aware of, and can easily obtain, copies of any rules.

The charity trustees may from time to time make such reasonable and proper rules or bye-laws as they may deem necessary or expedient for the proper conduct and management of the CIO, but such rules or bye-laws must not be inconsistent with any provision of this constitution. Copies of any such rules or bye-laws currently in force must be made available to any member of the CIO on request.

27. **Disputes**[47]

If a dispute arises between members of the CIO about the validity or propriety of anything done by the members under this constitution, and the dispute cannot be resolved by agreement, the parties to the dispute must first try in good faith to settle the dispute by mediation before resorting to litigation.

28. **Amendment of constitution**[48]

As provided by clauses 224–227 of the Charities Act 2011:
(1) This constitution can only be amended:
  (a) by resolution agreed in writing by all members of the CIO; or
  (b) by a resolution passed by a 75% majority of those voting at a general meeting of the members of the CIO called in accordance with clause 19 (General meetings of members).
(2) Any alteration of clause 3 (Objects), clause [29] (Voluntary winding up or dissolution), this clause, or of any provision where the alteration would provide authorisation for any benefit to be obtained by charity trustees or members of the CIO or persons connected with them, requires the prior written consent of the Charity Commission.
(3) No amendment that is inconsistent with the provisions of the Charities Act 2011 or the General Regulations shall be valid.
(4) A copy of any resolution altering the constitution, together with a copy of the CIO's constitution as amended, must be sent to the Commission within 15 days from the date on which the resolution is passed. The amendment does not take effect until it has been recorded in the Register of Charities.

29. **Voluntary winding up or dissolution**[49]

---

[47] It is good practice to include provisions for dealing with any disputes that arise between members of the CIO. Litigation can be expensive, and litigation about the internal affairs of a charity would almost certainly constitute "charity proceedings", which can be taken only with the Commission's authority. We would usually require the parties to a dispute to have tried mediation first.

[48] This reflects the CIOs' statutory power of amendment in sections 224–227 of the Charities Act 2011. A CIO's constitution **should** include these provisions for ease of reference. The constitution of a CIO cannot override the statutory power of constitutional amendment, but the General Regulations provide that you **may** include additional restrictions in some or all cases, for example requiring a longer period of notice before the meeting, or a higher majority, for certain changes. Additional restrictions are not provided for in this model and if you are considering this, we recommend that you take appropriate advice. To request the Commission's consent to an amendment or to inform the Commission of an amendment, please complete our online form which is available at http://forms.charitycommission.gov.uk/contact-us/get-our-permission/change-your-governing-document/amend-governing-document/.

[49] This clause reflects the provisions of the Charities Act 2011, the General Regulations and Dissolution Regulations. We recommend that it is included in the constitution for ease of reference. It also highlights that there are other requirements in the Dissolution Regulations

(1) As provided by the Dissolution Regulations, the CIO may be dissolved by resolution of its members. Any decision by the members to wind up or dissolve the CIO can only be made:
  (a) at a general meeting of the members of the CIO called in accordance with clause 19 (General meetings of members), of which not less than 14 days' notice has been given to those eligible to attend and vote:
    (i) by a resolution passed by a 75% majority of those voting, or
    (ii) by a resolution passed by decision taken without a vote and without any expression of dissent in response to the question put to the general meeting; or
  (b) by a resolution agreed in writing by all members of the CIO.
(2) Subject to the payment of all the CIO's debts:
  (a) Any resolution for the winding up of the CIO, or for the dissolution of the CIO without winding up, may contain a provision directing how any remaining assets of the CIO shall be applied.
  (b) If the resolution does not contain such a provision, the charity trustees must decide how any remaining assets of the CIO shall be applied.
  (c) In either case the remaining assets must be applied for charitable purposes the same as or similar to those of the CIO.[50]
(3) The CIO must observe the requirements of the Dissolution Regulations in applying to the Commission for the CIO to be removed from the Register of Charities, and in particular:
  (a) the charity trustees must send with their application to the Commission:
    (i) a copy of the resolution passed by the members of the CIO;
    (ii) a declaration by the charity trustees that any debts and other liabilities of the CIO have been settled or otherwise provided for in full; and
    (iii) a statement by the charity trustees setting out the way in which any property of the CIO has been or is to be applied prior to its dissolution in accordance with this constitution;
  (b) the charity trustees must ensure that a copy of the application is sent within seven days to every member and employee of the CIO, and to any charity trustee of the CIO who was not privy to the application.
(4) If the CIO is to be wound up or dissolved in any other circumstances, the provisions of the Dissolution Regulations must be followed.[51]

---

that the trustees must comply with, as there are offences for non-compliance. To inform the Commission of your CIO's dissolution, please complete our online form.

[50] The constitution **must** contain directions about how its property will be applied if it is wound up. Any assets remaining after the payment of debts **must** be applied for charitable purposes that are similar to those of the CIO.

[51] It is essential for trustees to be aware that if the CIO is unable to meet its financial obligations in full when it is wound up, the provisions in sub-clauses (1)-(3) do not apply, and the relevant

30. Interpretation[52]
    In this constitution:

    "connected person" means:
    (a) child, parent, grandchild, grandparent, brother or sister of the charity trustee;
    (b) the spouse or civil partner of the charity trustee or of any person falling within sub-clause (a) above;
    (c) a person carrying on business in partnership with the charity trustee or with any person falling within sub- clause (a) or (b) above;
    (d) an institution which is controlled –
        (i) by the charity trustee or any connected person falling within sub-clause (a), (b), or (c) above; or
        (ii) by two or more persons falling within sub-clause (d)(i), when taken together.
    (e) a body corporate in which –
        (i) the charity trustee or any connected person falling within sub-clauses (a) to (c) has a substantial interest; or
        (ii) two or more persons falling within sub-clause (e)(i) who, when taken together, have a substantial interest.

    Section 118 of the Charities Act 2011 apply for the purposes of interpreting the terms used in this constitution.
    "General Regulations" means the Charitable Incorporated Organisations (General) Regulations 2012.
    "Dissolution Regulations" means the Charitable Incorporated Organisations (Insolvency and Dissolution) Regulations 2012.
    The "Communications Provisions" means the Communications Provisions in [Part 10, Chapter 4] of the General Regulations.
    "charity trustee" means a charity trustee of the CIO.
    A "poll" means a counted vote or ballot, usually (but not necessarily) in writing.

---

provisions of the Dissolution Regulations must be followed. Failure to do so is not only an offence, but it could lead to personal liability for the trustees.

[52] This clause explains some terms used in the rest of the constitution.

APPENDIX

The following provisions do not form part of the 'Association' model constitution but are available as options under clauses 19 (General meetings of members) and 22 (Use of electronic communications). For CIOs intending to include these powers in their constitutions, we recommend that you use the following wording. Notes on these clauses are included with the explanatory notes accompanying the clauses in the model.

19. **General meetings of members**
    (7) **Proxy voting**
      (a) Any member of the CIO may appoint another person as a proxy to exercise all or any of that member's rights to attend, speak and vote at a general meeting of the CIO. Proxies must be appointed by a notice in writing (a "proxy notice") which:
         (i) states the name and address of the member appointing the proxy;
         (ii) identifies the person appointed to be that member's proxy and the general meeting in relation to which that person is appointed;
         (iii) is signed by or on behalf of the member appointing the proxy, or is authenticated in such manner as the CIO may determine; and
         (iv) is delivered to the CIO in accordance with the constitution and any instructions contained in the notice of the general meeting to which they relate.
      (b) The CIO may require proxy notices to be delivered in a particular form, and may specify different forms for different purposes.
      (c) Proxy notices may (but do not have to) specify how the proxy appointed under them is to vote (or that the proxy is to abstain from voting) on one or more resolutions.
      (d) Unless a proxy notice indicates otherwise, it must be treated as:
         (i) allowing the person appointed under it as a proxy discretion as to how to vote on any ancillary or procedural resolutions put to the meeting; and
         (ii) appointing that person as a proxy in relation to any adjournment of the general meeting to which it relates as well as the meeting itself.
      (e) A member who is entitled to attend, speak or vote (either on a show of hands or on a poll) at a general meeting remains so entitled in respect of that meeting or any adjournment of it, even though a valid proxy notice has been delivered to the CIO by or on behalf of that member.
      (f) An appointment under a proxy notice may be revoked by delivering to the CIO a notice in writing given by or on behalf of the member by whom or on whose behalf the proxy notice was given.

(g) A notice revoking a proxy appointment only takes effect if it is delivered before the start of the meeting or adjourned meeting to which it relates.

(h) If a proxy notice is not signed or authenticated by the member appointing the proxy, it must be accompanied by written evidence that the person who signed or authenticated it on that member's behalf had authority to do so.

(8) **Postal Voting**

(a) The CIO may, if the charity trustees so decide, allow the members to vote by post or electronic mail ("email") to elect charity trustees or to make a decision on any matter that is being decided at a general meeting of the members.

(b) The charity trustees must appoint at least two persons independent of the CIO to serve as scrutineers to supervise the conduct of the postal/email ballot and the counting of votes.

(c) If postal and/or email voting is to be allowed on a matter, the CIO must send to members of the CIO not less than [21] days before the deadline for receipt of votes cast in this way:

(i) a notice by email, if the member has agreed to receive notices in this way under clause [22] (Use of electronic communications), including an explanation of the purpose of the vote and the voting procedure to be followed by the member, and a voting form capable of being returned by email or post to the CIO, containing details of the resolution being put to a vote, or of the candidates for election, as applicable;

(ii) a notice by post to all other members, including a written explanation of the purpose of the postal vote and the voting procedure to be followed by the member; and a postal voting form containing details of the resolution being put to a vote, or of the candidates for election, as applicable.

(d) The voting procedure must require all forms returned by post to be in an envelope with the member's name and signature, and nothing else, on the outside, inside another envelope addressed to 'The Scrutineers for [name of CIO]', at the CIO's principal office or such other postal address as is specified in the voting procedure.

(e) The voting procedure for votes cast by email must require the member's name to be at the top of the email, and the email must be authenticated in the manner specified in the voting procedure.

(f) Email votes must be returned to an email address used only for this purpose and must be accessed only by a scrutineer.

(g) The voting procedure must specify the closing date and time for receipt of votes, and must state that any votes received after the closing date or not complying with the voting procedure will be invalid and not be counted.

(h) The scrutineers must make a list of names of members casting valid votes, and a separate list of members casting votes which were invalid. These lists must be provided to a charity trustee or other person overseeing admission to, and voting at, the general meeting. A member who has cast a valid postal or email vote must not vote at the meeting, and must not be counted in the quorum for any part of the meeting on which he, she or it has already cast a valid vote. A member who has cast an invalid vote by post or email is allowed to vote at the meeting and counts towards the quorum.

(i) For postal votes, the scrutineers must retain the internal envelopes (with the member's name and signature). For email votes, the scrutineers must cut off and retain any part of the email that includes the member's name. In each case, a scrutineer must record on this evidence of the member's name that the vote has been counted, or if the vote has been declared invalid, the reason for such declaration.

(j) Votes cast by post or email must be counted by all the scrutineers before the meeting at which the vote is to be taken. The scrutineers must provide to the person chairing the meeting written confirmation of the number of valid votes received by post and email and the number of votes received which were invalid.

(k) The scrutineers must not disclose the result of the postal/email ballot until after votes taken by hand or by poll at the meeting, or by poll after the meeting, have been counted. Only at this point shall the scrutineers declare the result of the valid votes received, and these votes shall be included in the declaration of the result of the vote.

(l) Following the final declaration of the result of the vote, the scrutineers must provide to a charity trustee or other authorised person bundles containing the evidence of members submitting valid postal votes; evidence of members submitting valid email votes; evidence of invalid votes; the valid votes; and the invalid votes.

(m) Any dispute about the conduct of a postal or email ballot must be referred initially to a panel set up by the charity trustees, to consist of two trustees and two persons independent of the CIO. If the dispute cannot be satisfactorily resolved by the panel, it must be referred to the Electoral Reform Services.

22. **Use of electronic communications**
    (2) **To the CIO**
    Any member or charity trustee of the CIO may communicate electronically with the CIO to an address specified by the CIO for the purpose, so long as the communication is authenticated in a manner which is satisfactory to the CIO.
    (3) **By the CIO**

(a) Any member or charity trustee of the CIO, by providing the CIO with his or her email address or similar, is taken to have agreed to receive communications from the CIO in electronic form at that address, unless the member has indicated to the CIO his or her unwillingness to receive such communications in that form.

(b) The charity trustees may, subject to compliance with any legal requirements, by means of publication on its website –
  (i) provide the members with the notice referred to in clause 19(2) (Notice of general meetings);
  (ii) give charity trustees notice of their meetings in accordance with clause 15(1) (Calling meetings); [and
  (iii) submit any proposal to the members or charity trustees for decision by written resolution or postal vote in accordance with the CIO's powers under clause 18 (Members' decisions), 18(4) (Decisions taken by resolution in writing), or [[the provisions for postal voting] (if you have included this optional provision, please insert the correct clause number here)].

(c) The charity trustees must:
  (i) take reasonable steps to ensure that members and charity trustees are promptly notified of the publication of any such notice or proposal;
  (ii) send any such notice or proposal in hard copy form to any member or charity trustee who has not consented to receive communications in electronic form.

APPENDIX G

CHARITABLE OBJECTS

Reproduced with the kind permission of the Charity Commission
https://www.gov.uk/government/publications/example-charitable-objects

ADVANCEMENT OF EDUCATION

- To advance the education of the public in the subject of [insert subject to be studied].
- To advance the education of the pupils at [the name of the school] by providing and assisting in the provision of facilities [not required to be provided by the local education authority] for education at the school.
- For the public benefit to promote the education (including social and physical training) of people [under the age of 25 years] in [place] in such ways as the charity trustees think fit, including by:
  1. awarding to such persons scholarships, maintenance allowances or grants tenable at any university, college or institution of higher or further education;
  2. providing their education (including the study of music or other arts), to undertake travel in furtherance of that education or to prepare for entry to any occupation, trade or profession on leaving any educational establishment.
- To assist in such ways as the charity trustees think fit any charity in [place] whose aims include advancing education of persons under the age of 25 years by developing their mental, physical and moral capabilities through leisure time activities.
- For the public benefit to promote learning for pleasure by people no longer in full time employment through the continued development of their individual capabilities, competencies, skills and understanding in subjects of educational value.
- To advance the education of the public in general (and particularly amongst scientists) on the subject of particle physics and to promote research for the public benefit in all aspects of that subject and to publish the useful results.

ADVANCEMENT OF RELIGION

- To advance the [insert basis of faith] [faith] [religion] for the benefit of the public in accordance with [the statements of belief appearing in the schedule] [the following doctrines: ...].
- The advancement of the [insert basis of faith] religion mainly, but not exclusively, by means of broadcasting [insert basis of faith] messages of an evangelistic and teaching nature.
- To advance the [insert basis of faith] religion in [insert area of benefit] for the benefit of the public through the holding of prayer meetings, lectures [public celebration of religious festivals] producing and/or distributing literature on [insert basis of faith] to enlighten others about the [insert basis of faith] religion.

ADVICE AND COUNSELLING

- The relief of the physical and mental sickness of persons in need by reason of addiction to [substance], in particular by the provision of counselling and support.
- The relief of financial hardship by the provision of free legal advice and assistance to persons who, through lack of means, would otherwise be unable to obtain such advice.
- To relieve the mental and physical sickness of persons resident in [area of benefit] suffering from bereavement or loss by the provision of counselling and support for such persons.

ANIMAL CHARITIES

- For the benefit of the public to relieve the suffering of animals in need of care and attention and, in particular, to provide and maintain rescue homes or other facilities for the reception, care and treatment of such animals.
- To promote humane behaviour towards animals by providing appropriate care, protection, treatment and security for animals which are in need of care and attention by reason of sickness, maltreatment, poor circumstances or ill usage and to educate the public in matters pertaining to animal welfare in general and the prevention of cruelty and suffering among animals.

Activities a charity for these purposes might be carrying out:

Offering shelter or sanctuary for animals which are in need of medical attention; providing medical treatment for animals; actively seeking new homes for 'rescued' animals.

NB: it is not charitable to offer sanctuary to fit and healthy animals.

CARERS

NB: There is an approved standard governing document for the Crossroads Care Attendant Scheme.

- To relieve people who are elderly or disabled resident in [parish/place] by the provisions of carers and by the provision of support and training to such carers.
- The relief of elderly people and those in poor health resident in [parish/place] (not being resident in an institution or nursing home as defined by the National Assistance Act 1948 or the Chronically Sick and Disabled Act 1970) by the provision of a sitting service to relieve those who are caring for or nursing them.
- To relieve financial hardship and sickness among persons who are caring for or nursing a person with a physical or mental disability in any place other than an Institution or Nursing Home as defined by the National Assistance Act 1948 and Chronically Sick and Disabled Persons Act 1970, and the relief of people who are chronically sick or disabled by the provision of training and advice for those responsible for their care.
- To preserve and protect the health of those caring for people with physical, mental or sensory impairment within the family or home by offering a respite service through the provision of community based care attendants and, at the discretion of the [Management Committee/Trustees] and in exceptional circumstances, to provide such care attendants for disabled people living alone.

See also example objects for charities for the relief of sickness.

Activities a charity for these purposes might be carrying out:

Providing approved training for carers; grants to carers to enable them to 'take a break'; replacement carers where the usual carer is absent.

COMMUNITY AMATEUR SPORTS CLUBS

- The promotion of community participation in healthy recreation in particular by the provision of facilities for the playing of [particular sports].

- The promotion of community participation in healthy recreation [for the benefit of the inhabitants of x] by the provision of facilities for playing [insert sport(s)].

Activities a charity for these purposes might be carrying out:

Please refer to the Charity Commission publication: *Charitable Status and Sport (RR11)*.

COMMUNITY CAPACITY BUILDING

- To develop the capacity and skills of the members of the [socially and economically] [socially] disadvantaged community of [insert place] in such a way that they are better able to identify, and help meet, their needs and to participate more fully in society.

Activities a charity for these purposes might be carrying out:

Please refer to the Charity Commission publication: *The Promotion of Community Capacity Building (RR5)*.

COMMUNITY CENTRE

To further or benefit the residents of [area of benefit] and the neighbourhood, without distinction of sex, sexual orientation, race or of political, religious or other opinions by associating together the said residents and the local authorities, voluntary and other organisations in a common effort to advance education and to provide facilities in the interests of social welfare for recreation and leisure time occupation with the objective of improving the conditions of life for the residents.

In furtherance of these objects but not otherwise, the trustees shall have power:

To establish or secure the establishment of a community centre and to maintain or manage or co-operate with any statutory authority in the maintenance and management of such a centre for activities promoted by the charity in furtherance of the above objects.

Activities a charity for these purposes might be carrying out:

Please refer to the Charity Commission publication: *Village Halls and Community Centres (RS9)RS9a.*

COMMUNITY TRANSPORT

- To provide transport facilities in [insert place] for people who have special need of such facilities because they are elderly, poor or disabled, people with young children or those living in isolated areas where there are no adequate public transport facilities.

Activities a charity for these purposes might be carrying out:

Operating a regular bus service using adapted vehicles between areas not otherwise served by public transport and local towns.

CONCILIATION AND MEDIATION

- To provide, for the benefit of the public, assistance through conciliation for couples whose relationships appear to be breaking down, and where such relationships have already broken down, to advise and help in the settlement of differences or potential differences over associated matters such as custody and access to children, and financial matters.

See also example objects for charities for the promotion of the law, police and crime prevention.

Activities a charity for these purposes might be carrying out:

Counselling (by trained counsellors), advice and information on legal rights or obligations; signposting to other forms of help; providing a safe 'neutral' place for couples to talk to each other with a view to reconciliation or agreement.

CONSERVATION OF THE ENVIRONMENT

- To promote for the benefit of the public the conservation protection and improvement of the physical and natural environment [by promoting biological diversity].

It is also acceptable for environmental charities to have an additional object of advancing the education of the public where appropriate.

- To advance the education of the public in the conservation, protection and improvement of the physical and natural environment.

Activities a charity for these purposes might be carrying out:

Please refer to the Charity Commission publication: *Preservation and Conservation Charities (RR9)*.

DISASTERS

- The relief of financial need and suffering among victims of natural or other kinds of disaster in the form of money (or other means deemed suitable) for persons, bodies, organisations and/or countries affected [including the provision of medical aid].
- The relief and assistance of people in any part of the world who are the victims of war or natural disaster, trouble, or catastrophe in particular by the supply of medical aid to such persons.

Activities a charity for these purposes might be carrying out:

Arranging for the purchase and delivery of aid to such areas; co-operating with others to get aid to the right place; identifying the real needs of those affected by disaster and ways of meeting those needs.

ELDERLY PEOPLE

- To relieve elderly people resident in [insert place] who are in need, by providing specially designed or adapted housing, and items, services or facilities calculated to relieve the needs of such persons.
- To relieve financial hardship, sickness and poor health amongst elderly people.

Activities a charity for these purposes might be carrying out:

Making adapted accommodation available to elderly people; making grants to elderly people to enable them to buy goods or services to help them overcome the debilities of old age.

Note: Extra facilities can be provided either in housing owned or managed by the charity or in the home of the elderly person.

EQUALITY AND DIVERSITY

- The promotion of equality and diversity for the public benefit by [for example]:
  (a) the elimination of discrimination on the grounds of race, gender, disability, sexual orientation or religion;
  (b) advancing education and raising awareness in equality and diversity;
  (c) promoting activities to foster understanding between people from diverse backgrounds;
  (d) conducting or commissioning research on equality and diversity issues and publishing the results to the public;
  (e) cultivating a sentiment in favour of equality and diversity.

Activities a charity for this purpose might be carrying out:

Please refer to the Charity Commission guidance on *The Promotion of Equality and Diversity for the Benefit of the Public*.

THE ESTABLISHMENT AND MAINTENANCE OF A MUSEUM AND/OR ART GALLERY

- To establish and maintain a museum and/or art gallery for the benefit of the public.
- To promote art for the benefit of the public by the establishment and maintenance of a [museum] [art gallery].
- To advance education by the establishment and maintenance of a museum.
- To advance education in the arts by the establishment and maintenance of an art museum or art gallery.

Activities a charity for these purposes might be carrying out:

Please refer to the Charity Commission publication: [Museums and art galleries (RR10) (http://www.charitycommission.gov.uk/media/95113/rr10text.pdf)

FAMILY PLANNING

- To educate young people in matters of sex and contraception and to develop amongst them a sense of responsibility in regard to sexual behaviour with the aim of preventing and mitigating of the suffering caused by unwanted pregnancy.

-
    (i) To preserve and protect the good health both mental and physical of parents, young people and children and to prevent the financial hardship, caused by unwanted conception;
    (ii) to educate the public in the field of procreation, contraception, and health with particular reference to personal responsibility in sexual relationships and to the consequences of population growth;
    (iii) to give medical advice and assistance in cases of involuntary sterility or of difficulties connected with the marriage relationship or sexual problems for which medical advice or treatment is appropriate.

- To promote education and research in the subject of fertility and pregnancy and the termination of pregnancy and into its effects on women, whether physical, medical, psychological or social; to provide advice treatment and assistance for women who are suffering from any physical or mental illness or distress as a result of fertility or infertility.

Activities a charity for these purposes might be carrying out:

Direct help: advice, education and guidance about and access to various types of contraception or fertility treatment; Indirect: supporting academic research into the causes and effects of unwanted pregnancy or new methods of fertility treatment and publishing that research.

PROMOTION OF THE LAW, POLICE AND CRIME PREVENTION

- To facilitate the administration of the law by the promotion of arbitration, mediation and conciliation services to settle civil disputes in [stipulated area].

- To promote for the benefit of the public in the [insert place] and its neighbourhood with a view to the preservation of public order, the provision of services for mediation and conciliation between people, organisations and groups who are involved in disputes or interpersonal conflicts where that dispute or conflict results from or may lead to acts of nuisance, vandalism, racial abuse or breach of the peace.

- To promote for the benefit of the public in [insert place] the provision of services for mediation and conciliation between victims of crime and offenders, with a view to the preservation of public order, and for the preservation and protection of the well-being of such victims and the rehabilitation of such offenders.

- To promote, for the benefit of the public, the efficiency of the police in [insert area] and to promote good citizenship and greater public participation in the prevention and solution of crime in the area.

- To promote for the benefit of the public in [insert specified Division of named County Police Constabulary], in partnership with the police, the protection of people and property from, and the prevention of, criminal acts.

Activities a charity for these purposes might be carrying out:

Educational programmes in the community; promoting Neighbourhood Watch schemes; liaising with the police on addressing the causes of crime in the area; providing a conciliation service; providing advice and support to victims and offenders.

PROMOTION OF HUMAN RIGHTS

To promote human rights (as set out in the Universal Declaration of Human Rights and subsequent United Nations conventions and declarations) throughout the world by all or any of the following means:

- monitoring abuses of human rights;
- obtaining redress for the victims of human rights abuse;
- relieving need among the victims of human rights abuse;
- research into human rights issues;
- providing technical advice to government and others on human rights matters;
- contributing to the sound administration of human rights law;
- commenting on proposed human rights legislation;
- raising awareness of human rights issues;
- promoting public support for human rights;
- promoting respect for human rights among individuals and corporations;
- international advocacy of human rights;
- eliminating infringements of human rights.

In furtherance of that object but not otherwise, the trustees shall have power.

To engage in political activity provided that the trustees are satisfied that the proposed activities will further the purposes of the charity to an extent justified by the resources committed and the activity is not the dominant means by which the charity carried out its objects.

Activities a charity for these purposes might be carrying out:

Please refer to the Charity Commission publication: *The Promotion of Human Rights (RR12)*.

RACIAL HARMONY

The promotion of racial harmony for the public benefit by: (for example)

(a) promoting knowledge and mutual understanding between different racial groups;

(b) advancing education and raising awareness about different racial groups to promote good relations between persons of different racial groups;

(c) working towards the elimination of discrimination on the grounds of race.

RECREATIONAL CHARITIES ACT 1958

- To promote for the benefit of the inhabitants of [insert place] and the surrounding area the provision of facilities for recreation or other leisure time occupation of individuals who have need of such facilities by reason of their youth, age, infirmity or disablement, financial hardship or social and economic circumstances or for the public at large in the interests of social welfare and with the object of improving the condition of life of the said inhabitants.

- To provide or assist in the provision of facilities in the interests of social welfare for recreation or other leisure time occupation of individuals who have need of such facilities by reason of their youth, age infirmity or disability, financial hardship or social circumstances with the object of improving their conditions of life.

Activities a charity for these purposes might be carrying out:

Please refer to the Charity Commission publication: *The Recreational Charities Act 1958 (RR4)*.

RECYCLING

- The protection and preservation of the environment for the public benefit by: (for example)
  (a) the promotion of waste reduction, re-use reclamation, recycling, use of recycled products and the use of surplus;
  (b) advancing the education of the public about all aspects of waste generation, waste management and waste recycling.
- The relief of financial hardship by the recycling and provision of furniture, clothes and other household items.

REFUGEES / THOSE SEEKING ASYLUM

- To advance education and relieve financial hardship amongst those seeking asylum and those granted refugee status particularly by the provision of legal and other advice.
- The relief of financial hardship amongst those granted refugee status and their dependants living (temporarily or permanently) in [...] and the surrounding area.
- To preserve and protect the physical and mental health of those granted refugee status and their dependants.
- To advance the education and training of those granted refugee status and their dependants in need thereof so as to advance them in life and assist them to adapt within a new community.
- To advance the education of the public in general about the issues relating to refugees and those seeking asylum.
- The provision of facilities for recreation or other leisure time occupation with the object of improving the conditions of life of those persons who have need of such facilities by reason of their youth, age, infirmity or disablement, financial hardship or social and economic circumstances.
- The relief of sickness and financial hardship amongst those seeking asylum in the United Kingdom or who are refugees, and who reside in [insert area of benefit].
- The relief of unemployment of those granted refugee status and those seeking asylum in the United Kingdom, and in particular [insert area of benefit], by the provision of vocational and skills training, advice and support.

Activities a charity for these purposes might be carrying out:

Training in basic skills to help find work; general education including language skills; temporary accommodation; access to leisure facilities to facilitate integration and understanding within the wider community.

RELIEF OF FINANCIAL HARDSHIP

- The relief of financial hardship among people living or working in [stipulated area] [by providing such persons with [goods/services] which they could not otherwise afford through lack of means].
- The relief of financial hardship, either generally or individually, of people living in [the area of benefit] by making grants of money for providing or paying for items services or facilities.
- The relief of the sick-poor living in [insert place] either generally or individually through the provision of grants, goods or services.

RELIEF OF POVERTY

- The prevention or relief of poverty in [insert geographical area of operation] by providing: grants, items and services to individuals in need and/or charities, or other organisations working to prevent or relieve poverty.
- To relieve poverty [or financial hardship] among refugees, asylum seekers, migrant workers and their dependants living in [insert geographical area] by providing interpreting/translating/advocacy/ health/housing advice and education.
- The prevention or relief of poverty [or financial hardship] anywhere in the world by providing or assisting in the provision of education, training, healthcare projects and all the necessary support designed to enable individuals to generate a sustainable income and be self-sufficient.
- To prevent or relieve poverty through undertaking and supporting research into factors that contribute to poverty and the most appropriate ways to mitigate these.
- To prevent or relieve poverty by awarding a 'fair trade mark' to products, the sale of which relieves the poverty of producers by ensuring they receive at least a fair price for their goods and advising such producers of the best ways in which to engage in the trading process.
- To relieve the poverty of young people by the provision of grants to enable them to participate in healthy recreational activities that they could not otherwise afford.

Please refer to the Charity Commission publication: *The Prevention or Relief of Poverty for the Public Benefit.*

RELIEF OF SICKNESS

- The relief of sickness and the preservation of health among people residing permanently or temporarily in [specified area of benefit].

- To assist in the treatment and care of persons suffering from mental or physical illness of any description or in need of rehabilitation as a result of such illness, by the provision of facilities for work and recreation.

- To promote and protect the physical and mental health of sufferers of [insert medical condition] in [insert area of benefit] through the provision of financial assistance, support, education and practical advice.

- To advance the education of the general public in all areas relating to [insert medical condition].

- To relieve sickness, poor health and old age amongst people living in [stipulated area] by providing a local broadcasting service for hospitals, residential homes and similar institutions.

- To relieve sickness and to preserve the health of the patients of [name of surgery] at [place] by providing or assisting in the provision of equipment, facilities and services [[not normally provided by the statutory authorities] [ancillary to those provided by the doctors]].

- To preserve and protect the health of patients of the [description of medical practice] by providing and assisting in the provision of facilities, support services and equipment not normally provided by the statutory authorities. To advance the education of the public in health care by the provision of lectures, and by the publication of newsletters devoted to healthcare.

RELIEF OF UNEMPLOYMENT

- The relief of unemployment for the benefit of the public in such ways as may be thought fit, including assistance to find employment.

Activities a charity for these purposes might be carrying out:

Please refer to the Charity Commission publication: *Charities for the Relief of Unemployment (RR3)*.

RELIGIOUS HARMONY

- The promotion of religious harmony for the benefit of the public by: [for example]
  (a) educating the public in different religious beliefs including an awareness of their distinctive features and their common ground to promote good relations between persons of different faiths;
  (b) promoting knowledge and mutual understanding and respect of the beliefs and practices of different religious faiths.

SOCIAL INCLUSION

- To promote social inclusion for the public benefit by preventing people from becoming socially excluded, relieving the needs of those people who are socially excluded and assisting them to integrate into society.

    For the purpose of this clause 'socially excluded' means being excluded from society, or parts of society, as a result of one of more of the following factors: unemployment; financial hardship; youth or old age; ill health (physical or mental); substance abuse or dependency including alcohol and drugs; discrimination on the grounds of sex, race, disability, ethnic origin, religion, belief, creed, sexual orientation or gender re-assignment; poor educational or skills attainment; relationship and family breakdown; poor housing (that is housing that does not meet basic habitable standards; crime (either as a victim of crime or as an offender rehabilitating into society).

- To promote social inclusion for the public benefit by preventing people from becoming socially excluded, relieving the needs of those people who are socially excluded and assisting them to integrate into society.

    Being excluded from society, or part of society, as a result of being a member of a socially and economically deprived community.

- To promote social inclusion for the public benefit by working with people in (insert geographical area of operation) who are socially excluded on the grounds of their ethnic origin, religion, belief or creed (in particular, members of the Muslim community) to relieve the needs of such people and assist them to integrate into society, in particular by:
    1. providing a local network group that encourages and enables members of the Muslim community to participate more effectively with the wider community;
    2. increasing, or co-ordinating, opportunities for members of the Muslim community to engage with service providers, to enable those providers to adapt services to better meet the needs of that community.

- The promotion of social inclusion for the public benefit amongst people between the ages of 16 to 30 who are socially excluded by providing them with an opportunity to build capacity by establishing and growing a business to relieve the needs of those people and assist them to integrate into society.

    (For the purposes of this clause 'socially excluded' means 'young people between the ages of 16 to 30 years of age who are excluded from society, or parts of society, as a result of one or more of the following factors: unemployment; financial hardship; race; gender; poor educational or skills attainment; disability; ethnic origin; or who are within, or have experienced, the public care or penal system').

- The promotion of social inclusion among deaf parents and their children who are socially excluded from society, or parts of society, as a result of being deaf by:
    1. providing education and information to support and enable deaf parents to maximise educational opportunities for their children;

2. raising public awareness of the issues affecting deaf parents and their children, both generally and in relation to their social exclusion;
3. providing workshops, forums, advocacy and general support;
4. providing recreational facilities and opportunities for deaf and hearing people.

- The promotion of social inclusion among elderly persons who are excluded from society because they are house-bound, or who are unable to drive or easily access public transport, by the provision of:
  1. a transport service to and from recreational and public services;
  2. outings and social trips including transport to and from home;
  3. information technology at home to enable them to access the internet.

- The promotion of social inclusion among single parents and their children, who are excluded from society, or parts of society, due to their social and economic position by the provision of a crèche, play scheme and drop in support and education centre to enable single parents and their children to develop and gain new skills.

- The promotion of social inclusion for the public benefit among people who are refugees and asylum seekers who are socially excluded on the grounds of their social and economic position, by providing:
  1. education and training in the English language and in vocational skills;
  2. social and recreational facilities and events involving the local community.

Please refer to the Charity Commission publication: *The Promotion of Social Inclusion*.

SUSTAINABLE DEVELOPMENT

- To promote sustainable development for the benefit of the public by: [include as applicable]
  (a) the preservation, conservation and the protection of the environment and the prudent use of resources;
  (b) the relief of poverty and the improvement of the conditions of life in socially and economically disadvantaged communities;
  (c) the promotion of sustainable means of achieving economic growth and regeneration.
- To advance the education of the public in subjects relating to sustainable development and the protection, enhancement and rehabilitation of the environment and to promote study and research in such subjects provided that the useful results of such study are disseminated to the public at large.

The following definition should always be included:

Sustainable development means 'development which meets the needs of the present without compromising the ability of future generations to meet their own needs.'

Activities a charity for these purposes might be carrying out:

Please refer to the Decision of the Charity Commissioners made on 24 January 2003 in respect of the application for registration of The Environment Foundation.

URBAN OR RURAL REGENERATION

(NB: you must select at least 3 from sub-clauses (a)–(m))

- The promotion for the benefit of the public of urban or rural regeneration in areas of social and economic deprivation (and in particular in [specify area]) by all or any of the following means:
    (a) the relief of financial hardship;
    (b) the relief of unemployment;
    (c) the advancement of education, training or retraining, particularly among unemployed people, and providing unemployed people with work experience;
    (d) the provision of financial assistance, technical assistance or business advice or consultancy in order to provide training and employment opportunities for unemployed people in cases of financial or other charitable need through help: (i) in setting up their own business, or (ii) to existing businesses;
    (e) the creation of training and employment opportunities by the provision of workspace, buildings, and/or land for use on favourable terms;
    (f) the provision of housing for those who are in conditions of need and the improvement of housing in the public sector or in charitable ownership provided that such power shall not extend to relieving any local authorities or other bodies of a statutory duty to provide or improve housing;
    (g) the maintenance, improvement or provision of public amenities;
    (h) the preservation of buildings or sites of historic or architectural importance;
    (i) he provision of recreational facilities for the public at large or those who by reason of their youth, age, infirmity or disablement, financial hardship or social and economic circumstances, have need of such facilities;
    (j) the protection or conservation of the environment;
    (k) the provision of public health facilities and childcare;
    (l) the promotion of public safety and prevention of crime;
    (m) such other means as may from time to time be determined subject to the prior written consent of the Charity Commissioners for England and Wales.

Activities a charity for these purposes might be carrying out:

Please refer to the Charity Commission publication: *Promotion of Rural and Urban Regeneration (RR2)*.

VILLAGE HALLS

The provision and maintenance of a village hall for the use of the inhabitants of [area of benefit] without distinction of political, religious or other opinions, including use for:

(a) meetings, lectures and classes, and

(b) other forms of recreation and leisure-time occupation, with the object of improving the conditions of life for the inhabitants.

Activities a charity for these purposes might be carrying out:

Please refer to the Charity Commission publication: *Village Halls and Community Centres (RS9)RS9a*.

YOUNG PEOPLE

- To advance in life and [relieve needs of] [help] young people through:
  (a) The provision of recreational and leisure time activities provided in the interest of social welfare, designed to improve their conditions of life;
  (b) Providing support and activities which develop their skills, capacities and capabilities to enable them to participate in society as mature and responsible individuals.
- To help young people, especially but not exclusively through leisure time activities, so as to develop their capabilities that they may grow to full maturity as individuals and members of society.
- To act as a resource for young people up to the age of [age] living in [area of benefit] by providing advice and assistance and organising programmes of physical, educational and other activities as a means of:
  (a) advancing in life and helping young people by developing their skills, capacities and capabilities to enable them to participate in society as independent, mature and responsible individuals;
  (b) advancing education;
  (c) relieving unemployment;
  (d) providing recreational and leisure time activity in the interests of social welfare for people living in the area of benefit who have need by reason of their youth, age, infirmity or disability, poverty or social and economic circumstances with a view to improving the conditions of life of such persons.

APPENDIX H

MODEL ANNUAL REPORT FOR AN UNINCORPORATED CHARITY

Reproduced with the kind permission of the Charity Commission
https://www.gov.uk/government/uploads/system/uploads/attachment_data/file/350991/arwbyc.pdf

Commentary on the model Trustees' Annual Report and accounts: Westbeach Youth Club

This example is for a charity preparing receipts and payments accounts.

The youth club charity had an income of £47,476 in the year and is eligible for independent examination. As the charity is below the audit threshold it may also prepare a simple annual report (refer to CC15a Charity Reporting and Accounting: The essentials and the Charities (Accounts and Reports) Regulations 2008). An example report by the charity's the independent examiner (see 'CC32- Independent Examination of Charity Accounts' for further examples of examiner's reports) is also included.

Reporting Public Benefit

This example also addresses the new public benefit reporting requirements that applies to all charities reporting for financial years beginning on or after 1 April 2008. As a small charity, below the Charities Act's audit threshold, the report focuses on the main activities undertaken by the charity to further its charitable purposes for the public benefit. The **'Summary of the main activities undertaken'** provides a brief summary of activities undertaken together with a confirmation that the trustees have had regard to our guidance on public benefit when planning the charity's activities. Further information about the success of these activities is provided in a **'Summary of the main achievements'**.

The annual report also addresses the two key principles by which we will assess public benefit:

> 1) There must be an identifiable benefit or benefits – the trustees explaining the value to the young people of the charity's work.
> 2) Benefit must be to the public, or a section of the public – the trustees explaining that any young person aged 11 to 18 is eligible to benefit from the charity's activities.

The Pro forma CC16b Trustees' Annual Report

Trustees do not have to use the pro forma to write their annual report but the form includes all the information trustees must provide and gives an opportunity to provide further optional information if the trustees so wish.

In this example additional voluntary information is provided about the contribution made by volunteers, collaboration with other organisations and details of the charity's main policies and future plans. In addition, the report confirms that the trustees received no remuneration or other benefits from the charity. We do recommend that information is provided about any remuneration or other benefits received by the trustees either directly or though arrangements entered into with related parties. This information can be disclosed by way of a note, or in the trustees' annual report.

The accounts CC16a pro forma (in original form as a separate excel document)

The accounts pro forma is suitable for comparatively straight forward accounts. Before using the pro forma please read the completion notes. We also recommend that a bank reconciliation is prepared to reconcile the closing balance at bank before completing the form. Also charities with several restricted funds or more complex affairs may need to summarise their information before using the pro forma or alternatively use it as a tool to assist in the design of their own accounts.

In the example gift aid recovered from HM Revenue and Customs is shown separately. The charity has a small restricted fund, called the Youth Aid Appeal, associated with the awards scheme and has undertaken fundraising, the proceeds of which were restricted for the awards only. The acquisition of functional fixed assets is shown separately on row A4.

The statement of assets and liabilities includes cash at bank and also identifies an outstanding gift aid claim relating to the year which was not received by the 31st December 2009. Similarly there is an invoice from PC Services which has not been paid relating to work undertaken prior to the year end.

The minibus, office and computer equipment are listed under the section 'assets retained for the charity's own use' and the trustees have provided voluntary information about their estimate of the residual value of the minibus.

Model Annual Report for an Unincorporated Charity 253

Trustees' annual report for the period

From	Period start date			To	Period end date		
	Day 01	Month 01	Year 2009		Day 31	Month 12	Year 2009

Reference and administration details

Charity name	Westbeach Youth Club
Other names charity is known by	WYC
Registered charity number (if any)	999xx9
Charity's principal address	Room 5
	Westbeach, Community Centre
	Westbeach, Seatown
Postcode	ST11 2ZZ

Names of the charity trustees who manage the charity

	Trustee name	Office (if any)	Dates acted if not for whole year	Name of person (or body) entitled to appoint trustee (if any)
1	Janet West	Chair		
2	Frank Doyle			
3	Robert Cox	Fundraising Secretary		
4	Suzan Rich		From 1 January until 18 July 2009	
5	Judith Rich		From 18 July 2009	
6				
7				
8				
9				
10				
11				
12				
13				
14				
15				
16				
17				

Names of the trustees for the charity, if any, (for example, any custodian trustees)

Name	Dates acted if not for whole year

Names and addresses of advisors (Optional information)

Type of advisor	Name	Address
Bank	Our Bank PLC	210 High Street, Seatown, ST1 4AB

Name of chief executive or names of senior staff members (Optional information)

Part time youth workers Andrew Able and Sophie Dancer

Structure, governance and management

Description of the charity's trusts

Type of governing document (eg. trust deed, constitution)	Constitution adopted 4th March 2000
How the charity is constituted (eg. trust, association, company)	Association consisting of 40 members
Trustee selection methods (eg. appointed by, elected by)	Trustees are appointed or reappointed annually at the Annual General Meeting held in July

Additional governance issues (Optional information)

You **may choose** to include additional information, where relevant, about: • Policies and procedures adopted for the induction and training of trustees • The charity's organisational structure and any wider network with which the charity works • Relationship with any related parties • Trustees' consideration of major risks and the system and procedures to manage them	There is a child protection policy in place. Criminal Records Bureau checks are carried out prior to commencement of employment or trusteeship. These checks are carried out again every two years in line with statutory requirements. WYC is a member of Youth Clubs of Great Britain confederation which provides helpful advice and opportunities for joint programmes. WYC is also partnered with the community association with whom we jointly undertake the summer activity programme and from whom we rent the rooms for the IT suite and Junior and Senior club activities. All trustees give their time voluntary and received no remuneration or other benefits.

Model Annual Report for an Unincorporated Charity

Objectives and activities

Summary of the objects of the charity set out in its governing document	*To advance the mental, physical and spiritual welfare of Young People by promoting a scheme of awards and their personal development.*
Summary of the main activities undertaken for the public benefit in relation to these objects	*In planning our activities for the year we kept in mind the Charity Commission's guidance on public benefit at our trustee meetings.* *The focus of our activities remains the Duke of Edinburgh awards scheme, the design of personal development plans and a programme of youth orientated events and activities. This benefits young people by developing their self-confidence and social skills alongside practical IT skills and life skills. We welcome all young people regardless of personal background, faith, gender or personal circumstances and we believe this philosophy of openness to all enriches everyone through the sharing of the skills, aptitudes and life experiences of our young people aged 11 to 18 and volunteers.*

Additional details of objectives and activities (Optional information)

You **may choose** to include further statements, where relevant, about: • Policy on grantmaking • Policy programme related investment • Contribution made by Volunteers	*A great contribution is made by member volunteers. We are grateful for the many hours volunteers have spent listening and encouraging our young people and working with our youth workers. Without this valuable contribution of time, energy and expertise we would not have been able to achieve so much.* *Any surplus funds which are not likely to be needed to pay for activities are placed on deposit to earn interest.*

Achievements and performance

Summary of the main achievements of the charity during the year.

Spring
The new Monday Junior and Senior Clubs were in full swing with much enjoyment from the play station, pool table, games music and table tennis. The Wednesday Duke of Edinburgh group began map work, cycling and training for the great adventure of their expeditions. The Tuesday, Wednesday and Thursday Junior sections met regularly for games and training. Following the purchase of the second hand minibus in 2008, WYC has undertaken a broader range of activities and at Easter there was great excitement as Dartmoor appeared out of the mist on the road up from Yelverton as we headed out on a field trip.

Summer
The next event was the 'do it yourself' Cotswolds long weekend cycle event. This was followed by more training and map work. The Duke of Edinburgh group went windsurfing in Cornwall, with a visit to a Tin Mine and to Lands End. Quality Camping skills were much in evidence.

Autumn
The half term event was a success. Training in map work was carried out with great dedication from all those involved. The Silver and Gold group passed with flying colours.

Extras
The keyboard tuition classes have been attended by over a dozen members who have shown a great interest and are now looking into other instruments.
Following the purchase this year of new computer equipment, the IT suite is now upgraded to the new Windows product suite with 12 operational computers, and a qualified lecturer. The local Council has agreed in principle to renew funding for a further 3 years.

Fundraising
A member suggested a charity car wash, where she and others raised hundreds of pounds for club funds. Tombola, Raffles, jumble Sales have also produced small but useful sums for funds. Local businesses donated office furniture.

Financial review

Brief statement of the charity's policy on reserves	We hold cash at bank of £12,000, all of which is unrestricted funds. These funds are held in order to meet any unforeseen expenditure that may occur, for example vehicle repairs. We aim to hold at least £10,000 and no more than £15,000 in reserves at the year end.
Details of any funds materially in deficit	Not applicable

Further financial review details: (Optional information)

You **may choose** to include additional information, where relevant about: • The charity's principal sources of funds (including any fundraising). • How expenditure has supported the key objectives of the charity. • Investment policy and objectives including any ethical investment policy adopted.	Our main source of funds this year has been grant funding and entrance fees for participants in the award programme. We hold a small fund to help families who would otherwise struggle to meet the cost of entrance fees. We rely on the local community and our local council for their continuing support. Seatown District Council provided a further grant of £20,000 towards the running costs the charity. The majority of income is applied to the awards and clubs related activity. With the main costs incurred being, award entrance fees, Staff costs and transport costs We try to keep staff costs down by employing seasonal staff.

Other optional information

<u>Future Plans</u>
The coming year will see a continued emphasis on the use of the Duke of Edinburgh Awards and other structured activities to build and deepen the confidence and capability of our young people.

Declaration

The trustees declare that they have approved the trustees' report above.

Signed on behalf of the charity's trustees

Signature(s)	J West	
Full name(s)	Janet West	
Position (eg secretary, chair, etc)	Chair	
Date	31st January 2010	

Independent examiner's report on the accounts

Report to the trustees/ members of	Charity Name: *Westbeach Youth Club*
On accounts for the year ended	*31st December 2009*
Set out on pages	*9 and 10*
Respective responsibilities of trustees and examiner	The charity's trustees consider that an audit is not required for this year (under section 43(2) of the Charities Act 1993 (the Act)) and that an independent examination is needed. It is my responsibility to • examine the accounts (under section 43 of the Act), • to follow the procedures laid down in the General Directions given by the Charity Commission (under section 43(7)(b) of the Act), and • to state whether particular matters have come to my attention.
Basis of independent examiner's report	My examination was carried out in accordance with General Directions given by the Charity Commission. An examination includes a review of the accounting records kept by the charity and a comparison of the accounts presented with those records. It also includes consideration of any unusual items or disclosures in the accounts, and seeking explanations from you as trustees concerning any such matters. The procedures undertaken do not provide all the evidence that would be required in an audit, and consequently no opinion is given as to whether the accounts present a 'true and fair' view and the report is limited to those matters set out in the statement below.
Independent examiner's statement	In the course of my examination, no matter has come to my attention 1. which gives me reasonable cause to believe that in, any material respect, the requirements: • to keep accounting records in accordance with section 41 of the Act; and • to prepare accounts which accord with the accounting records and comply with the accounting requirements of the 1993 Act; have not been met; or 2. to which, in my opinion, attention should be drawn in order to enable a proper understanding of the accounts to be reached.
Signed: *Eric Scrivner*	Date: April 4th 2011
Name:	Eric Scrivner
Relevant professional qualification(s) or body (if any):	
Address:	*124 Home Farm Street* *Little Town* *Middleshire, QQ1 4MP*

Model Annual Report for an Unincorporated Charity

Disclosure section

Only complete if the examiner needs to highlight material problems.

Give here brief details of any items that the examiner wishes to disclose.

None to report

Charity Name	No (if any)
Westbeach Youth Club	999xx9

Receipts and payments accounts

CC16a

for the period	Period start date	To	Period end date
	01/01/2009		31/12/2009

Charity Name

Section A Receipts and payments

	Unrestricted funds to the nearest £	Restricted funds to the nearest £	Endowment funds to the nearest £	Total funds to the nearest £	Last year to the nearest £
A1 Receipts					
Grants & Donations	36,250	-	-	36,250	35,255
Membership subscriptions	1,090	-	-	1,090	979
Fundraising: 'Youth Aid' Appeal	-	677	-	677	1,528
Award and Activity entrance fees	5,531	-	-	5,531	11,419
Interest	378	-	-	378	352
Gift aid receipts	3,550	-	-	3,550	4,014
Sub total	46,799	677	-	47,476	53,547
A2 Asset and investment sales, etc.	-	-	-	-	
Total receipts	46,799	677	-	47,476	53,547
A3 Payments					
Awards and Activity Costs	13,342	777	-	14,119	12,847
Room Hire	1,709		-	1,709	1,359
Minibus expenses	4,182	-	-	4,182	8,759
Training/Affiliation	609	-	-	609	762
Staff Remuneration	9,905	-	-	9,905	8,250
Insurance	1,309	-	-	1,309	1,252
New Garden Project	-	-	-	-	5,624
Administration	1,726	-	-	1,726	1,126
Norlands Loft Activity Centre hire	-	-	-	-	4,375
Sub total	32,782	777	-	33,559	44,354

A4 Asset and investment purchases, etc.	4,784	-	-	4,784	10,500
Total payments	37,566	777	-	38,343	54,854
Net of receipts/(payments)	9,233	(100)	-	9,133	(1,307)
A5 Transfers Between Funds	-	-	-	-	-
A6 Cash funds last year end	2,767	100	-	2,867	4,174
Cash funds this year end	12,000	-	-	12,000	2,867

Section B Statement of assets and liabilities at the end of the period

Categories	Details	Unrestricted funds to nearest £	Restricted funds to nearest £	Endowment funds to nearest £
B1 Cash funds	*Cash at Bank*	12,000	-	
		-	-	
	Total cash funds (agree balances with receipts and payments account(s))	12,000	-	
B2 Other monetary assets	*Final gift aid claim*	726	-	
		-	-	

		Fund to which asset belongs	Cost (optional)	Current value (optional)
B3 Investment assets			-	
			-	

		Fund to which asset belongs	Cost (optional)	Current value (optional)
B4 Assets retained for the charity's own use			-	
	Minibus	*Unrestricted*	-	8,350
	Donated office furniture	*Unrestricted*		
	Computer Equipment	*Unrestricted*	-	

		Fund to which liability relates	Amount due (optional)	When due (optional)
B5 Liabilities	*PC Services invoice due*	*Unrestricted*	529	
			-	

APPENDIX I

MODEL ANNUAL REPORT FOR A LARGER CHARITABLE COMPANY

Reproduced with the kind permission of the Charity Commission https://www.gov.uk/government/uploads/system/uploads/attachment_data/file/350985/arddacpb.pdf

Commentary on the model Trustees' Annual Report and accounts: Dorsetshire Drugs Advice Centre

This example is for a company limited by guarantee that provides drugs rehabilitation and prevention programmes. Its activities include operating a café and a charity shop. The company has to comply with the Companies Act 1985 (the accounting provisions of the Companies Act 2006 applying to period starting on or after 6 April 2008), the SORP and new public benefit reporting requirements. The majority of its funding is received from the County Council and the local Primary Care Trust.

The charity meets the Companies Act 1985 definition of a small company and does not exceed the Companies Act 1985 audit threshold. The trustees, in this example, may therefore claim exemption from an audit under subsection (1) of section 249A of the Companies Act 1985 provided the audit exemption statement required by 249B (4) is made on the balance sheet. However, if exemption is claimed from an audit under the Companies Act then an audit of the charity's accounts will be required under the Charities Act 1993. The trustees, in this example, have therefore chosen not to claim audit exemption under the Companies Act and therefore no audit exemption statement is provided on the balance sheet. The accounts are therefore audited the Companies Act 1985 and no audit is then required under the Charities Act 1993. Auditors can find further guidance on the format of charity audit reports on the Auditing Practices Boards website - www.frc.org.uk/apb/publications/pub1891.html

The Trustees' Annual Report

The report does not follow the order set out in the SORP and demonstrates how the order of presentation of the annual report can be varied. Paragraph headings continue to highlighting each key disclosure required by the SORP, including trustee induction and training.

The annual report has been updated for new public benefit reporting requirements. In particular, the report explains how the trustees have used our public benefit guidance and explains in more detail which groups used and benefited from the charities services.

The report includes a *risk management statement* which also refers to compliance with the applicable national standards. The charity's objects, aim, strategy and major activities undertaken are summarised in the *objectives and activities* section. The *achievements and performance* section provides a detailed information about the nature of the activities undertaken, including performance information, for each of the main areas of charitable activity. These areas of charitable activity map to note 4 to the accounts.

Note the *reserves policy* includes an explanation of the target level of reserves, the reserves held, and the charity's plans to increase its reserves (paragraph 55).

The report concludes with a statement of trustees' responsibilities in relation to the financial statements which has been included in accordance with APB Audit Standards, although this statement is not a requirement of the SORP. The example is amended to include the disclosure of information to auditors.

Business Review

Where the charity does not qualify as a small company, the trustees should, when preparing a combined Trustees' and company charity Director's annual report (SORP paragraph 40), ensure that the report covers the mandatory disclosures required for the Business Review section of that report.

The Accounts

The Statement of Financial Activities reports the charitable activities as single line with an expanded analysis in note 4 to the accounts (paragraph 89).

Governance costs and support costs and their allocation is analysed in note 4.

On the face of the balance sheet, the types of fund are disclosed including designated funds with the revaluation fund shown separately, as required by Company Law.

dorsetshire
drugs advice centre

Dorsetshire Drugs Advice Centre
(A company limited by guarantee)

**Report and Financial Statements
For the Year Ended 31 March 2009**

**Charity number 1253687
Company number 1032145**

Dorsetshire Drugs Advice Centre
(A company limited by guarantee)

Financial Statements
For the Year Ended 31 March 2009

Contents	Page
Legal and Administrative Information	
Report of the Management Committee	
Statement of Financial Activities	
Balance Sheet	
Notes forming part of the financial statements	

Model Annual Report for a Larger Charitable Company

Dorsetshire Drugs Advice Centre
Report of the Management Committee for the year ended 31 March 2009

The Management Committee presents its directors' report and audited financial statements for the year ended 31 March 2009.

Reference and Administrative Information

Charity Name:	Dorsetshire Drugs Advice Centre
Charity registration number:	1253687
Company registration number:	1032145
Registered Office and operational address:	10 High Street, Dorchester, Dorsetshire. BA1 6PR

Management Committee

Mr P Smith	Chair	
Mrs L Jones	Vice Chair	
Mrs M Haliwell	Treasurer	
PC N Francis		
Mr J Blackmore		
Mrs S Thorne	(resigned 24 September 2008)	
Mr T Forester	(resigned 11 November 2008)	
Mr G Peterson	(appointed 22 October 2008)	
Miss C Snow		

Secretary

Miss L Gupta

Senior Management Team

Mrs V Hunter	Chief Executive
Mr R Snick	Services Manager
Mrs C Cash	Finance and Administration Manager

Auditors - Risk & Co, 10 Poole Street, Dorchester, Dorsetshire BA2 1CE

Bankers - Petty Cash, 33 Wimborne Street, Dorchester, Dorsetshire, BA2 7PC

Solicitors - Ivor Deed & Co, 26 Chesil Road, Dorchester, Dorsetshire B22 1L

Our Aims and objectives

Purposes and Aims

Our charity's purposes as set out in the objects contained in the company's memorandum of association are to:

- benefit the public by promoting the prevention of drug misuse, and
- to treat those suffering from drugs misuse within the area covered by Dorsetshire.

The aims of our charity are to reduce the levels of drug dependency within the county and to educate young people about the risks involved in the use of recreational drugs. Our aims fully reflect the purposes that the charity was set up to further.

Ensuring our work delivers our aims

We review our aims, objectives and activities each year. This review looks at what we achieved and the outcomes of our work in the previous 12 months. The review looks at the success of each key activity and the benefits they have brought to those groups of people we are set up to help. The review also helps us ensure our aim, objectives and activities remained focused on our stated purposes. We have referred to the guidance contained in the Charity Commission's general guidance on public benefit when reviewing our aim and objectives and in planning our future activities. In particular, the trustees consider how planned activities will contribute to the aims and objectives they have set.

The focus of our work

Our main objectives for the year continued to be the promotion and prevention of the misuse of drugs and the rehabilitation of those drug users. The strategies we used to meet these objectives included:

- Providing a range of services which are reflective of relevant quality standards and address the potential problems related to drug misuse.
- Focussing upon limiting the harm which comes with drug abuse, not only for the individual but also their family and friends and the wider community of Dorsetshire.
- Working towards applying national standards of service and the implementation of the National Occupational Standards.
- Working in partnership with other agencies to secure the widest range of services is available that best matches the needs of its client population.

How our activities deliver public benefit

Our main activities and who we try to help are described below. All our charitable activities focus on the prevention and treatment of drug abuse and are undertaken to further our charitable purposes for the public benefit.

Who used and benefited from our services?

Our objects and funding limit the services we provide to those resident in Dorsetshire. The number of Problematic Drug Users in Dorsetshire is estimated at some 2700 (0.8% of total population) and the number of people accessing Structured Treatment across Dorset is estimated at

dorsetshire
drugs advice centre

approximately1250. Our funding limits those we can help, for example, our counselling service can only deal with 50 individual clients at any time. Demand for our services is limited by giving priority to referrals from medical and social services sources and is also based an initial assessment of an individual's personal commitment to seeking help. All our services are provided free to our clients.

Equal access to our services is an important issue for us. In addition to our current monitoring of access to our services by gender, disability and sexual orientation next year will see the publication of our first ethnicity monitoring study. We are aware from a baseline study undertaken this year, using data available on the Neighbourhood Statistics website, that Black and minority ethic communities are disproportionately represented in deprived areas of our county. We believe equal access to our services is vital to our success and that successful outcomes must be shared by all communities that use our services.

The peak age for injecting drug users is late 20's with arrests peaking in the 20-25 year age group. It is estimated that males represent 72 per cent of drug users. Our monitoring suggests those that we are able to help broadly reflect these statistics. Our information services are targeted at those between the ages 15 and 30 who are regarded as the age group primarily at risk and represent 18 per cent of Dorsetshire's population. Further information about who benefits directly from our services is explained in the analysis of performance and achievements below.

However, the impact of our work goes far beyond those we help directly and includes reducing the distress suffered by the families and friends of users through to impact on crime where it is estimated that in Dorsetshire up to 40 per cent of crime is drug related.

Some areas of our work, for example the needle exchange programme, gave rise to some local concern last year. Our active liaison with local community group and with local councillors has helped significantly in reducing these concerns and has created better local understanding of our work.

The main areas of charitable activity are the provision of counselling, advice and information; outreach work; and the operation of a café as a training project for former drugs users. These activities and the achievements that flow from our work are described below.

Counselling, Advice and Information

The Counselling, Advice and Information (CAI) project is based at the central office and provides help and advice to drug users, teachers, social workers and others wanting to know more about the effects of drug use. Funding for the CAI project is primarily provided by the Dorsetshire County Council and is sufficient to employ 4 members of staff. The mainstay of our service remains our volunteers who provide advice and distribute information leaflets. In the year under review over 2,000 volunteer hours were donated.

We produced two new leaflets on cocaine use and the dangers of ecstasy in addition to the existing leaflets on cannabis, amphetamines, substance abuse and tranquiliser abuse. Leaflets are made available in doctors' surgeries, Dorsetshire Royal Infirmary, the Citizens' Advice Bureau, the Magistrates' Courts and Probation and Youth Offending Services offices. Feedback from Doctor's surgeries, teachers and social workers is that the plain English style has helped in both giving advice and stimulating conversation and debate. Only through understanding can those at risk and the vulnerable realise the dangers and avoid the pitfalls. Over 5,000 leaflets were distributed in the year.

Individual advice is provided at drop-in times and also by special appointment. Some 220 people regularly used the drop in service during the year with over 1200 individual counselling sessions being held. In addition to breaking social exclusion and stigma, we aim to provide a friendly face and a sympathetic ear. We were able to help in a variety of tangible ways and where appropriate can also arrange referrals to our partners where assistance is needed in relation to housing, debt, or social service related issues. Often drug abuse leads to a life apart from society with associated

dorsetshire
drugs advice centre

problems of depression, crime and poverty. We are pleased that by working with our partners we can offer a holistic approach to the problems arising from drug abuse. Our counselling service is partly funded by Dorsetshire Primary Care Trust on the basis of a performance related grant which is restricted to our counselling work.

As a result of the advice service, a parents' support group has been set up on the Dorchester Green Estate. Over 40 families are currently involved in this project and the demand continues to grow. In addition to providing information, with some 600 leaflets distributed, the group is an opportunity for parents to share experiences and learn about how best to connect with their children. This sharing has reduced the sense of hopelessness and all the families have been able to talk openly with their children in a supported environment. Although success in stopping abuse to date has been limited, 25 children have agreed to undergo treatment or seek medical advice for a variety of drug abuse problems as a result of this work.

The receipt of a donation from the Berrow Estate Charitable Trust, specifically to assist in the provision of counselling services has enabled the purchase of a new computer and database software to be used to organise information and make it more easily accessible for volunteer counsellors.

Outreach

The outreach work of the charity provides support to young people who are vulnerable or falling into drug misuse. This work continued to expand in the year under review. At the beginning of the year, we had set a target to reach 150 young people and to make our other services available to them. Although due to difficulties in recruiting staff our target could not be reached, we were nevertheless able to directly help 118 young people through our programme during the year. Our strategy is to complement the social services and youth worker roles by providing specific staff trained in recognising and talking to young people suffering a drug problem. By a mixture of personal approaches, referrals and partnership working we hope to create the trust needed for children and young people abusing drugs to talk about their problem and seek help without feeling that they are being blamed, or at risk of prosecution. By explaining the services available to them and by developing support networks of former drug abusers we hope to change and rescue lives from the misery of drug abuse.

The outreach service also runs a health clinic including a needle exchange programme and the provision of laundrette facilities. Infection, including HIV, is a significant health issue. By providing clean needles and a laundrette, we reduce the likelihood of infection and avoid the risk of shared needles. Over 6000 needles were issued and collected in the period.

We continue to work in close co-operation with Dorsetshire County Council Social Services department in operating this outreach project. We are grateful for their support. Again, the grant funding received is restricted specifically to this project.

The training project continues to be focused on the operation of the café and drop in centre. This enterprise was initially funded through a contract with Dorsetshire County Council but is now self-funding. The café continues to provide a bright and cheerful atmosphere and hosts all sorts of activities, including art exhibitions, jazz evenings and other theme evenings.

The café has a paid manager and is staffed primarily by former drug users. The disruption to life caused by prolonged abuse often destroys a person's self esteem and life skills and coupled with the stigma of being a former addict, it is often difficult for former drug users to gain employment. The danger is that by being socially disadvantaged coupled with poverty and poor housing, the temptation to relapse into substance abuse and crime is great. The café enables people to regain their life skills and provides a stepping off point into the world of work. To date 12 people have found new work after a spell in the café.

Financial Review

Against the backdrop of limited resources and insecurities over funding, it has continued to be difficult to plan or develop services. Nevertheless the charity, with the aid of sound financial management and the support of both its staff and volunteers generated a very positive financial outcome for the period with a net increase in funds of just over £54,000. Its success in obtaining new funding for 2009/10 from the Dorsetshire Probation Service and Youth Offending Service, to reflect the referrals from these services, will provide much needed additional resources.

Principal Funding Sources

Aside from the income generated by the charity shop, the principal funding sources for the charity are currently by way of grant and contract income from Dorsetshire County Council and the Dorsetshire Primary Care Trust. As a result of increasing constraints on local authority expenditure, the charity has to seek funding from a much broader group of agencies. The involvement of the charity with the Drug Action team (DAT) and the Dorsetshire Drugs Reference Action Group (DDRAG) is proving particularly useful in identifying possible opportunities for a much wider range of funding for the future.

Investment Policy

Aside from retaining a prudent amount in reserves each year most of the charity's funds are to be spent in the short term so there are few funds for long term investment. Having considered the options available, the Management Committee has decided to invest the small amount that it has available in commercial common investment funds. Grants received in advance are invested on the money market. The Management Committee consider the overall return on long term investments and deposits together, at over 4% in the year, to be disappointing. A review of investment policies is therefore planned early in the new financial year.

Reserves Policy

The Management Committee has examined the charity's requirements for reserves in light of the main risks to the organisation. It has established a policy whereby the unrestricted funds not committed or invested in tangible fixed assets held by the charity should be between 3 and 6 months of the expenditure. Budgeted expenditure for 2009/10 is £550,000 and therefore the target is £137,500 to £275,000 in general funds. The reserves are needed to meet the working capital requirements of the charity and the Management Committee are confident that at this level they would be able to continue the current activities of the charity in the event of a significant drop in funding. Whilst income funds stand at £56,792 a designation of £20,000 has been set aside for the purchase of equipment for the training project and a further £22,500 funds the office equipment of the charity. The present level of reserves available to the charity of £14,292 therefore falls significantly short of this target level. Although the strategy is to continue to build reserves through planned operating surpluses, the Management Committee is well aware that it unlikely that the target range can be reached for at least five years. In the short term the Management Committee has also considered the extent to which existing activities and expenditure could be curtailed, should such circumstances arise.

Plans for Future Periods

The charity plans continuing the activities outlined above in the forthcoming years subject to satisfactory funding arrangements. Plans are also being developed to work on a number of schemes with local employers and local job centres to place rehabilitated drug users who have been through our training projects on mentoring schemes which it is hoped will lead to long-term gainful employment.

The charity will also continue to work towards the QuADS Standard (Quality Assurance for Drug and Alcohol Services). Developed jointly by Alcohol Concern and DrugScope, it provides a set of quality standards for organisations in the sector. Widely used by alcohol and drug treatment services, they are endorsed by the National Treatment Agency and Drug Action Teams. The charity will also work towards the continuing implementation of the Drugs and Alcohol National Occupational Standards (DANOS).

Structure, Governance and Management

Governing Document

The organisation is a charitable company limited by guarantee, incorporated on 8 August 1992 and registered as a charity on 8 September 1992. The company was established under a Memorandum of Association which established the objects and powers of the charitable company and is governed under its Articles of Association. In the event of the company being wound up members are required to contribute an amount not exceeding £10.

Recruitment and Appointment of Management Committee

The directors of the company are also charity trustees for the purposes of charity law and under the company's Articles are known as members of the Management Committee. Under the requirements of the Memorandum and Articles of Association the members of the Management Committee are elected to serve for a period of three years after which they must be re-elected at the next Annual General Meeting.

All member of the Management Committee give their time voluntarily and received no benefits from the charity. Any expenses reclaimed from the charity are set out in note 7 to the accounts.

Mr P Smith and Mrs L Haliwell retire by rotation and, being eligible, offer themselves for re-election.

Due to the nature of drug abuse much of the charity's work inevitably focuses upon young people. The Management Committee seeks to ensure that the needs of this group are appropriately reflected through the diversity of the trustee body. To enhance the potential pool of trustees, the charity has, through selective advertising in the Big Issue and networking with local medical practitioners, sought to identify rehabilitated drug addicts who would be willing to become members of the centre and use their own experience to assist the charity.

The more traditional business and medical skills are well represented on the Management Committee. In an effort to maintain this broad skill mix, members of the Management Committee are requested to provide a list of their skills (and update it each year) and in the event of particular skills being lost due to retirements, individuals are approached to offer themselves for election to the Management Committee.

Trustee Induction and Training

Most trustees are already familiar with the practical work of the charity having been encouraged to take up the "Cooks Tour" of the Advice Centre and the Outreach Work offered as part of the two "charity membership open days" that are run each year.

Additionally, new trustees are invited and encouraged to attend a series of short training sessions (of no more than an hour) to familiarise themselves with the charity and the context within which it operates. These are jointly led by the Chair of the Management Committee and the Chief Executive of the charity and cover:

- The obligations of Management Committee members.

- The main documents which set out the operational framework for the charity including the Memorandum and Articles.
- Resourcing and the current financial position as set out in the latest published accounts.
- Future plans and objectives.

A Question & Answer pack has also been prepared drawing information from the various Charity Commission publications signposted through the Commission's guide "the Essential Trustee" as a follow up to these sessions. This is distributed to all new trustees along with the Memorandum and Articles and the latest financial statements. Feedback from new trustees about their induction has been very positive.

Risk Management

The Management Committee has conducted a review of the major risks to which the charity is exposed. A risk register has been established and is updated at least annually. Where appropriate, systems or procedures have been established to mitigate the risks the charity faces. Significant external risks to funding have led to the development of a strategic plan which will allow for the diversification of funding and activities. Internal control risks are minimised by the implementation of procedures for authorisation of all transactions and projects. Procedures are in place to ensure compliance with health and safety of staff, volunteers, clients and visitors to the centre. The continuing implementation of the Drugs and Alcohol National Occupational Standards (DANOS) and the adoption of the QuADS Standard (Quality Assurance for Drug and Alcohol Services) ensure a consistent quality of delivery for all operational aspects of the charity. These procedures are periodically reviewed to ensure that they continue to meet the needs of the charity.

Organisational Structure

The Dorsetshire Centre has a Management Committee of up to 8 members who meet quarterly and are responsible for the strategic direction and policy of the charity. At present the Committee has seven members from a variety of professional backgrounds relevant to the work of the charity. The Secretary also sits on the Committee but has no voting rights.

A scheme of delegation is in place and day to day responsibility for the provision of the services rest with the Chief Executive along with the Services and Finance and Administration Managers. The Chief Executive is responsible for ensuring that the charity delivers the services specified and that key performance indicators are met. The Services Manager has responsibility for the day to day operational management of the Centre, individual supervision of the staff team and also ensuring that the team continue to develop their skills and working practices in line with good practice.

Related Parties

In so far as it is complimentary to the charity's objects, the charity is guided by both local and national policy. At a national level drug treatment is steered by the ten year strategy "Tackling Drugs to Build a Better Britain" and the Updated Drug Strategy 2005. Drug Action Teams (DATs) are the local partnerships charged with responsibility for delivering the National Drug Strategy and commissioning services at the local level and includes representatives from amongst others, the local authority, health and voluntary sector agencies. The Chairman of Dorsetshire Drugs Advisory Centre is also the chair of the Dorsetshire Drug Reference Action Group (DDRAG). This is a multi agency group with Dorsetshire as its focus. The representation of local organisations within this group has proved invaluable to the charity in establishing improved links within the community and identifying relevant policy developments and prospective funding.

Responsibilities of the Management Committee

Company law requires the Management Committee to prepare financial statements for each financial year which give a true and fair view of the state of the affairs of the charitable company as at the balance sheet date and of its incoming resources and application of resources, including income and expenditure, for the financial year. In preparing those financial statements, the management committee should follow best practice and:

- select suitable accounting policies and then apply them consistently;
- make judgements and estimates that are reasonable and prudent; and
- prepare the financial statements on the going concern basis unless it is not appropriate to assume that the company will continue on that basis.

The Management Committee is responsible for maintaining proper accounting records which disclose with reasonable accuracy at any time the financial position of the charitable company and to enable them to ensure that the financial statements comply with the Companies Act 1985. The Management Committee is also responsible for safeguarding the assets of the charitable company and hence for taking reasonable steps for the prevention and detection of fraud and other irregularities.

Members of the Management Committee

Members of the Management Committee, who are directors for the purpose of company law and trustees for the purpose of charity law, who served during the year and up to the date of this report are set out on page 3.

In accordance with company law, as the company's directors, we certify that:

- so far as we are aware, there is no relevant audit information of which the company's auditors are unaware; and
- as the directors of the company we have taken all the steps that we ought to have taken in order to make ourselves aware of any relevant audit information and to establish that the charity's auditors are aware of that information.

Auditors

Risk & Co were re-appointed as the charitable company's auditors during the year and have expressed their willingness to continue in that capacity.

This report has been prepared in accordance with the Statement of Recommended Practice: Accounting and Reporting by Charities (issued in March 2005) and in accordance with the special provisions of Part VII of the Companies Act 1985 relating to small entities.

Approved by the Management Committee on 13 September 2009 and signed on its behalf by:

Mr P Smith (Director)

Dorsetshire Drugs Advice Centre
Statement of Financial Activities (including Income & Expenditure Account) for the year ended 31 March 2009

	Notes	Unrestricted Funds 2009 £	Restricted Funds 2009 £	Total Funds 2009 £	Total Funds 2008 £
Incoming resources					
Incoming resources from generated funds:					
Voluntary income:					
Donations and grants	2	4,900	10,000	14,900	13,592
Activities for generating funds:					
Shop income		34,030	-	34,030	34,484
Investment income		1,800	1,530	3,330	2,648
Incoming resources from charitable activities:	3				
Grants & contracts		-	300,000	300,000	252,264
Café and drop-in centre		191,070	-	191,070	162,344
Total incoming resources		231,800	311,530	543,330	465,332
Resources expended					
Costs of generating funds					
Costs of generating voluntary income	4	2,950	-	2,950	3,786
Fundraising trading: cost of goods sold and other costs	4	23,748	-	23,748	22,450
Charitable activities	4	173,000	273,298	446,298	353,596
Governance costs	4	17,332	-	17,332	14,744
Total resources expended		217,030	273,298	490,328	394,576
Net income for the year. (Net incoming resources before other recognised gains)		14,770	38,232	53,002	70,756
Other recognised gains					
Gain on revaluation of investments	10	1,524	-	1,524	404
Net movement in funds		16,294	38,232	54,526	71,160
Reconciliation of funds					
Total funds brought forward		40,498	2,632	43,130	(28,030)
Total funds carried forward		56,792	40,864	97,656	43,130

The statement of financial activities includes all gains and losses in the year. All incoming resources and resources expended derive from continuing activities.

Dorsetshire Drugs Advice Centre

Balance Sheet as at 31 March 2009

	Notes	2009 £	2009 £	2008 £
Fixed Assets				
Tangible assets	9		22,500	20,000
Investments	10		23,308	21,784
			45,808	41,784
Current Assets				
Stock		334		108
Debtors	11	15,336		11,148
Cash at bank and in hand		52,946		7,594
		68,616		18,850
Creditors: amounts falling due within one year	12	(16,768)		(17,504)
Net Current Assets			51,848	1,346
Net Assets	12		97,656	43,130
Unrestricted funds	14			
⋅ Designated funds		20,000		–
⋅ Revaluation funds		3,658		2,134
⋅ General funds		33,134		38,364
			56,792	40,498
Restricted funds	14		40,864	2,632
Total Funds			97,656	43,130

These accounts are prepared in accordance with the special provisions of Part VII of the Companies Act 1985 relating to small entities.

Approved by the management committee on 13 September 2009 and signed on its behalf by:

M Haliwell, Treasurer

Notes forming part of the Financial Statements for the year ended 31 March 2009

1. **Accounting Policies**

   The principal accounting policies are summarised below. The accounting policies have been applied consistently throughout the year and in the preceding year.

   (a) **Basis of accounting**

   The financial statements have been prepared under the historical cost convention, as modified by the inclusion of fixed asset investments at market value, and in accordance with the Companies Act 1985 and the Statement of Recommended Practice : Accounting and Reporting by Charities issued in March 2005.

   (b) **Fund accounting**

   - Unrestricted funds are available for use at the discretion of the trustees in furtherance of the general objectives of the charity. Unrestricted funds include a revaluation reserve representing the restatement of investment assets at market values.

   - Designated funds are unrestricted funds earmarked by the Management Committee for particular purposes.

   - Restricted funds are subjected to restrictions on their expenditure imposed by the donor or through the terms of an appeal.

   (c) **Incoming resources**

   All incoming resources are included in the statement of financial activities when the charity is entitled to, and virtually certain to receive, the income and the amount can be quantified with reasonable accuracy. The following policies are applied to particular categories of income:

   - Voluntary income is received by way of grants, donations and gifts and is included in full in the Statement of Financial Activities when receivable. Grants, where entitlement is not conditional on the delivery of a specific performance by the charity, are recognised when the charity becomes unconditionally entitled to the grant.

   - Donated services and facilities are included at the value to the charity where this can be quantified. The value of services provided by volunteers has not been included in these accounts.

   - Clothing and other items donated for resale through the charity's shop are included as incoming resources within activities for generating funds when they are sold.

   - Investment income is included when receivable.

   - Incoming resources from charitable trading activity are accounted for when earned.

   - Incoming resources from grants, where related to performance and specific deliverables, are accounted for as the charity earns the right to consideration by its performance.

   (d) **Resources expended**

   Expenditure is recognised on an accrual basis as a liability is incurred. Expenditure includes any VAT which cannot be fully recovered, and is reported as part of the expenditure to which it relates:

dorsetshire
drugs advice centre

- Costs of generating funds comprise the costs associated with attracting voluntary income and the costs of trading for fundraising purposes including the charity's shop.

- Charitable expenditure comprises those costs incurred by the charity in the delivery of its activities and services for its beneficiaries. It includes both costs that can be allocated directly to such activities and those costs of an indirect nature necessary to support them.

- Governance costs include those costs associated with meeting the constitutional and statutory requirements of the charity and include the audit fees and costs linked to the strategic management of the charity.

- All costs are allocated between the expenditure categories of the SoFA on a basis designed to reflect the use of the resource. Costs relating to a particular activity are allocated directly, others are apportioned on an appropriate basis e.g. floor areas, per capita or estimated usage as set out in Note 4.

(e) **Fixed assets**

Fixed assets (excluding investments) are stated at cost less accumulated depreciation. The costs of minor additions or those costing below £1,000 are not capitalised. Depreciation is provided at rates calculated to write off the cost of each asset over its expected useful life, which in all cases is estimated at 4 years. Impairment reviews are carried out as and when evidence comes to light that that the recoverable amount of a functional fixed asset is below its net book value due to damage, obsolescence or other relevant factors.

Investments held as fixed assets are revalued at mid-market value at the balance sheet date and the gain or loss taken to the Statement of Financial Activities.

2. **Donations**

	Unrestricted £	Restricted £	2009 Total £	2008 Total £
Berrow Estate Charitable Trust	-	10,000	10,000	-
Donations	4,900	-	4,900	13,592
	4,900	10,000	14,900	13,592

3. **Incoming Resources from Activities to further the Charity's Objects**

	Unrestricted £	Restricted £	2009 Total £	2008 Total £
Dorsetshire County Council:				
Advice & information	-	140,000	140,000	120,000
Outreach	-	110,000	110,000	132,264
Dorsetshire PCT:				
Counselling	-	50,000	50,000	-
Training Project:				
Income from Café	191,070	-	191,070	162,344
	191,070	300,000	491,070	414,608

Model Annual Report for a Larger Charitable Company   279

dorsetshire drugs advice centre

4. Total Resources Expended

	Basis of allocation	Voluntary income	Charity shop	Advice & Information	Outreach Work	Café Training Project	Governance	2009 Total	2008 Total
Costs directly allocated to activities		£	£	£	£	£	£	£	£
Staff costs	Direct	-	-	115,797	115,493	138,486	-	369,776	295,464
Café supplies	Direct	-	-	-	-	10,420	-	10,420	10,000
Recruitment	Direct	-	-	-	2,852	-	-	2,852	5,634
Travel	Direct	-	-	648	964	792	332	2,736	1,912
Volunteer expenses	Direct	-	3,046	1,728	-	2004	-	6,778	5,040
Audit fees	Direct	-	-	-	-	-	4,000	4,000	3,600
Annual report	Direct	-	-	-	-	-	5,124	5,124	3,650
Support costs allocated to activities									
Premises	Floor Area	2,180	20,560	3,072	7,662	4,168	-	37,642	31,124
General office and finance staff	Staff Time	642	-	7,843	5,643	8,498	3,756	26,382	23,758
Communications	Staff Time	106	-	1,188	1,538	3,000	1,358	7,190	5,632
Consultancy	Usage	--	-	2,000	2,000	2,000	212	6,212	-
Legal & Professional	Usage	-	-	780	766	930	24	2,500	2,858
Depreciation	Usage	-	-	1,250	1,250	2,500	2,500	7,500	5,000
Bank charges	Transactions	22	142	422	402	202	26	1,216	904
Total resources expended		2,950	23,748	134,728	138,570	173,000	17,332	490,328	394,576

5. Net Incoming Resources for the Year

This is stated after charging:	2009 £	2008 £
Depreciation	7,500	5,000
Auditors' remuneration re external scrutiny	4,000	3,600

	£	£
Salaries and wages	360,144	288,494
Social security costs	36,014	30,728
Total	396,158	319,222

No employee received emoluments of more than £60,000.

The average number of employees during the year, calculated on the basis of full time equivalents, was as follows:

	2009 Number	2008 Number
Chief Executive	1	1
Counselling, advice and information	4	4
Outreach work	4	3
Training project	6	5
Administration and support	1	1
Total	16	14

The charity does not operate any pension scheme for its employees but does administer contributions to a stakeholder pension scheme for 5 (2008 – 4) staff. The charity makes no contributions to this scheme.

7. Trustee Remuneration & Related Party Transactions

No members of the management committee received any remuneration during the year. Travel costs amounting to £332 (2008 - £368) were reimbursed to 4 (2008 – 5) members of the management committee.

No trustee or other person related to the charity had any personal interest in any contract or transaction entered into by the charity during the year (2008 – Nil).

8. Taxation

As a charity, Dorset Drugs Advice Centre is exempt from tax on income and gains falling within section 505 of the Taxes Act 1988 or s256 of the Taxation of Chargeable Gains Act 1992 to the extent that these are applied to its charitable objects. No tax charges have arisen in the Charity.

9. Tangible Fixed Assets

	Office Equipment £
Cost	
At 1 April 2008	30,000
Additions	10,000
At 31 March 2009	40,000
Accumulated Depreciation	
At 1 April 2008	10,000
Charge for the year	7,500
At 31 March 2009	17,500
Net book value	
At 31 March 2009	22,500
At 31 March 2008	20,000

10. Investments

	2009 £	2008 £
Charityfund Unit Trust at mid-market value:		
At 1 April 2008	21,784	21,380
Unrealised gain on investments	1,524	404
At 31 March 2009	23,308	21,784

11. Debtors

	2009 £	2008 £
Trade Debtors - contract income receivable	13,084	9,180
Other debtors and prepayments	2,252	1,968
Total	15,336	11,148

12. Creditors: Amounts Falling Due within One Year

	2009 £	2008 £
Taxation and social security	8,916	7,792
Other creditors and accruals	7,852	9,712
Total	16,768	17,504

13. Analysis of Net Assets Between Funds

	General Funds £	Designated Funds £	Restricted Funds £	Total Funds £
Tangible fixed assets	15,000	-	7,500	22,500
Investments	19,650	3,658	-	23,308
Current assets	10,340	20,000	38,276	68,616
Current liabilities	(11,856)	-	(4,912)	(16,768)
Net assets at 31 March 2006	33,134	23,658	40,864	97,656

14. Movements in Funds

	At 1 April 2008 £	Incoming Resources (inc.gains) £	Outgoing Resources £	Transfers £	At 31 March 2009 £
Restricted funds:					
Computer equipment – counselling service	-	10,000	(2,500)	-	7,500
Counselling, Advice and information	2,632	140,000	(134,016)	-	8,616
Outreach	-	161,530	(136,782)	-	24,748
Total restricted funds	2,632	311,530	(273,298)	-	40,864
Unrestricted funds:					
Designated training project equipment fund	-	-	-	20,000	20,000
Designated revaluation fund	2,134	1,524	-	-	3,658
General funds	38,364	231,800	(217,030)	(20,000)	33,134
Total unrestricted funds	40,498	233,324	(217,030)	-	56,792
Total funds	43,130	544,854	(490,328)	-	97,656

Purposes of Restricted Funds

Computer equipment: This was a grant for computer equipment used in conjunction with database software to organise information and make it accessible for volunteer counsellors. The balance is reducing as the computers depreciate.

Advice and Information: The fund is for the advice and information activity as explained in the trustees' report.

Outreach: This is a fund for outreach work with young people who are vulnerable or falling into drug misuse. The balance arose from a delay in using grants which were given for the purpose of appointing new staff. Staff were appointed late in the year and all the fund will be utilised in forthcoming months.

Purposes of Designated Funds

Training Project Equipment: The Management Committee has designated funds for purchase of new equipment in the training project.

Revaluation Reserve Fund: The revaluation reserve fund is required by the Companies Act 1985 and represents the amount by which investments exceed their historical cost.

INDEX

References are to paragraph numbers.

Academic institutions	4.9.2
training	4.9.2
Accounting	3.1, 3.2, 3.2.1, 3.2.2, 3.2.3, 3.2.4, 3.2.5, 3.3, 3.4, 3.4.1, 3.4.2, 3.4.3, 3.4.4, 3.4.5, 3.4.6
audit	3.3
independent audit	3.3
rates	3.4, 3.4.1
property used for charitable purposes	3.4.2
tax	3.4, 3.4.1, 3.4.2, 3.4.3, 3.4.4, 3.4.5, 3.4.6
Accounts	3.2
annual report	3.2.4
achievements and performance	3.2.4
financial review	3.2.4
objectives and activities	3.2.4
reference and administrative details	3.2.4
structure, governance and management	3.2.4
branches	3.2.5
formats	3.2.3
small charities	3.2.2
structure	3.2.1
Amalgamation	2.7, 2.7.1, 2.7.1.1, 2.7.1.2
transfer of assets	2.7.1
scheme	2.7.1.2
statutory power	2.7.1.1
Annual report	3.2.4
Applications for assistance	3.8.2, 3.8.3
Articles of association	2.6.1
changing	2.6.1
Audit	3.3
Branches	3.2.5
accounts	3.2.5
Buildings	3.7
Capital gains tax	3.4.1
CEDAG	5.5
Certificate of incorporation	3.7.1.1
Charitable purposes	1.1.1, 1.1.5
Charitable status	1.4
examples	1.4
Charity	1.1, 1.1.1, 1.1.2, 1.1.5, 1.3.5, 2.1
constitutional requirements	2.1
meaning	1.1, 1.1.1, 1.1.2, 1.1.5
England and Wales	1.1.1, 1.1.5
Scotland	1.1.2

Charity—*continued*	
reputation	1.3.5
Charity Commission	2.3, 2.3.1, 2.3.2, 2.3.3, 2.3.4, 2.3.5, 2.3.6, 4.10.6.2
inquiry	4.10.6.2
registration	2.3
excepted charities	2.3.2
exempt charities	2.3.1
name of charity	2.3.4
number	2.3.5
registration pack	2.3.3
significance	2.3.6
Charity consultants	4.5.4
Charity trustee	1.2, 1.3, 1.3.1, 1.3.2, 1.3.3, 1.3.4, 1.3.5
contracts with third parties	1.3.4
delegation	1.3.3
duties	1.3.5
meaning	1.2
responsibilities	1.3
conflict	1.3.2
public trust	1.3.1
Committee of Permanent Representatives	5.3.2
Committee of the Regions	5.3.9
Common investment funds	3.6.1
Compensation	4.10.5
Computers	
equipment	4.7, 4.7.1
Conflict of duties	
charity trustee	1.3.2
Constitution	2.6, 2.6.1, 2.6.3, 2.6.4, 2.6.4.1, 2.6.4.2, 2.6.4.2.1, 2.6.4.2.2, 2.6.4.3, 2.6.5, 2.6.6
changing	2.6, 2.6.1
alternative procedures	2.6.4, 2.6.4.1, 2.6.4.2, 2.6.4.2.1, 2.6.4.2.2, 2.6.4.3, 2.6.5
cy-près doctrine	2.6.4.2.2
express power	2.6.3
new governing instrument	2.6.6
procedure	2.6.4.2.1
reviewing aims and procedures	2.6.5
scheme	2.6.4.2, 2.6.4.3
England and Wales	2.6.4.2, 2.6.4.2.1, 2.6.4.2.2
Scotland	2.6.4.3
statutory power	2.6.4, 2.6.4.1
Constitutional requirements	2.1
Continuing education	4.9

Contract culture	4.5.2
Contracts	1.3.4
third parties	1.3.4
Council of Europe	5.3.12
Council of Ministers	5.3.1
Cy-près doctrine	2.9
changing constitution	2.6.4.2.2
examples	2.9
Decisions	5.2.4
Declaration of trust	2.2
Directives	5.2.3
Director	4.4.11
relationship with trustees	4.4.11
Directorates General	5.3.5
Economic and Social Committee	5.3.8
Emergencies	4.10.1
Employees	1.3.3, 4.4, 4.4.1, 4.4.2, 4.4.3, 4.4.4, 4.4.5, 4.4.6, 4.4.7, 4.4.8, 4.4.10, 4.9.5
encouragement or praise when deserved	4.4.4
fairness	4.4.7
freedom from annoyance	4.4.3
freedom from insecurity	4.4.2
health and safety legislation	4.4.10
interviewing	4.4.1
opportunities	4.9.5
pension rights	4.4.8
policy guidelines	1.3.3
remuneration	4.4.8
support for weaknesses	4.4.5
training	4.4.6
Equipment	4.6, 4.6.1
computers	4.7
social media	4.7.1
websites	4.7.1
Europe	5.1, 5.1.1, 5.5
associations	5.1
foundations	5.1
networks	5.5
umbrella bodies	5.5
European Commission	5.3.4, 5.4.1
functions	5.4.1
European Council	5.3.3
European Foundation	5.3.10, 5.4.4
functions	5.4.4
European Foundation Centre	5.5
European institutions	5.3, 5.4, 5.4.1, 5.4.2, 5.4.3, 5.4.4, 5.4.5
Committee of Permanent Representatives	5.3.2
Council of Europe	5.3.12
Council of the European Union	5.3.1
Directorates General	5.3.5
European Commission	5.3.4, 5.4.1
European Council	5.3.3
European Foundation	5.3.10, 5.4.4
European Parliament	5.3.6, 5.3.7, 5.3.8, 5.3.9, 5.4.2
European Social Committee	5.4.3
interaction	5.4

European institutions—*continued*	
non-governmental organisations	5.4.5
European law	5.2, 5.2.1, 5.2.2, 5.2.3, 5.2.4, 5.2.5
Decisions	5.2.4
Directives	5.2.3
Opinions	5.2.5
Recommendations	5.2.5
Regulations	5.2.2
treaties	5.2.1
European Parliament	5.3.6, 5.4.2
Committee of the Regions	5.3.9
committees	5.3.7
Economic and Social Committee	5.3.8
functions	5.4.2
European Social Committee	5.4.3
functions	5.4.3
European Union	5.1, 5.1.1
social economy	5.1, 5.1.1
social tourism	5.1.1
Exclusively charitable purposes	1.1.5
Exempt charities	2.3.1, 2.3.2
Formation of charity	2.1, 2.2
Act of Parliament	2.1
charitable incorporated association	2.1
choosing legal form	2.2
company limited by guarantee	2.1
declaration of trust	2.1, 2.2
industrial and provident society	2.1
Royal Charter	2.1
unincorporated charitable association	2.1
will	2.1
Formation of trust	
Scotland	2.2
Fundraising	3.9, 3.9.1, 3.9.2, 3.9.3, 3.9.4, 3.9.5, 3.12.2
agreements	3.9.5
managing	3.9.1
methods	3.9.2
records	3.9.4
restrictions on	3.9.3
trading for purpose of	3.12.2
General charitable intention	3.10.2.2
Gift aid	3.4.3
Gifts	3.10, 3.10.1, 3.10.2, 3.10.2.1, 3.10.2.2, 3.10.2.3, 3.10.3
accepting	3.10
failure of purpose	3.10.2.1, 3.10.2.2, 3.10.2.3
avoiding	3.10.3
general charitable intention	3.10.2.2
identifiable donors	3.10.2.3
refusal to accept	3.10.1
subject to conditions	3.10.2, 3.10.2.1
failure of purpose	3.10.2.1
general charitable intention	3.10.2.2
identifiable donors	3.10.2.3
Grants	3.8, 3.8.1, 3.8.2, 3.8.3
applications for assistance	3.8.2
objective of	3.8.1

Index

Grants—*continued*
    policy guidelines   3.8.3

Health and safety legislation   4.4.10

Income tax   3.4.1, 3.4.3, 3.4.4, 3.4.5, 3.4.6
Independent audit   3.3
Insurance   3.5, 3.5.1, 3.5.2, 3.5.3, 3.5.4, 3.5.5, 3.5.6, 3.5.7, 3.5.8, 4.10.2
    damage   3.5.1
    employer's liability   3.5.3, 3.5.4
    fidelity   3.5.5
    fire   3.5.1
    liability   3.5.7
    limited liability company   3.5.8
    particular risks   3.5.6
    public liability   3.5.3, 3.5.4
    terrorism   3.5.2
    theft   3.5.1
    vandalism   3.5.2
International Society for Third Sector Research   5.5
Investment   3.6, 3.6.1, 3.6.2, 3.6.2.1, 3.6.3, 3.6.3.1, 3.6.4, 3.6.4.1
    advice on   3.6.3
    advisers   3.6.3.1
    common investment funds   3.6.1
    holding of investments   3.6.4
        incorporation   3.6.4.1
    powers   3.6.2, 3.6.4.1
        advice on   3.6.3
        advisers   3.6.3.1
        statutory powers   3.6.2.1
    statutory powers   3.6.2.1

Land   3.7, 3.7.1, 3.7.1.1, 3.7.1.2, 3.7.2, 3.7.2.1, 3.7.2.2, 3.7.3
    exchange   3.7.2, 3.7.2.1
        formalities   3.7.2.2
    holding   3.7.1
        certificate of incorporation   3.7.1.1
        land vested in Official Custodian   3.7.1.2
    leasing   3.7.2, 3.7.2.1
        formalities   3.7.2.2
    mortgage of   3.7.3
    sale   3.7.2, 3.7.2.1
        formalities   3.7.2.2
Legacies   3.10
    accepting   3.10
Limited liability company
    insurance   3.5.8
Listed buildings   4.8.3

Management   4.1, 4.5.1, 4.5.2, 4.5.4
    charity consultants   4.5.4
    coherence   4.5.3
    contract culture   4.5.2
    planning
        time   4.5.1
Mediation   4.10.7

Memorandum of association   2.6.1
    alteration   2.6.1
Money   3.1, 3.2, 3.2.1, 3.2.2, 3.2.3, 3.2.4, 3.2.5, 3.3, 3.4, 3.4.1, 3.4.2, 3.4.3, 3.4.4, 3.4.5, 3.4.6
Mortgage
    land, of   3.7.3

Name of charity   2.3.4
National Council for Voluntary Organisations   5.5
National Lottery   3.9
    Big Lottery Fund   3.9
    Heritage Lottery Fund   3.9
    UK Sport   3.9
Negligence   4.10.3
Neighbours   4.8.5
Non-governmental organisations   5.4.5

Official Custodian   3.7.1.2
    land vested in   3.7.1.2
Opinions   5.2.5
OSCR   4.10.6.3
    powers   4.10.6.3

Patrons   3.11
Payroll Giving Scheme   3.4.4
Pension rights
    employees   4.4.8
Planning
    time   4.5.1
Premises   4.8, 4.8.1, 4.8.2, 4.8.3, 4.8.4, 4.8.5
    appearance   4.8.1
    listed buildings   4.8.3
    moving   4.8.4
    neighbours   4.8.5
    regulations   4.8.2
Professional advisers   4.3, 4.3.1, 4.3.1.1, 4.3.1.2, 4.3.2, 4.3.3, 4.3.4, 4.3.5, 4.3.6
    barristers   4.3.5
    beauty parades   4.3.6
    charity consultants   4.3.5
    choosing   4.3.1
    communication with   4.3.2
    effectiveness   4.3.2
    fees   4.3.1.1
    mistakes to avoid   4.3.4
    paralegals   4.3.5
    particular specialists   4.3.5
    problems with   4.3.3
    relationship with trustees   4.3.1.2
    solicitors   4.3.5
Property   3.1, 3.2, 3.2.1, 3.2.2, 3.2.3, 3.2.4, 3.2.5, 3.3, 3.4, 3.4.1, 3.4.2, 3.4.3, 3.4.4, 3.4.5, 3.4.6
Public trust   1.3.1
    responsibilities of trustees   1.3.1

Rates	3.4, 3.4.1
property used for charitable purposes	3.4.2
Recommendations	5.2.5
Record-keeping	3.2, 3.3, 3.4, 3.4.1, 3.4.2, 3.4.3, 3.4.4, 3.4.5, 3.4.6
branches	3.2.5
formats	3.2.3
small charities	3.2.2
structure	3.2.1
Register of Charities	1.4
Registered office	4.8
Registration	2.3, 2.3.1, 2.3.2, 2.3.3, 2.3.4, 2.3.5, 2.3.6, 2.4
Charity Commission	2.3
excepted charities	2.3.2
exempt charities	2.3.1
name of charity	2.3.4
number	2.3.5
registration pack	2.3.3
significance	2.3.6
Scotland	2.4
Regulations	5.2.2
Remuneration	
employees	4.4.8
Reviewing aims and procedures	2.6.5
Running out of money	4.10.6.1
Self-help	4.9.1
Small charities	3.2.2
accounts	3.2.2
Social economy	5.1, 5.1.1
Social media	4.7.1
Social tourism	5.1.1
Sponsors	3.11
Stationery	4.6, 4.6.1
legal requirements	4.6, 4.6.1
Tax	3.4, 3.4.1, 3.4.2
capital gains	3.4.1
gift aid	3.4.3
gifts	3.4.5
HM Revenue and Customs guidance	3.4.6
income	3.4.1
payments from supporters	3.4.3
payroll deduction scheme	3.4.4
property used for charitable purposes	3.4.2
Technical skills	4.9.3
training	4.9.3
Tenants	4.10.4
defaults	4.10.4
Time	
management	4.5.1
Trading	3.12, 3.12.1, 3.12.2
activities as adjunct to charitable purpose	3.12.1
fundraising, for	3.12.2
Training	4.9, 4.9.1, 4.9.2, 4.9.3, 4.9.4, 4.9.5, 4.9.6
academic institutions	4.9.2, 4.9.3
continuing education	4.9

Training—*continued*	
informal	4.9.6
in-house	4.9.6
opportunities for staff	4.9.5
self-help	4.9.1
special courses	4.9.4
Trustee Training Unit	4.9.6
Transfer of assets	2.7.1
scheme	2.7.1.2
statutory power	2.7.1.1
Treaties	5.2.1
Troubleshooting	4.10, 4.10.1, 4.10.2, 4.10.3, 4.10.4, 4.10.5, 4.10.6, 4.10.6.1, 4.10.6.2, 4.10.6.3, 4.10.7
Charity Commission inquiry	4.10.6.2
compensation	4.10.5
emergencies	4.10.1
insurance	4.10.2
mediation	4.10.7
negligence	4.10.3
OSCR's powers	4.10.6.3
problems	4.10.6
running out of money	4.10.6.1
tenants' defaults	4.10.4
Trustee meetings	4.2, 4.2.1, 4.2.2, 4.2.3, 4.2.4, 4.2.5
Trustee Training Unit	4.9.6
Trustees	4.1, 4.2, 4.2.1, 4.2.2, 4.2.3, 4.2.4, 4.2.5, 4.3, 4.3.1, 4.3.1.1, 4.3.1.2, 4.3.2, 4.3.3, 4.3.4, 4.3.5, 4.3.6, 4.4.11
characteristics	4.1
choosing	4.1
meetings	4.2
chairmanship	4.2.3
frequency	4.2.5
minutes	4.2.4
preparation	4.2.1
quorum	4.2.2
professional advisers	4.3, 4.3.1, 4.3.1.1, 4.3.1.2, 4.3.2, 4.3.3, 4.3.4, 4.3.5, 4.3.6
qualities	4.1
relationship with director	4.4.11
Volunteers	4.4, 4.4.1, 4.4.2, 4.4.3, 4.4.4, 4.4.5, 4.4.6, 4.4.7, 4.4.10
encouragement or praise when deserved	4.4.4
fairness	4.4.7
freedom from annoyance	4.4.3
freedom from insecurity	4.4.2
health and safety legislation	4.4.10
interviewing	4.4.1
support for weaknesses	4.4.5
training	4.4.6
Winding up	2.8, 2.8.1, 2.8.2, 2.8.3
CIO	2.8.3
express power	2.8.1
statutory power	2.8.2